THE GLOBAL HISTORY SERIES

Leften Stavrianos, *Northwestern Un........,*
General Editor

This series aims to present history in global perspective, going beyond
national or regional limitations, and dealing with overriding trends
and forces. The various collections of original materials span the globe,
range from prehistoric times to the present, and include anthropology,
economics, political science, and religion, as well as history.

George Lenczowski, the editor of this volume, is Professor of Political
Science, University of California at Berkeley, and Director, Middle
East Research Project, American Enterprise Institute for Public Policy
Research, Washington, D.C. He is the author of *Russia and the West
in Iran, The Middle East in World Affairs,* and *Oil and State in the
Middle East.*

Also in the Global History Series

Africa in the Days of Exploration, *edited by Roland Oliver and Caro-
line Oliver,* S-123

The Americas on the Eve of Discovery, *edited by Harold E. Driver,*
S-93

Asia on the Eve of Europe's Expansion, *edited by Donald F. Lach and
Carol Flaumenhaft,* S-125

Christianity in the Non-Western World, *edited by Charles W. Forman,*
S-150

The Decline of Empires, *edited by S. N. Eisenstadt,* S-154

European Expansion and the Counter-Example of Asia, *edited by
Joseph R. Levenson,* S-170

Man Before History, *edited by Creighton Gabel,* S-92

The Muslim World on the Eve of Europe's Expansion, *edited by
John J. Saunders,* S-144

The Political Awakening in India, *edited by John R. McLane,* S-211

The Political Awakening of Africa, *edited by Rupert Emerson and
Martin Kilson,* S-124

World Migration in Modern Times, *edited by Franklin D. Scott,* S-185

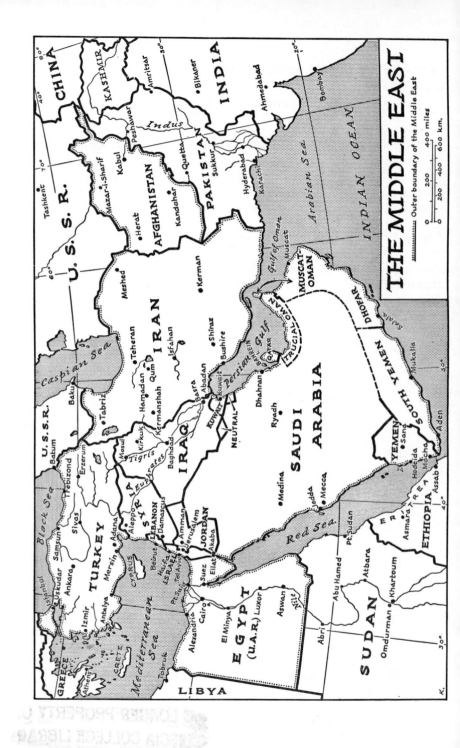

THE MIDDLE EAST

.... Outer boundary of the Middle East

0   200   400   miles
0   200   400   600 km.

THE POLITICAL AWAKENING
IN THE MIDDLE EAST

EDITED BY GEORGE LENCZOWSKI

Prentice-Hall, Inc. / *Englewood Cliffs, N.J.*

To my wife

© 1970 by Prentice-Hall, Inc.,
Englewood Cliffs, New Jersey.

A SPECTRUM BOOK.

C–13-684704-8
P–13-684696-3

Library of Congress Catalog Card Number 79-79450.

Printed in the United States of America.

Current printing (last number):
10   9   8   7   6   5   4   3   2   1

PRENTICE-HALL INTERNATIONAL, INC. (*London*)
PRENTICE-HALL OF AUSTRALIA PTY. LTD. (*Sydney*)
PRENTICE-HALL OF CANADA, LTD. (*Toronto*)
PRENTICE-HALL OF INDIA PRIVATE LIMITED (*New Delhi*)
PRENTICE-HALL OF JAPAN, INC. (*Tokyo*)

PREFACE

The purpose of this book is to present, through the medium of selected readings, the political transition of the Middle East from traditionalism to modernism. The process of transition (or awakening) is traced historically and topically. Taking the traditional structures of the Ottoman and Persian Empires as the base, the book endeavors to reveal such significant departures from this base as have occurred in the fields of administration and military affairs, Islamic thought, political institutions and processes, and ideology. The process of modernization has not been uniform; on the contrary, it has followed different paths depending on the historical period, environment, characteristics of a given ethnic group, and the genius of its leaders; correspondingly, the main variants of this process are reflected in the chapters and sections of this volume. Both primary and secondary materials are included, the chief criteria of their selection being their relevance to the main theme under review and the clarity with which they treat the subject matter. In view of the focus of this book on the process of change within the predominantly Islamic societies, Israel as a new political phenomenon, whose birth and growth has not been organically connected with the surrounding area, is not included.

The editor would like to acknowledge with gratitude the services consecutively rendered him during the preparation of this volume by two doctoral candidates at the University of California at Berkeley, Mr. M. A. Loutfi, currently on the faculty of McGill University, and Mr. Ralph H. Magnus, formerly assistant cultural attaché at the American Embassy in Kabul. Similarly, thanks are due to Mrs. Florence C. Myer for her patience and thoughtful attention to detail in typing the manuscript.

CONTENTS

THE POLITICAL AWAKENING
IN THE MIDDLE EAST

INTRODUCTION

I

Readings selected for this volume are grouped into chapters and sections corresponding to the phases of the process of awakening as outlined in the following synopsis of Middle Eastern history. They are composed of three broad categories: (a) accounts of reformist and revolutionary movements and policies excerpted from specialized works and monographs; (b) "portrait" type descriptions of certain political and religious leaders who had made a major impact upon the course of modernization in their countries; and (c) speeches, pronouncements, excerpts from programs, charters, resolutions, and other primary documents reflecting various approaches to the process of change in the Middle East.

The Middle East cannot be defined in purely geographic terms. While it is possible to say that it comprises the area situated at the junction of Asia, Europe, and Africa, its limits have to be primarily set according to cultural and political criteria. It is in the Middle East that the ancient civilizations of Mesopotamia and the Nile Valley grew and flourished. It is in this area that mankind's first notions of codified law, alphabet, and monotheism were born. And it is there that the first imperial concepts were developed in succession by the Babylonian, Assyrian, Persian, Greek, Roman, Byzantine, Arab, and Ottoman Empires.

The contemporary Middle East is, culturally, a predominantly Moslem area. Islam, however, expanded beyond its Middle Eastern origin into such diverse regions as India, the Far East, and the northern and central parts of Africa. These far-flung extensions of Islam should not be lumped together with the Middle East, partly because of their different cultural background—with a possible exception of North Africa—and primarily because of a vastly different political history. Politically, the main point of difference could be attributed to the fact that these lands have been subjected to direct colonial control of Western powers. By contrast, the Middle East has been a region of two independent empires, the Ottoman and the Persian. While in the nineteenth century both suffered a decline and a corresponding intervention and partial occupation by European powers, neither lost its formal sovereign status.

Always a rich mosaic of races, cultures, and languages, the Middle East has comprised three principal ethnic and cultural groups: the Iranian, the Arab, and the Turkish. Each of them was an heir to a different tradition and each possessed its own distinctive language. Cradle of a splendid civilization, ancient Iran developed, through its early Zoroastrian religion, the concept of the permanent struggle between light and darkness, symbolized by its deities of Ormuzd and Ahriman. Its first Achaemenian Empire had a universalist vision; the Empire's imprint upon the vast regions beyond Iran proper was profound; even today, the *kyrie eleison* in the Catholic mass can be traced to Cyrus the Great whose name—through its Greek adaptation—had become synonymous with the notion of lordship; so can the German, Turkish, and Arabic monetary terms of *Groschen, kuruš,* and *girsh.* Iran, land of refined artistic expression, of monumental yet delicately designed architecture typified by the palaces and temples of Persepolis, of miniature painting, bronze and silver crafts, and exquisite rug-weaving, has also produced immortal epic and lyrical literature to become a country in whose national Pantheon the poets may lay claim of precedence over the generals.

Reared in the dual environment of the desert and the merchant cities of the old spice route, Arabs have partly inherited the legacy of earlier Semitic civilizations. As the latecomer in the long history of the Semites, they made their most significant contribution by giving the world the religion and law of Islam. The message of Islam served as a powerful catalyst in mobilizing a hitherto scattered and disorganized Arab community; it substituted a higher loyalty to that of family, clan, and tribe; and it endowed the new Arab polity with sufficient energy to build an empire stretching from the borders of China to the Atlantic. Islam was both militant and tolerant. It destroyed old religions and empires; it imposed its beliefs upon vast non-Arab populations; but it also absorbed and adopted much of the culture of the conquered peoples. The caliphs' courts in Baghdad, Cairo, and Cordova became famous cosmopolitan seats of learning. By the tenth century of the Christian era, the Arab world radiated culture and refinement. Mathematics, astronomy, medicine, and philosophy flourished under the patronage of Arab rulers. In comparison, early medieval Europe was "underdeveloped."

The last to arrive on the scene were the Turkish tribes, natives of

Central Asia, initially employed as soldiers and bodyguards at the Abbasid court in Baghdad. Their early history remained largely unrecorded because neither their nomadic life nor their home ground of the steppes was conducive to the erection of durable monuments. Their first exposure to higher civilization occurred upon their incursions into the Arab empire. By the tenth century, from slaves and mercenaries they turned into generals and rulers. Converted to Islam, they became not only its staunch defenders but also assumed the role of its militant propagators. By 1071 they established themselves firmly on the formerly Byzantine-controlled soil of Anatolia. By 1453, with the fall of Constantinople, they put an end to the Byzantine power and built an empire of their own. Subsequent conquest of the Arab lands of Syria, Egypt, Mesopotamia, Arabia, and North Africa made them heirs to the most important centers of Islam. Turkish-Ottoman sultans claimed the legitimacy of caliphial succession and, like their Arab predecessors, ruled a vast cosmopolitan area which contained the Greek Acropolis, the Byzantine Haghia Sophia, the Mosque of Omar and the Holy Sepulchre of Jerusalem, the old ruins of Nineveh and Babylon, the Pyramids of Giza, the Al-Azhar University in Cairo, the Leptis Magna monuments in Libya, and the Holy Kaaba of Mecca. Although they inherited an already mature civilization of Islam from the Arabs, the Turks left their own indelible imprint on it. Their martial talents, discipline, and organization launched them upon an imperial career of five hundred years' duration.

II

These, then, were—and still are—the three dominant ethnic groups in the Middle East. While each of these has its own proud legacy, they have the common link of Islam which, without erasing older customs, overshadowed many of their inherited differences. Islam gave all three groups not only a common faith, but also a set of attitudes and customs. While politically the world of Islam experienced much turmoil, socially and culturally it exhibited solid continuity and stability over many centuries. But what initially had been a source of strength in due time became a source of weakness. Stability turned into immobility. Strength of convictions degenerated into stubborn resilience against the influx of new ideas. In the meantime, with the passing of the Middle Ages, the outside world was changing. Europe became stronger in the fields of technology, economics, military science, and statecraft. And, inevitably, major European powers began the process of encroachment upon the domain of Islam. This process was particularly accelerated in the nineteenth century. By 1914 most of the lands of Islam were either under direct European control or under Europe's overwhelming influence. France was entrenched in North Africa, Italy in Libya, and

Britain in Egypt, at both extremities of the Red Sea, and in the Persian Gulf. An international administration controlled the Ottoman debt payments, while Russia and Britain carved out spheres of influence in Iran.

Certain Moslem rulers perceived Islam's inferior power position as compared with Europe's as early as the late eighteenth and the early nineteenth century. Ottoman Sultans Selim III (1789–1807) and Mahmud II (1808–39) clearly grasped the fact of European military superiority and directed their efforts at the reform and improvement of their own military establishment and administrative machinery. Their unfinished task was later taken up by their successors in what came to be known as the *Tanzimat* reform movement. Similarly, Egypt's Albanian ruler, Mohammed Ali (1805–48), launched a radical program of reform which gave his adopted country sound finances, better judicial administration, and an efficient army capable of achieving victories over the Ottoman forces and extending Egypt's dominion over Syria, Arabia, and the Sudan.

The *Tanzimat* and Mohammed Ali's reform constituted the first major break with tradition in the Islamic states. The old immobility was shaken; a conscious effort to introduce new techniques and organizational devices was made. Changes thus introduced were important and sometimes far-reaching. But they did not as yet constitute a true socio-political revolution. They were instituted from above by the rulers themselves, virtually singlehandedly in Egypt and by a small court-affiliated elite in Constantinople. Their object was not to replace one political order by another, but to *strengthen* the existing one by making it more efficient through the adoption of rational Western methods in the military, financial, and administrative sectors. A more basic institutional reform had to wait until more propitious circumstances, both domestic and international, would make it possible. Thus, the early Ottoman and Egyptian reforms had an aura of superficiality about them: by not coming to grips with the more profound motive forces in human society, by not penetrating the depth of the relationship of man to man and man to God, they were doomed to touch merely the externals. As such, the rulers' work was imperfect and incomplete.

III

The task of deeper penetration into the inner springs of human action fell upon the shoulders of those whose natural business it was to ask questions about man's destiny and his role in the world—namely, the religious leaders of Islam. So long as the traditional Islamic society maintained a modicum of inner harmony while living in a state of relative isolation from the outside world, no major challenge confronted Islam's religious leadership. But this static condition could not persist indefinitely. The end of the eighteenth and the beginning of the nineteenth centuries brought about too many new developments and released too many new forces in the world to allow the domain of Islam to remain untouched.

As a religion and a system of ethics, Islam of that era was characterized by strict dogmatism, formal ritualism, and strong discouragement of independent inquiry by the well-entrenched establishments of the *ulema*. Its rigid immobility paralleled the immobility of the Islamic society and intertwined with it. To deeper theological thinkers it was becoming clear that unless a profound reform was effected within Islam as a religion, prospects for improvement within Islam as a polity would be doomed to failure. But whereas certain religious leaders felt the urgency of reform, they lacked unanimity as to remedy for the ills. Ultimately, two major trends emerged. One, fundamentalist, followed the thesis that Islam needed to be purified from the accumulation of practices, superstitions, and impious innovations which obscured and distorted its original meaning in the course of the centuries. Mohammed ibn Abdul Wahhab in the Nejd (1703–92) and Sayyid Mohammed ibn Ali as-Senussi in Cyrenaica (1787–1859) launched puritan movements that strived to restore Islam's pristine quality by rejecting anything which did not conform to the letter of the Koran and the Tradition. Both reformers gave proof of charismatic leadership and succeeded in drawing to themselves devoted followers. Each expanded his activities in the desert hinterlands of Arabia and Libya, respectively. Both created a state-within-a-state: Abdul Wahhab by allying himself with the House of Saud; Senussi by establishing a well-organized religious order, of which he became grand master and dynastic founder. Due to the combination of spiritual fervor, skillful organization, and leadership abilities of their founders and successors, both structures survived the Ottoman Empire and European imperialism to emerge in the twentieth century as independent kingdoms and mainstays of puritan Islamic orthodoxy.

While the adherents of the fundamentalist formula sought to reform Islam by turning its back to secular ideas from the West and recapturing the spirit of the early classical era of Islamic history, the teeming urban centers of Egypt spawned another school of reformers who looked forward rather than backward. The modernist movement initiated by Jamaluddin al-Afghani (1838–97) and his disciple, Mohammed Abduh (1849–1905), aimed at rediscovering the real meaning of Islam and reconciling it with the needs of modern society. It rebelled against the petrified principle of *taqlīd*, i.e., reliance on authority for proper understanding of the faith, and called instead for the "reopening of the gate of *ijthihād*," i.e., for the revival of individual interpretation and individual striving to discover the truth of Islam. Exposed to foreign environments and influences in the course of their stormy careers, both Afghani and Abduh were in a position to draw comparisons between their own and the European societies. These comparisons drew mixed responses from both of them. Although they gave acknowledgment to Europe's superiority in the secular sphere, they refused it to the spiritual realm. Both in his debates with Ernest Renan and in his *Refutation of the Materialists,* Afghani defended the spiritual superiority of Islam; he was concurrently exhorting his fellow Moslems to revive and reform Islam by infusing it with additional content likely to assure greater enlightenment and justice to the Moslem society. As a thinker, Afghani was eclectic, combined elements of fundamentalism with modernism, and viewed Islamic reform as a reform not only of religion but as one of polity as well.

While not altogether neglecting the political and international aspects of reform, Abduh's outlook was more consistent than that of Afghani, and focused concern primarily on the reform of Islam as a religious, ethical, and educational system. This, in his view, deserved priority. Once the fundamentals were attended to, Moslems could look forward with greater confidence to the solution of more mundane problems. Thus, it was with considerable hesitation that, after initial resistance, Abduh gave his support to the Egyptian nationalist rebellion of Ahmed Urabi (1881).

The work begun by Afghani and Abduh was left unfinished. Perhaps it was in the very nature of their message that its appeal should remain as a permanent memento. As Rector of Al-Azhar University, Abduh was instrumental in reforming and modernizing its curriculum. But unless the flame of progress was to burn continuously, reforms carried out by one generation were bound to appear as obsolete to later generations.

By the mid-1930s Egypt was again facing a period of spiritual and political unrest, compounded by international complications. While, by that time, concern for reform was given expression in the writings and activities of secularly minded political leaders, preoccupation with the spiritual reform of Islam was far from extinguished. It found a new exponent in the person of Hasan al-Banna (1906–49), a schoolteacher of modest background. In launching his Moslem Brotherhood, Banna continued Afghani's tradition of simultaneous concern for the spiritual and the political. And, like Afghani, he was eclectic in his ideas, combining fundamentalism with awareness of the social problems of modern urban society. Unlike Afghani, however, he was a good organizer: his Moslem Brotherhood became a tightly knit political machine that survived not only its founder but also the collapse of

Egypt's multiparty system and the repeated acts of suppression it was subjected to by Nasser's dictatorship.

IV

While the religious leaders were concerning themselves with regeneration of Islam, groups of civil and military laymen in the Ottoman Empire initiated a movement aimed at changing the institutions of the state. The objectives of the Young Turk movement went beyond the reform of the military and the administrative branches. The movement focused its attention on the transformation of Sultan Abdul Hamid II's (1876–1909) police state into a constitutional monarchy. The Young Turkish Committee of Union and Progress succeeded in seizing power in 1908. One of its first acts was to restore the so-called Midhat Pasha Constitution, a basic law that was issued in 1876 but suspended during the subsequent thirty years. Under the restoration, the nationally diverse groups of people of the Empire were to be treated on an equal basis. The obsolete allegiance to the despotic sultan-caliph, who was propped by the army and the religious establishment, was to be replaced by "Ottomanism," a loyalty to the multinational state that would dispense equal justice to all its citizens. In this early flush of enthusiasm about freedom and equality, Arabs were invited to share in the work of progress with their fellow Turks, and an organization called the Ottoman-Arab Fraternity came into being, symbolic of the new spirit.

The politically articulate younger Arabs in the Empire welcomed the Young Turk revolution as opening a new era in which the hitherto suppressed Arab national rights could be achieved. Thus, while in the center the revived constitutionalism was interpreted in a broad libertarian sense by the Young Turks, in the Arab provinces it was viewed primarily as a vehicle that would enable the promotion of Arab nationalism. The latter reaction could be traced to a politico-cultural movement known as the "Arab Awakening" that occurred during the last quarter of the nineteenth century. Initially, Arab expectations did not go beyond the assurance of full equality to the Arabs. According to the early concepts this equality was to be secured either by appropriate decentralization or by the creation of a dual Turkish-Arab monarchy that was to be similar in pattern to the Austro-Hungarian Empire. However, before long these restrained ideas gave place to demands for far-reaching autonomy and even for complete independence. Intensification of Arab demands resulted partly from the inner dynamics of the Arab nationalist movement and partly as a response to the ruling Young Turks' abandonment of the idea of Ottomanism in favor of the nascent Turkish nationalism.

The early constitutionalism and nationalism in the Ottoman Empire found a parallel development in Persia during the years 1905 to 1909. Like the Young Turks, the Persian constitutionalists wanted to put an end to the despotic rule of the Shah but maintain the monarchy. While their emphasis was on popular representation and effective parliamentary control of legislation and finances, their movement also had strong nationalistic aspects that reflected the belief that the Shah was subjected to undue influence of foreign powers. Although the Persian movement was free from the complications inherent in the Arab-Turkish relationship in the Ottoman Empire, it had its own complexities that stemmed, on the one hand, from its own heterogeneous composition and, on the other, from Russia's hostile intervention.

V

The work of institutional modernization undertaken by the Turks and the Persians was interrupted by World War I. When modernization was resumed in the 1920s, it had to be carried out under vastly different circumstances. The Ottoman Empire had crumbled, and had been replaced by a Turkish Republic founded on an ethnic-nationality basis. Persia was subjected to the ravages of war, anarchy, famine, and foreign invasion that, due to her weakness, she was unable to prevent. The traditional state structures of both countries were utterly discredited. In Turkey, a powerful nationalist upsurge put an end to the institutions of the sultanate and the caliphate. Broadly based, representing spontaneous popular revulsion against the evils of the past, the Turkish nationalist movement found a leader of great ability in the person of Kemal Atatürk. Kemal's reforms launched Turkey on the path of secularism and modernization. These reforms were carried out under the joint tutelage of the Republican People's Party and Kemal himself. The one-party system under which Turkey endeavored to modernize her life and institutions constituted a deviation from the Western models that the new Turkish constitution had set out to emulate. Yet the existence of a strong and genuine political party modified what otherwise could have become merely a personal dictatorship, and gave the reformist regime a continuity which permitted it to survive Kemal's death.

By contrast, Iran's King-reformer, Reza Shah, chose the path of personal leadership without the benefit of a strong supporting party organization. Consequently, although his reforms were often drastic, Iran's process of modernization was more erratic and superficial than that of Turkey. Eschewing a popularly based party organization, Reza Shah succeeded in integrating only a part of Iran's reformist-minded intelligentsia, alienated the other part, and thus paved the way for the considerable political turmoil that followed his forced abdication.

VI

While Turkey and Iran were thus modernizing themselves within the framework of full sovereignty, the Arab world was partly under a newly imposed Western control in the form of mandates (and a temporary protectorate in Egypt), and thus had its attention divided between reform and liberation from imperialism. The preoccupation with the struggle for independence, which was characteristic of Egypt, Iraq, Syria, and Lebanon in the interwar period, did not prevent the elites of these countries from experimenting with new political institutions and processes. Educated Arab intelligentsia tended to be Western-oriented. Egypt and the countries of the Fertile Crescent that were under British and French control adopted Western-patterned constitutions and electoral laws in the 1920s and 1930s. While this choice partly reflected the dominant presence of the two Western tutelary Powers, it also corresponded to the Arab elites' genuine ideas about the most desirable forms of government. They believed that the alternatives were either a traditional Eastern state, with Islam providing the basis of its institutions and processes, or a modern secular state. That the latter would have to follow parliamentary representative patterns was taken for granted by the modernizers in those years. Yet their ideas were not universally accepted: the traditionalist Islam-oriented opposition engaged in heavy rear-guard battles. The Westernizers, such as Khalid M. Khalid, Taha Hussein, and Boutros Ghali, had to argue and persuade, particularly in Egypt, where—after the formal achievement of independence in the 1930s— many schools of thought were fiercely competing for supremacy.

In the meantime, political life in the Arab democracies underwent an evolution. During the period of foreign control, the prevalent trend had been toward the emergence of the dominant parties which, even though they embraced a wide spectrum of political orientations, united under the slogan of struggle for independence. Once independence was achieved, the old liberation slogans became insufficient. The dominant parties (such as the Wafd in Egypt and the National Bloc in Syria) suffered disintegration that resulted in the formation of splinter groups. Furthermore, they encountered competition from other political parties which hitherto had either been dormant or non-existent. The dominant party system thus gave way to a multiparty system and the latter, in turn, experienced considerable polarization that was due to the impact of such external influences as the European totalitarian ideologies, World War II, and the creation of the State of Israel. In addition to the established conventional parties, the late 1930s and 1940s saw the birth and growth of non-conventional ideological movements. Though greatly varying in ultimate objectives and programs, these new movements shared common rejection of the legitimacy of the existing state and alienation from its "establishment."

VII

Demands for radical change were not limited to ideologically oriented civilian groups; they also began to be voiced by younger army officers, who were frustrated by the 1948 defeat in Palestine and resentful of the corruption and inefficiency of professional politicians. The emancipation of several Arab countries from foreign control offered new vistas for the military. The use of force to bring down a civilian government could now be contemplated with a much greater likelihood of success than could have been hoped for when the presence of foreign troops acted as a deterrent. Less than a year after the Palestine defeat, army officers in Syria struck the first blow at the conventional-parliamentary fabric of the state. The result was the establishment of a military dictatorship under Colonel Husni Zaim, which was followed by the successive, coup-engendered regimes of Colonels Sami Hinnawi and Adib Shishakli. These successful challenges to constitutional legitimacy released and emboldened other non-conventional forces; of particular interest is the Baath Party, whose program called for liberation from bourgeois-dominated system, for Arab unity, and for socialism. Even the restoration of Syria's parliamentary democracy in 1954 did not fully free this nation from the military's constant interference with the governing process. At the same time, polarization between the radical left (Socialist and Communist) and the radical right had a highly unsettling effect on the parliamentary constitutionalism of the country.

While Syria was thus suffering from disruption and radical challenges to established values, Colonel Gamal Abdul Nasser overthrew Egypt's constitutional monarchy in 1952. Initially a *coup d'état* that merely expressed the Free Officers' protest against the evils of feudalism, corruption, and imperialism, the movement grew into a real revolution which effected major changes in the Egyptian society and made a profound impact upon the Arab world. In contrast to the Syrian-based Baath Party which paid considerable attention to ideological questions since its founding in 1947, the ruling *junta* in Egypt was pragmatically oriented. Nasser's initial ideas were expressed in his *Philosophy of the Revolution* (1953). In it he spoke of three concentric circles—Arab, Islamic, and African—in which Egypt was to play a central role; urged eradication of evils in the Egyptian society; and mused on the "role in search of a hero" in Arab history. These were significant but generalized statements that permitted a wide latitude of interpretation and practical application. No detailed program for economic and social action was yet offered, no blueprint for a political organization of the state was drawn. However, as his pragmatic actions were subjected to trial and error, his government gradually formulated an ideology. By 1956, the regime had moved from fulminations against the old ills to the slogan of a "socialist, cooperative, and democratic society." Simultaneously, major emphasis on Arab unity began to overshadow the concern for domestic reform. Egypt's merger with Syria in 1958 constituted the apogee of the Pan-Arab drive. It was a period of the pragmatic Pan-Arab offensive that was expressed in the interventions in Lebanon and Jordan, and in a militant unionist activity—legal and illegal—in most other Arab states. Syria's defection in 1961 compelled Egypt's revolutionary leadership to rethink its earlier assumptions and attempt to crystallize its ideology in the light of this experience. Adoption of the National Charter in the spring of 1962 was the result. The Charter defined the objectives of "Arab Socialism" and outlined, with greater precision, a revolutionary program to be followed in the domestic, intra-Arab, and foreign sectors.

One of the countries which was visibly affected by the revolutionary thought and action emanating from Cairo was Iraq. Having long resisted the Egyptian iconoclastic ideas while under the leadership of powerful Nuri Said, this stronghold of conservatism crumbled in July, 1958, giving place to a series of military dictatorships. The pragmatic approach of the first dictator, Abdul Karim Kassem, could be compared to that of Nasser in the early stages of his revolution. Emphasis was put on elimination and punishment of old-time political figures through police action and revolutionary court proceedings; on agrarian reform and some hastily conceived development projects; and on anti-imperialism and neutralism in foreign policy. Kassem obviously enjoyed the amenities of power, and neither he nor his most influential generals were in a hurry to unite with Egypt. A suggestive slogan of an "eternal Iraqi Republic" was to serve as an antidote to idealistic unionist schemes. Pan-Arabism had to await Kassem's overthrow by the Iraqi branch of the Baath to be restored to official respectability and socialism, as a pragmatic series of measures, was not introduced until 1964, the sixth anniversary of the revolution. Even at that time, socialism represented not so much an ideological commitment as an opportunistic policy of a new dictator, Abdul Salaam Aref, who was eager to please Cairo and secure its support for his vacillating regime. Under his successor, Abdur Rahman Aref, Iraq tried to follow the Egyptian organizational patterns more closely, primarily by attempting to set up a single government-controlled party, to be called, like its Egyptian prototype, the Arab Socialist Union. But in ideological formulations, it trailed behind both Cairo and Damascus. Yet, in spite of this "retardation," Iraq had in many ways broken its ties to the past and joined the Arab revolutionary camp. Though less clear and less consistent than those by Nasser, pronouncements of its successive leaders deserve our attention as another variety of Arab radicalism.

VIII

Our review of the "awakening" of the Middle East would be incomplete if we ignored those reformist endeavors that may best be given the generic name of "White Revolutions." The main features of these undertakings could be summed up as follows: a purposeful socioeconomic reform aimed at elimination of traditional class privileges; planned economic development in both the private and the public sectors, with a friendly bias toward free enterprise; promotion of education and social mobility; all of these steps carried out by an authoritarian or semi-authoritarian government, but within the framework of traditional political legitimacy and without the coercion typical of radical regimes. It was the Shah of Iran, Western-educated Mohammed Reza Pahlavi (1941–   ) who, after two decades of conservative-feudal supremacy alternating with revolutionary nationalism, launched a program of controlled reform that in some ways represented a radical departure from the past but also assured the continuity of the basic institutions of the state. Furthermore, it was he who not only coined the slogan of "White Revolution" but also articulated his ideas in two books published in the 1960s.

It may be debatable whether Saudi Arabia under King Faisal (1964–   ) should be included in the same category as Iran under its Shah. That major differences exist between the old sophisticated culture of Iran and the traditional patriarchalism of the Saudi Kingdom, there is no doubt. However, it may be argued that some important similarities link the two systems, and that the two follow parallel lines in their transitions from the old to the new. Saudi Arabia's ruler has an intelligent appreciation of the need for change; like the Shah of Iran, he encounters entrenched vested interests in certain traditional groups who resent and oppose reform; and he is aware of the aspirations of the growing numbers of Western-educated Saudi intelligentsia who, in the course of their travels and studies, have formed new ideas about economy, society, and government. His program of reform, enunciated in 1962 when he was Crown Prince and Premier, was designed to satisfy these aspirations in a way that would spare his country a revolutionary upheaval. Like the Shah's, his experiment has not yet been concluded; the results will await the verdict of history. If they succeed, their techniques will provide a valid alternative to the more turbulent methods of change embraced by the revolutionary centers of the Middle East.

I / ADMINISTRATIVE AND MILITARY REFORM

INTRODUCTION

The three selections in this chapter contain accounts of the early reforms in the Ottoman Empire and in its autonomous province of
Egypt, as well as a statement of the traditional concepts of government in Afghanistan. This choice has been dictated by the desire to
acquaint the reader, on the one hand, with the contrast between traditional thought and modern innovations in the world of Islam and,
on the other, with the sequence and scope of the initial changes
brought about by purposeful action of the Ottoman and Egyptian
rulers in the nineteenth century.

In his smoothly flowing narrative, the renowned British author
Sir Harry Luke presents the story of the first break with tradition
that was carried out under the energetic and imaginative leadership
of two remarkable Ottoman sultans, Selim III and Mahmud II, and
follows it up with a systematic description of the chain of reforms
known as the *Tanzimat*. The reader is introduced to the major obstacles that were faced by the modernizer-sultans, the foremost of which
was the opposition of the well-entrenched Corps of Jannissaries. This
Corps was suspicious of any move that was likely to reduce its coercive
power over the state and was ready to rebel to safeguard its privileged
position. The creation of a new, Western-patterned army, the curbing
of the feudal "lords of the valley" (the derebeys), and the purge from
the Ottoman court of the parasite officeholders are vividly described.
In a subsequent section, Sir Harry Luke gives an account of the
Tanzimat reforms and the impact they had upon the multiracial and
multireligious population of the Ottoman Empire. The tenor and
consequences of the two major rescripts, the *Hatt-i-Sherif* and the
Hatt-i-Humayun are presented and analyzed; so are other reformist measures that were taken between these two major legislative acts.

In his book, *The Economic Development of Modern Egypt*, A. E.
Crouchley gives what is possibly the most systematic description of

the domestic reforms of Mohammed Ali. This erstwhile, illiterate Albanian officer, who had landed in Egypt with the Ottoman troops sent to fight the invading army of Napoleon, not only succeeded in assuming supreme power in his adopted country and achieving its acknowledgment by the Turkish sultan but also was to have historians evaluate him as a radical reformer who shook the land of the Nile out of its centuries-old lethargy and placed it firmly on the political map of the modern world. There was something mysterious and fascinating about Mohammed Ali: his iron will power, his imaginative planning, his imperial ambitions, and his special charisma that inspired more fear than love, made him one of the most colorful and outstanding figures of the nineteenth century, worthy of keeping company with Napoleon, Frederick the Great of Prussia, and Disraeli. To do full justice to his entire personality would require a comprehensive biography. In selecting excerpts from Crouchley's book, our objective has been more modest: to give the reader an understanding and appreciation of the reforms this extraordinary man had carried out in Egypt, where he was faced with traditional inertia and grave international complications.

The third selection is taken from an authentic document, an autobiography of Abdur Rahman, Emir of Afghanistan. The excerpted sections deal with the ruler's ideas about government and representation. It is a statement in which the Emir tried to graft certain modern concepts upon the traditional base of an essentially tribal society.

1 / THE OTTOMAN EMPIRE:
THE FIRST BREAK WITH TRADITION

The forerunner of the two bold reformers among the Sultans, Selim III and Mahmud II, was Selim's uncle Abdul Hamid I, whose inauspicious reign from 1773 to 1789 was marked by the treaty of Küchük Qainarji and the advance of Russia at Turkey's expense. . . . Abdul Hamid was, as has been said, a well-intentioned ruler and, albeit weak both in character and intellect, had sufficient sense to perceive that the Empire could be regenerated from the state of decay into which it had sunk only by a reform of the part which was at once the rottenest and the most vital, the army. So he imported some French officers in the hope that these might succeed in reorganizing the Janissaries, and thus took the first step towards the Westernization of his country. In one other respect he made a notable departure from the habits of his predecessors by refusing to observe the usual practice (of which he

From Sir Harry Luke, *The Old Turkey and the New: From Byzantium to Ankara*, rev. ed. (London: Geoffrey Bles, Ltd., 1955), pp. 30–43, 44–50. Excerpted and reprinted by permission of the executors.

himself was a conspicuous victim) of immuring the heir to the throne in that outwardly beautiful but carefully guarded kiosk in the Seraglio which bore and still bears the sinister name of the *Qafes,* "the cage." On the contrary, he treated Selim with every mark of trust and affection and allowed him complete liberty.

When Selim succeeded to the throne, he brought to the government of his to all outward appearances tottering Empire a type of mind unusual among the rulers of Turkey. Not only had he enjoyed the unwonted privilege of freedom both intellectual and physical during the reign of his predecessor; he was well educated, a poet and a musician; he was alert, enterprising and untrammelled by prejudice or tradition. It was not altogether without significance that the beginning of his reign coincided with the beginnings of the French Revolution, and Selim was one of the first of the sovereigns of Europe to recognize the Republic.

Sharing his uncle's views as to the urgent necessity for reforming the army and with the ability and determination that were lacking in the ineffective Abdul Hamid I, Selim III established military schools, secured European officers to act as instructors, bought model ships from England for his navy, and imported shipwrights from France. He modernized his frontier fortresses, remodelled the whole artillery system, adopted the calibre of the French cannon, and began to build the cannon foundry which has given its name to the well-known Top-khané quarter of Galata. He created a corps of engineers and caused a work of Vauban to be translated into Turkish. Selim III and Mahmud II were the first [two] Ottoman sovereigns possessing any strength of character and individuality since Murad IV (1623–1640), the conqueror of Baghdad and the last Sultan to return to his capital victorious from a campaign which he had led in person. Under them the Empire made a new start.

Selim's reforms, affecting in particular the departments of war and finance, went by the general name of *Nizam-i-Jedid,* a term which may be translated "the new organization" or "the new institutions." The most significant single item of the reforms was the establishment of a new military force, drilled on Western lines and clothed in a distinctive uniform, to serve as a counterpoise to the Janissaries, for Selim realized that an effective reform of that corps was out of the question. . . .

Mahmud II, who had a French mother and is described by Halidé Edib Khanum[1] as the Peter the Great of the Ottoman Empire, was determined to pursue the policy of his cousin and preceptor, but his experiences impressed upon him the need to wait until he was master of the situation. . . .

If Mahmud can be compared with Peter the Great (although the

[1] *Turkey faces West* [New Haven, Conn., Yale University Press], 1930.

two monarchs were confronted with widely different conditions), he may be compared no less justly with Louis XI. When he came to the throne, the Ottoman Empire seemed to most observers both inside and outside its frontiers to be on the verge of collapse. Powerful and ambitious provincial governors were preparing their plans for carving out for themselves hereditary dominions from the body of the expiring Empire; some of the feudal Deré-beyis[2] of the rich valleys of Anatolia were seeking to consolidate their ancestral possessions. Mahmud had to cope not only with rebellious Moslem vassals such as Ali Pasha of Yanina, Husein Agha of Gradishka ("the Dragon of Bosnia"), Pasvanoghlu, Pasha of Vidin, Abdallah, Pasha of Acre and the yet more formidable Pasha of Egypt, Mohammed Ali, and his son Ibrahim. He was faced with such far-flung revolts as those of the Greeks in the Morea and the Wahhabis in Arabia, combined with the unsuccessful war with Russia that ended with the Peace of Adrianople in 1829. . . .

But we are not concerned here so much with Mahmud's external relationships and his foreign campaigns as with the revolution which he brought about in the internal organization of his dominions. Of this, the central factor was the suppression of the Janissaries, which, as he came to realize after seventeen years of experience of their lawlessness, could be effected only by their literal extermination. During these years, Mahmud was patiently preparing his stroke, partly by acquiring with gifts and appointments the goodwill of some of the Janissaries' supporters, partly by causing individual Janissaries of importance to be secretly put away. . . .

In 1811, his vassal Mohammed Ali set him an example by the massacre of the Mamluks, which the determined Pasha of Egypt caused to be carried out before his own eyes. We have already seen how the Janissaries had enforced the suppression of Selim III's well conceived "new model army." In 1825 Mahmud II felt himself strong enough to repeat the experiment of creating a force of trained regular troops, taking the precaution on this occasion to obtain from the Sheikh ul-Islam a *fetva* to the effect that it was the duty of Moslems to acquire military knowledge. . . .

The Janissaries reacted in the traditional manner. On the 12th June, 1826, were held the first drills under the new order. On the 16th June the Janissaries overturned their cauldrons. Mahmud, who was at Beshik-Tash on the other side of the Golden Horn, crossed the water

---

[2] Lit. "Lords of the Valley": the vassal dynasties which from the beginning of the 18th century grew up in some of the provinces of Asia Minor, descended from tribal chieftains or high Ottoman officials. Some of these dynasties, especially that of the Karaosmanoghlu, who from their capital of Mánissa (Magnesia) controlled the hinterland of Smyrna, maintained benevolent, efficient and popular administrations.

to the Seraglio and produced the standard of the Prophet from its place of custody and displayed it to the people. He filled the city with faithful troops and called upon the Janissaries to submit to the new dispensation. The *ulema,* consulted by the Sultan, issued the following fetva: "If unjust and violent men attack their brethren, fight the aggressors and send them before their natural judge." The Janissaries remaining defiant, war was now formally declared on the breakers of the public peace and guns were trained on the Et-meidan, the square in which they habitually mustered. Ibrahim Agha, the Commandant of the Artillery, known by the nickname of Kara Jehennem ("Black Hell"), made a last appeal to them to surrender. On their refusal he opened fire, and by the following day this once renowned body had ceased to exist and the Sheikh ul-Islam had formally proclaimed its extinction. . . .

With the destruction of the Janissaries Mahmud was able to resume into his own hands the supreme power in his somewhat though not drastically shrunken Empire, a power which had been severely limited in the previous reigns by that of the Janissaries and of powerful Grand Viziers. The Seraglio was now once more the fountain of authority and not, as had been the case for close on two centuries, the Porte. Mahmud restored that Palace government which was to become so marked a feature of the reign of his grandson Abdul Hamid II. Indeed, it was his success in this direction that saved Mahmud, whose passion for Westernization led him far in advance of public opinion, from the disaster that overtook Amanullah of Afghanistan a century later. Many of his reforms dealt with externals and sometimes offended his Moslem subjects without necessarily effecting equivalent advantages. Such a case occurred in 1834, when he struck coins bearing his portrait and thereby brought upon himself an insurrection which was suppressed, indeed, with a loss of 4,000 lives but in the event led to the recall of the issue. . . .

The effect of these reforms and of the abolition of the corps of the Janissaries was to make an end of mediaeval Turkey; and it was inevitable that there should disappear amid much that was bad much also that was picturesque.[3] One of the most conspicuous outward changes was that of the official dress of state functionaries from the floating oriental robes, with their silks, brocades and fur-lined pelisses, their embroidered sashes and their gigantic turbans, to a type of dress approximating to the European. . . . No more was the Seraglio to be the centre of the most lavish court in history, with its thousands

---

[3] But not, apparently, the respect paid to the science of astrology. The Khatt i-Sherif of 1834 reorganizing the departments of State was dated Tuesday, "the 26th Shaban, at twenty minutes past four o'clock, being the hour adjudged to be the most propitious for its promulgation."

of palace guards and pages, its *bostanjis* and *paltajis,* its *chaushes* and its *solaqs.* No longer was it to support the charges of the *bülbüljibashi* (Chief Keeper of the Nightingales) and the *tutijibashi* (Chief Keeper of the Parrots), of the *dülbend-agha* (Keeper of the Turban) and the *ibriqdar-agha* (Keeper of the Ewer), of the *qapaniji* (Keeper of the Robe of State) and the *sorghuchji* (Custodian of the Heron's Plume).[4]

The exodus from the Seraglio of the host of parasites with their sonorous sinecures effected by Mahmud may be likened to the purge of the Manchu Court in the Forbidden City through the mass expulsion of the eunuchs carried out in 1923 by the young Hsuan Tung, the last Emperor of China, . . . Coinage, weights and measures, public holidays, the establishment of a Government Gazette, were among the many matters dealt with by the indefatigable reformer in addition to the simplification of the Court and the all-important task of recreating the armed forces. He [Mahmud] sent young officers to be trained in the military schools of Western Europe; he toured his provinces, a thing which no Sultan had done before except when riding at the head of his troops on a campaign; he gave some security to his officials by formally relinquishing the right enjoyed by himself and his predecessors to confiscate the property of deceased functionaries. And in the external appearance of his subjects Mahmud effected the greatest vestimentary change experienced by the Turkish people until the days of the Ankara Republic. It is one of the minor ironies of history that the fez, which Mustafa Kemal abolished as being a symbol of an effete and Islamic Orientalism which he wished to eradicate from the Turkish nation, should have been regarded by the Turks of Mahmud's day as one of the most obnoxious innovations of the *Giaur Sultan,* when he imposed on his *muslimin* this head-dress borrowed from the despised and rebellious Greek *rayahs.* . . . Mahmud II lost Greece, he lost Egypt in all but name, he was involved in conflict with England, with France and, above all, with Russia; he suffered, in the latter's favour, a reduction of his rights over to the Danubian Principalities; he had to concede autonomy to the Serbs. Nevertheless, when he died in 1839, he left his Empire stronger than he found it. For, with a tenacity astonishing in the face of the almost insuperable difficulties by which he was harassed without a respite from inside and outside his dominions, he had succeeded in making himself master in his own house. If that house was now a smaller one, it was on that account more compact and the more easily controlled. . . .

The changes wrought by Mahmud II in the fabric of the Turkish State were the precursors of the changes wrought in it a hundred years

---

[4] For a description of the Old Seraglio as it was at the end of the Sultanate *cf.* Chap. 7 of the present writer's *An Eastern Chequerboard,* Lovat Dickson, London, 1934.

later by the Government of Ankara. They constituted the first deliberate break with the traditions of Byzantium.

The Era of the Tanzimat

Thanks to the work of Selim III and Mahmud II, the Ottoman Empire had now begun to assume in part the semblance of a modern State administered on uniform lines. The autonomous or semi-autonomous dynasts in the Moslem districts had been eliminated, provincial government had been centralized within a symmetrical administrative framework, there was now something like an organized Civil Service. But in one important respect a wide gulf was still fixed between Turkey and the countries of the West, namely, that not all categories of the Sultan's subjects were equal before the law. The Moslems constituted the ruling and privileged caste, to which were attached, however, certain onerous obligations from which the *rayahs* were exempt; non-Moslems lay, despite advantages by no means to be underrated, in other respects under definite disabilities.

Even the diminished heritage to which Abdul Mejid succeeded on the death of his father, Mahmud II, embraced within its borders one of the most varied assemblages of race, custom, language, culture and civilization that have ever come under the control of a single Government. The new Sultan ruled in Europe over Turks, Greeks, Serbs, Bulgars, over Moldavians and Wallachians later to be welded into Rumanians, over Albanians, Bosnians, Jews, gypsies; in Africa, over Egyptians, Copts, Berbers, negroes of many stocks; in Asia, in addition to some of those already enumerated, over Armenians, Kurds, the ancient races and Churches of the Nestorians and the Jacobites who still speak the Syriac tongue, over devil-worshipping Yezidis, over the Sabaeans from the banks of the Tigris who constitute the only living link with the moon-worshippers of ancient Charran, over the tiny remnant of the Samaritans, over Druses with their mysterious amalgam of ill-assorted beliefs, over Lazes, who are a Moslem branch of the Georgian race; last, but not least in numbers or importance, over the Arabs.

And the Arabs under his sway were a microcosm in themselves, embracing every type of Arabic-speaking person from the pastoral inhabitants of the Arabian peninsula, organized in tribes with a natural tendency towards intertribal warfare, to the dwellers in the great cities of Syria and Iraq with their ancient civilizations; from the wild and nomad Bedouin in their black "tents of Kedar" to the settled *fellahin* in their stone-built villages and the lordly Effendis in the palaces of Damascus. . . .

It is doubly true to describe this anthropological and ethnographic collection as a mosaic of races; for, as in a mosaic each tessera is of one colour only, frequently distinct from the colour of the next, so its races met within the Ottoman Empire without mingling. So, too, did the *millet* system on which the State was based add constitutional and legal barriers to perpetuate the cleavage already established by differences of faith, social type and cultural aspirations and by the absence of elements making for uniformity and fusion. Not only were the non-Moslem *millets* alien to and in some cases antagonistic to the peoples embraced within the *millet* of Islam; they were alien to and generally antagonistic to one another. Nay more, there existed, as we shall see later, the sharpest antagonism between Slav and Hellene within the single *millet* of Rûm.

The keynote of the reigns of the brothers Abdul Mejid and Abdul Aziz, that is to say, of the years 1839 to 1876, was the continuation, at all events in theory, of the reforming work of their father by means of enactments aiming at the removal of the legal disabilities of the *rayah.* Mahmud's premature death had not left him the time to pass from the destruction of the old order to the completion of the new; but his elder son and successor, Abdul Mejid, proceeded without a break to the next stage. Ascending the throne in July, 1839, by November of the same year he had issued from the pavilion of Gül-Khané ("the Rose-Chamber") the Khatt-i-Sherif (Imperial Rescript) embodying the comprehensive reforms commonly known as the Tanzimat.[5]

The charter of the Tanzimat affected to remove the disabilities of the non-Moslem sections of the population by guaranteeing the lives, property and honour of the Sultan's subjects irrespective of creed or race, while it aimed at regularizing internal administration by reforming the incidence of taxation. It created a Council of State, a Penal Code and a State Bank; it provided for secondary education; it placed conscription on a more equitable footing and limited the period of military service; it abolished, ephemerally, the farming of taxes. It is interesting to speculate as to the probable course of Turkish history had the Khatt-i-Sherif of Gül-Khané and its sequel, the Khatt-i-Humayun, been carried into effect; but it was not altogether the young Sultan's fault that these reforms, so excellent in theory, proved largely abortive in practice.

In the first place, Abdul Mejid possessed none of his father's virile character and ruthless resolution. While liberal-minded, kindly and well-meaning, he was a feeble voluptuary lacking both the will-power and the physical and mental vigour necessary to impose his reforms on a reluctant population. For the Tanzimat pleased neither Moslem nor *rayah;* it was, for example, the opposition of the Christian *sarrafs* (money-changers) of Constantinople which broke down the attempt to abolish tax-farming. Furthermore, the new Sultan had, like his father,

---

[5] Plural of the Arabic *tanzim,* organization, ordering.

to cope with foreign complications. It was not until he had been two years on the throne that the problem of Mohammed Ali was liquidated by the grant to that turbulent satrap of the hereditary pashalik of Egypt with the transmission of the dignity to his descendants in the order of primogeniture, a keenly desired concession. In the later years of the reign he was faced with the renewed pressure of Russia, which culminated in the Crimean War. It was therefore to his credit, even though much of the impetus and pressure came from his Crimean allies, that he persisted with his reforming policy, reiterated in the Khatti-i-Humayun ("Illustrious Rescript"), which he issued on the 18th February, 1856.

This edict "confirmed and consolidated" the guarantees of security of personal property and of the preservation of their honour to all subjects of the Empire, without distinction of class or religion, promised in the Tanzimat; it confirmed the privileges and spiritual immunities granted by previous Sultans to the non-Moslem communities. Patriarchs were to be nominated for life, so that an end might be put to the scandal of frequent depositions; the ecclesiastical dues on which they and other heads of non-Moslem religious bodies had hitherto subsisted were abolished and replaced by fixed salaries, assessed according to the rank and dignity of the ecclesiastics concerned. Elective assemblies, partly clerical, partly lay, were set up for the temporal administration of the property of the *millets,* who were given permission to repair, when necessary, their churches, schools, hospitals and cemeteries "according to their original plan." Distinctions tending to make any class of the Sultan's subjects inferior to another class on account of their religion, language or race, were effaced from the administrative protocol. All forms of religion were to be freely professed; none could be compelled to change his faith, nor was any man's religion to be a bar to public employment. All legal proceedings were to be transacted in public; the evidence of witnesses was to be received in the courts without distinction of race or creed. Prison administration was to be reformed, torture abolished, the organization of the police "revised in such a manner as to give to all the peaceable subjects of my Empire the strongest guarantees for the safety both of their persons and property." It was made lawful for foreigners to acquire landed property. Taxes were to be levied without religious or racial discrimination; and—"the equality of taxes entailing equality of burdens"—Christians and members of other non-Moslem bodies were made subject to the obligations of the law of recruitment. Public works were to be undertaken in the provinces; an annual budget was to be drawn up and published; banks and other similar institutions were to be established and the monetary and financial system of the State to be overhauled.

It will be apparent, even from the above brief summary, that the Khatt-i-Humayun would have converted Turkey, had it been implemented, into something like a model State. But one of the outstanding features of the Ottoman Empire in its decadence has been the contrast between theory and practice in the working of its institutions. The statute-book might contain the most admirable provisions; their enforcement was another matter. Yet it would be going too far to regard the Tanzimat and the Khatt-i-Humayun as nothing more than window-dressing whereby Sultan and Viziers, determined that they should remain a dead letter, hoped to dupe and appease prying and critical Western Powers.

Many circumstances caused the reforms to fail, foremost among them the very nature of the Empire, whose essential characteristic had been the barriers between its component peoples. Other reasons were: lack of driving-power on the part of Abdul Mejid; the hostility of the conservatives, which paralysed the activities of the would-be reformers; and, as in the case of the Tanzimat, the dislike of some of the reforms on the part of the intended beneficiaries themselves. What the Orthodox hierarchy thought of the clause substituting fixed salaries for such dues as they had previously been able to extort from their flocks will be referred to in another chapter, while the provision admitting all sections of Ottoman subjects to the army was rendered abortive by the opposition of Moslems and Christians alike. The former asserted that their lives would be in danger if the Christians were armed; the latter declared that they would not fight under the standard of the Prophet or against other Christians. But the two charters of liberty of Abdul Mejid's reign were not wholly sterile. Ministries of Justice and Public Instruction were set up, the law was codified, judicial processes were improved, schools were opened, banks were founded. And it was something to have decreed, if only on paper, the equality in the eyes of the State and of the law of every class of the Sultan's subjects.

2 / MOHAMMED ALI OF EGYPT: AUTOCRATIC REFORMER

Chronological Survey

The departure of the French left Egypt in a very unsettled state. The Sultan, nominal master of the country, was not strong enough to assert his authority; the remnants of the Mamelukes came back and attempted, without success, to regain their former authority; the

From A. E. Crouchley, *The Economic Development of Modern Egypt* (London: Longmans, Green and Co., Ltd., 1938), pp. 40–44, 101–103. Reprinted by permission of the publisher.

English still had an army near Alexandria; and finally, numbers of foreign mercenaries, mainly Albanians, brought in during the war, were elements of disorder and unrest. There was a period of lawlessness, intrigue and factional fighting out of which a young Albanian captain, Mohamed Ali, by his ability and force of character hoisted himself to the position of power. By 1805 he had already succeeded in getting himself named Pasha. The next thirty-five years were to be spent in a struggle to keep, extend, and consolidate the position thus acquired. His clear intellect grasped the essential fact that his success in that struggle depended upon the strength he could draw from the potentially rich province of which he had made himself the temporary master. He set himself, with boundless energy and determination, to make of Egypt a country richer and stronger than its nominal master, Turkey. And in the struggle and effort of his reign modern Egypt was born.

Economically, the period of his reign divides itself into three main sections.

In the first period, from 1805 to 1816, Mohamed Ali dealt one by one with the English, the Turks, the Mamelukes and finally, the Albanians, who had helped him to power. By 1816, he thus had, apart from the latent jealousy and hostility of the Sultan, no serious challenge to his power.

In this same period, he reformed the system of taxation, abolished the Iltizam system of farming out the land tax, readjusted the basis of taxation and arranged for taxes to be paid direct to the government.

By successive steps, from 1808 to 1814, he swept away the privileged classes of landowners that had developed under the previous regime, gathered into his own hands the nominal ownership of all the land in the country, and imposed the miri, or land tax, on all cultivated land.

By firm discipline and ruthless suppression of revolts and disorders, the country was gradually pacified and subdued. Having thus asserted his dominion at home, Mohamed Ali turned to wider fields, and from 1811 to 1818 he was engaged in a war in Arabia, originally undertaken at the request of the Sultan, but destined in his own mind to bring Arabia under Egyptian domination.

The second period, 1816–1840, saw Mohamed Ali, in a great effort to achieve independence and empire, gather into his hands all the productive resources of Egypt and with indomitable will impose upon the people an almost incredible effort of development. To his ownership of all the land of the country, Mohamed Ali added the ownership of all the agricultural and manufactured products by declaring one after another of them government monopolies and ordering that all such products must be delivered to government storehouses. The products thus received were paid for at a tariff of prices fixed in advance by the government. These prices were very low, sometimes only one-half or one-third of the market value of the goods, and in the resale, particularly for export, Mohamed Ali drew large profits from these monopolies, which became, indeed, the keystone of his financial policy and the means of equipping his army and navy and paying for his military operations. At the same time a vast programme of agricultural, industrial, military and naval development was undertaken.

Chronologically, the period resolves itself into a number of alternating periods of warfare, during which the resources of the country were strained practically to breaking point, and periods of peace, during which the boundless energy of the Pasha was engaged in strengthening and developing the economic organisation of the country in preparation for the next struggle. In this way the war in Arabia, 1811–1815 and 1816–1818, was followed by the expeditions to the Soudan and Abyssinia, 1818 to 1820. In the meantime, from 1816 to 1820, Mohamed Ali monopolised the industries and the principal summer crops. To extend the cultivation of the latter, large numbers of canals were constructed in the Delta designed to carry water in summer for the purposes of irrigation. In 1819, the Mahmoudia Canal was built, joining Alexandria to the Nile at Atf, thus providing an outlet for the export of crops to Europe by way of Alexandria.

During this period, too, the new army of fellahin was started, and large-scale industry introduced.

In the short period of peace after 1820, the reforms introduced were carried on apace. The irrigation works in the Delta were rapidly extended, every possible effort was exerted to increase agricultural production and—event of capital importance—the cultivation of cotton on a large scale was undertaken. New factories were opened. The army and navy were increased. A great fleet was built up, with ships bought from abroad. The increased power at the command of the Pasha was revealed in the war in Greece, 1824–1826. It was during this war, under the stress of war conditions, that he was able finally to impose his new system of administration and monopoly on all branches of the economic life of the country.

After the disaster of Navarino, in 1827, where his fleet was destroyed, and the evacuation of Morea, there was a period of calm and relative prosperity. Mohamed Ali used it to undertake a big programme of development of public works destined to extend the cultivated area, to increase agricultural production and to develop his industries. In Alexandria, the Arsenal was established. The monopoly system was extended to crops consumed in the country itself. Hitherto the agricultural monopolies had been aimed at crops to be sold to foreign merchants, or in the towns.

The brief period of peace and prosperity soon gave way to war. In the first Syrian campaign, 1831–1833, all efforts were again directed to the prosecution of the war. During the war, as usual at such periods, finances were strained and various expedients were resorted to in order to obtain money. The salaries of government officials fell in arrears; loans were obtained from merchants on the security of crops for future delivery.

The successful termination of the first Syrian campaign, in 1833, was followed by a great burst of economic activity. In the great year of projects, 1834, work was started on two huge schemes, the Delta Barrage and the Cairo-Suez railway, neither of which, however, was destined to be completed for many years. In the same year a currency reform endowed Egypt with a system of national currency. The next few years saw a big increase in agricultural production and trade, though there was a commercial crisis in Alexandria in 1837, as a result of a sudden fall in the price of cotton.

This second period terminated with the second Syrian campaign in 1839–1840, the coalition of European powers against Mohamed Ali and the Treaty of London. The political aspects therein involved do not concern this study, except that in so far as the political status of Mohamed Ali as hereditary ruler of Egypt was formally established, an end was put to the strained conditions which had so markedly affected the economic progress of the country in the earlier period. His army, which by 1840 had risen to 200,000 men, was reduced to 18,000.

The Treaty of London, however, had most important economic effects. In particular, it made effective a commercial convention, passed in 1838, between England and the Porte. This convention allowed foreign merchants to enter freely into all parts of the Ottoman dominions, Egypt specifically included, and to buy from the inhabitants the products of the soil and industry of those regions. The application of this treaty meant the collapse of the whole system of monopolies erected by Mohamed Ali and a profound modification of the economic structure of the country. Henceforth the farmers were free, within limits, to cultivate what they pleased. The development of agriculture and the choice of crops to be grown became dependent upon the will of the farmers rather than the imposed orders of an autocratic government. The industries collapsed under the weight of their own top-heavy superstructure. The government, deprived of the profits drawn from the monopolies, was obliged to seek for other sources of revenue, in reformed taxation. Mohamed Ali, freed from the fear of war, turned again to the development of agriculture and, at the very end of his reign, again took up the plan for the Delta Barrage abandoned since 1836. A new start was made, but before it could be completed, the old Pasha died. . . .

3 / AFGHANISTAN: CONCEPTS OF GOVERNMENT

Though in every chapter of my book some advice or instruction has been given to my sons and successors, I have thought it important to give the above hints as a guide and foundation for the principles which he is to follow. I will now proceed to discuss another matter, the mode of administering and ruling Afghanistan, which ought to develop gradually but steadily, so that the kingdom may become a strong, self-governed kingdom.

The foundation stone of a Constitutional Government has been laid by me; though the machinery of Representative Government has not taken any practical shape as yet. It is necessary that every ruler should observe and consider the various modes of Government adopted in various countries, not jump at conclusions in a hurry, but apply the best modes of governing gradually, modifying them according to circumstances and the position of his country. In my belief, the best principle of governing was that laid down by the great lawgiver of Arabia, Mahomed, our Holy Prophet, may God bless Him. It was the system of a representative Government divided into two parties; the Muhagir and the Ansar. The Government was carried out on the principles of democracy; every member had the power of giving his vote and opinion; and the majority was to be followed. I have made the following arrangements for making Afghanistan into a Constitutional Government. There are three kinds of representatives who assemble in my court and audience for consulting with me about the supplies for war materials and various other state affairs. These three classes of people are called Sirdars (or aristocracy), Khawanin Mulki (Commons, or representatives of the people), and Mullahs (ecclesiastical heads and church representatives). The first of these take their seats in the court by hereditary right, subject to the approval of the sovereign. The second are elected from among the chiefs of the country who are chosen in the following manner. In every village or town there is one man elected by the citizens of that town who must have certain qualifications which I need not give here in detail. He is elected by the inhabitants of that village or town, and is called Malik or Arbab. These Maliks or Arbabs elect another man from among them, but one of greater influence and greater importance in their province or constituency, whom they call their Khan (or chief). Our House of Commons is composed of these Khans. But in the matter of electing the Khans the final authority rests with the Sovereign who judges of the suitability of the election of these persons for the post of Khan by

From Mahomed Khan, ed., *The Life of Abdur Rahman* (London: John Murray, 1900), II, 187–90. Reprinted by permission of the publisher.

their merits, their position, their loyalty, their services or the services of their fathers: these facts are considered as well as the fact that the candidate has been already chosen by the people. The third party consists of the Khan Alum (the head of religion), the Kazis (ecclesiastical judges), Muftis (ecclesiastical heads of churches and inferior courts), and Mullahs (the priests). The last-named people are the ecclesiastical heads, and rise to the position of holding their seats in the Parliament by passing examinations in religious studies and in the laws of the country, and by serving in the religious departments.

This constitutional body has not yet attained the ability nor the education to qualify it for being entrusted with authority of any importance for giving sanction to Bills or Acts of the Government. But in time they will perhaps have such authority, and in this way the people of Afghanistan will be governed for their own safety by themselves. I must strongly urge my sons and successors never to make themselves puppets in the hands of these representatives of Constitutional Government; they must always reserve to themselves the full power of organizing the army and keep it in their own hands, without admitting any right of interference by their constitutional advisers. And, further, they must keep the power of vetoing any reforms, schemes or bills passed and sanctioned by their Council or Durbar, or Parliament, as this body may be called.

My sons and successors should not try to introduce new reforms of any kind in such a hurry as to set the people against their ruler, and they must bear in mind that in establishing a Constitutional Government, introducing more lenient laws, and modelling education upon the system of Western universities; they must adopt all these gradually as the people become accustomed to the idea of modern innovations, so that they will not abuse the privileges and reforms given to them.

II / REFORM WITHIN ISLAM: FUNDAMENTALISM AND MODERNISM

INTRODUCTION

This chapter has reform of Islam as a religion as its principal focus. The five selections begin with what has become a classic in the contemporary literature on Islam: Sir Hamilton A. R. Gibb's *Modern Trends in Islam*. In the sections of the book chosen here, the author reviews two main streams of reformist thought in Islam, the fundamentalist and the modernist. With reference to the latter, he introduces the reader to the notions of the changing concept of *ijma* (consensus of the community) and stresses the role which the foremost spokesman of modernism, Mohammed Abduh, played in isolating "the religious element in the reform movement from the emotional influences of the revolutionary or nationalist program." "The effect of his teaching," points out Sir Hamilton, "was to separate the religious issues from the political conflict, so that (even though they might continue to be associated) they were no longer interdependent and each was set free to develop along its own appropriate lines."

Following this introduction, the next two selections (Nos. 5 and 6) deal with two principal varieties of fundamentalism in Islamic reform, the Wahhabi and the Senussi. Both were selected as excellent illustrations of how the fundamentalist variety of reform was producing, in contrast to Abduh's modernist approach, a close intertwining between the religious and the political spheres and how both have led to the creation of theocratic or divine nomocratic states which formed around the nucleus of the original religious organization. In his *Saudi Arabia*, H. St. John Philby, one of the foremost explorers and Arabists which England produced in modern times and a convert to Islam, gives us a vivid picture of the growth of the second Wahhabi empire under the leadership of the outstanding Arab of the twentieth century, Abdul Aziz ibn Saud. Similarly, in *The Sanusi of Cyrenaica*, E. E. Evans-Pritchard describes the nature of development of the Senussi order, discusses its similarities and differences with the Wahhabi movement, and points out the connection between the new order and the tribal organization of Cyrenaican bedouin.

The two last selections of the chapter (Nos. 7 and 8) focus on the Moslem Brotherhood as an ambivalent movement combining elements of fundamentalism and modernism. In her *Nationalism and Revolution in Egypt,* Christina Phelps Harris concentrates on the career, teachings, and program of the Brotherhood's founder, Hasan al-Banna. Relying on Banna's original writings, she reviews in some detail his ideas on government, law, society, culture, and economics. The next selection is excerpted from the book *Social Justice in Islam* by Sayed Kotb, one of the Brotherhood's most articulate and intellectual leaders, and is devoted entirely to its political theory. The picture that emerges is that this organization had a very fundamentalist concept of government. The mode of thinking brings the author closer to such classical theorists of the caliphate as Mawardi and Baghdadi than to modern political scientists. At the same time, Kotb is genuinely concerned with the achievement of such essentially modern aims of contemporary society as social justice, equality, limitation of power, and economic abundance.

4 / VARIETIES OF ISLAMIC REFORM

It may, I think, be granted, without taking an unduly pessimistic view of human nature, that if a state of equilibrium in any organism is accompanied by relaxation of tension, the usual consequence is that the organism tends insensibly to lower its standards. We have seen that the spread of Islam in the new territories to the east and south, in Asia and Africa, was largely the work of the Sufi brotherhoods and that the brotherhoods were in many cases tolerant of traditional usages and habits of thought which ran contrary to the strict practice of Islamic unitarianism. The upshot of this was that in the Muslim community as a whole the balance was gradually tilting against the high orthodox doctrine. The ulema were being dragged in the wake of the Sufis, and their resistance was being gradually transferred, so to speak, to a lower level. Theology was beginning to compromise with Sufi doctrine, the citadel was weakening from within. Sooner or later this downhill movement was bound to call out a reaction—bound to call it out, that is, if the Koran remained a living force in the life of the community—and because of the general declension the reaction, when it came, was formulated in more violent and uncompromising terms.

From H. A. R. Gibb, *Modern Trends in Islam* (Chicago: University of Chicago Press, 1947), pp. 25–29, 33, 43–45. Copyright 1947 by The University of Chicago. Reprinted with the permission of The University of Chicago Press.

It is significant that this reaction finally emerged in the Arab world, but less significant—as I see the facts at present—that it emerged in Arabia. The movement led by Muhammad Ibn Abd al-Wahhab in the middle of the eighteenth century was not, in principle, an Arabian movement. Its inspiration lay in the puritanical Hanbalite school, the school which recognized *ijma* only within the narrowest limits and produced Ibn Taimīya and which still, though much reduced in numbers, lived on in the Hijaz, Iraq, and Palestine.[1] Muhammad Ibn Abd al-Wahhab, in selecting his native central Arabia as the scene of his mission, was (whether consciously or unconsciously) adopting the same course as was taken by the leaders of similar reformist movements both before and after his time. This course was to seek out some region which was out of reach of an organized political authority, where there was, therefore, an open field for the propagation of his teaching and where, if he were successful, he might be able to build up a strong theocratic organization by the aid of warlike tribesmen. It was by such means that the early Shi'ites and the Berber empires of the Almoravids and the Almohads had gained their first successes; and so, too, Ibn Abd al-Wahhab achieved his initial purpose by alliance with the house of Saud in the fastnesses of Nejd.

The results of this first Wahhabi movement were, and still are, far reaching. In its original phase it shocked the conscience of the Muslim community by the violence and intolerance which it displayed not only toward saint-worship but also toward the accepted orthodox rites and schools. By holding them all guilty of infidelity to the pure transcendental ideal and excluding them from the status of true believers, the first Wahhabis repeated the error of the Kharijites (the uncompromising idealists of the first century of Islam), alienated the sympathy and support of the orthodox, and made themselves heretics. Ultimately, therefore, like all fighting minorities who reject any kind of co-operation with more powerful majorities, their opposition was, in a political sense, crushed. But in its ideal aspect, in the challenge which it flung out to the contamination of pure Islamic monotheism by the infiltration of animistic practices and pantheistic notions, Wahhabism had a salutary and revitalizing effect, which spread little by little over the whole Muslim world.

During the greater part of the nineteenth century, however, the revitalizing element in Wahhabism was obscured by its revolutionary theocratic aspect. It set an example of revolt against an "apostate"

---

[1] Even outside the ranks of the Hanbalis, there were individual cases of fundamentalist reaction before Ibn Abd al-Wahhab; see, e.g., Jabarti, I, 48–49, and the note on Muhammad b. Ismail as-San‘ani by J. Schacht in *Zeitschrift für Semitistik,* VI (Leipzig, 1928), 203, with which cf. Brockelmann, *Supplement,* II, 556.

Muslim government; and its example was the more eagerly followed in other countries as their Muslim governments fell more and more patently under European influence and control. At the beginning of the nineteenth century it inspired the Indian movements led by Shari'at Allah and Sayyid Ahmad against the decadent Mogul sultanate, the Sikhs, and the British. A few years later, in the middle and second half of the nineteenth century, the militant and reformist order founded by the Algerian shaikh, Muhammad Ibn Ali as-Sanūsi, in Cyrenaica set up a theocratic state in southern Lybia and equatorial Africa in protest against the secularist laxity of the Ottoman Sultans; and the Mahdist brotherhood was organized by Muhammad Ahmad as the instrument of revolt in the eastern Sudan against Turco-Egyptian rule and its European agents. Even in such distant regions as Nigeria and Sumatra, Wahhabi influence contributed to the outbreak of militant movements.

The same revolutionary theocratic impulse underlay the activity of the famous revivalist, Jamal ad-Din al-Afghani (d. 1897), but with a significant change in direction. By this time the current of European infiltration was swelling to a flood. Jamal ad-Din strove with all his energies to dam and, if possible, to sweep back the encroaching tide by means of the organized power of the existing Muslim governments. He brought inspiration and a popular program to the Pan-Islamic movement by restating the bases of the Islamic community in terms of nationalism. But though Pan-Islamism was, on the political side, aimed against European penetration, it had an internal reforming aspect also. Jamal ad-Din attacked with the same vigor the abuses which he saw within Islam and the evils of the Muslim governments. It was an essential element in his thought that the Muslim peoples should purify themselves from religious errors and compromises, that Muslim scholars should be abreast of modern currents of thought, and that the Muslim state should stand out as the political expression and vehicle of sound koranic orthodoxy.

Although these various attempts at revolutionary political action all ended in failure, when they are looked at from the outside, they had, nonetheless, strong and enduring effects in the religious sphere. They spread the Wahhabi emphasis on pure doctrine and the reassertion of koranic orthodoxy far and wide—not in the sense of preaching and popularizing the narrow tenets of Wahhabism but in the sense of recalling the great body of Muslims, learned and unlearned alike, to a fuller understanding of what Muslim faith demands and of the dangers with which it was menaced. Sir Muhammad Iqbal has suggested that if Jamal ad-Din's "indefatigable but divided energy could have devoted itself entirely to Islam as a system of human belief and conduct, the world of Islam, intellectually speaking, would have been on a much more solid ground today." [2] If, as he [Muhammad Iqbal] seems to imply by the context of this sentence, he means that Jamal ad-Din was a man who by his "deep insight into the inner meaning of the history of Muslim thought and life" would have been able to "rethink the whole system of Islam," then I confess that I find it difficult to agree with him. The time for "rethinking" was not yet come. The first and most urgent task, and the essential prerequisite for "rethinking the whole system of Islam," was to set Islam back again on its old solid foundations, so that the "new spirit" which Iqbal postulates should work upon principles clear, precise, and free from alloy of any kind. And Jamal ad-Din's sole published work, *The Refutation of the Materialists*,[3] does not by any means suggest a man of such intellectual capacity as Iqbal indicates.

Before a beginning could, in fact, be made with the reformulation of Islamic doctrine, it was necessary to isolate the religious element in the reform movement from the emotional influences of the revolutionary or nationalist program. This was the task taken up and to some extent accomplished by Jamal ad-Din's most influential pupil, the Egyptian shaikh, Muhammad Abduh, in the later period of his active career. The effect of his teaching was to separate the religious issues from the political conflict, so that (even though they might continue to be associated) they were no longer interdependent and each was set free to develop along its own appropriate lines. If he had been able to win more general support for this doctrine, he might indeed have created a revolution in the thought and outlook of the Muslim world. But among the main body of Muslims, whether conservatives or reformers, it has never been fully accepted. The conservatives rejected it—as they rejected almost all Muhammad Abduh's ideas—a priori and on principle; the modernists, who claim to be his followers, did not understand it and, for external reasons, fell back upon Jamal ad-Din's activism. Although Muhammad Abduh's influence remains alive and is continuing to bear fruit in present-day Islam, the immediate outward consequence of his activities was the emergence of a new fundamentalist school calling themselves the "Salafiya," the upholders of the tradition of the fathers of the Islamic church. . . .

In a prolific output of writings and lectures, Abduh dealt, of course, with a great variety of topics, some at length and some more cursorily. But the program which he bequeathed to the reform movement can be summed up under four main heads: (1) the purification of Islam

[2] *The Reconstruction of Religious Thought in Islam,* 2d ed. ([London:] Oxford [Univ. Press], 1934) , p. 92.

[3] A French translation of this work by Mlle. A.-M. Goichon was published at Paris in 1942.

from corrupting influences and practices; (2) the reformation of Muslim higher education; (3) the re-formulation of Islamic doctrine in the light of modern thought; and (4) the defense of Islam against European influences and Christian attacks. . . .

In Muhammad Abduh's own thought the purification of Islam was a wide concept, embracing many features of contemporary thought and practice. But the aspect which found the readiest and most widespread support was the campaign to eradicate the vices and distortions which permeated the religious life of the people. . . .

What impressed his lay readers was the spirit in which he approached questions of dogma and practice, and especially his forceful rejection of the traditional teaching that the doctrines of the Koran had been authoritatively expounded once for all by the doctors of the first three centuries of Islam, that their expositions had been confirmed by an irrevocable *ijma,* and that no free investigation of the sources could be tolerated.

> Islam has condemned blind imitation in matters of belief and the mechanical performance of religious duties. . . . Islam drew the intellect out of its slumber . . . and raised its voice against the prejudices of ignorance, declaring that man was not made to be led by the rein but that it was in his nature to guide himself by science and knowledge, the science of the universe and the knowledge of things past. . . . Islam turns us away from exclusive attachment to the things that come to us from our fathers. . . . It shows us that the fact of preceding us in point of time constitutes neither a proof of knowledge nor a superiority of mind and intellect, that ancestors and descendants are equal in critical acumen and in natural abilities. . . . Thus it delivered reason from all its chains, liberated it from the blind imitation that had enslaved it, and restored to it its domain in which it makes its own decision in accordance with its own judgment and wisdom. . . . Nevertheless, it must humble itself before God alone and stop at the limits set by the Faith; but within these bounds there is no barrier to its activity and there is no limit to the speculations which may be carried on under its aegis.[4]

The effect upon the rising generation of such passages, with their repeated emphasis upon the rights of reason within its own field, was further strengthened by his arguments that there can be no conflict between religion and physical science, that the Koran commands men to engage in scientific studies, and that "our first duty is to endeavour with all our might and main to spread the sciences in our country." [5]

The most encouraging feature in all this for the new Muslim pro-

[4] *Rissalat al-Tawhid,* trans. B. Michel and Moustapha Abdel Razik (Paris: 1925), pp. 107–109; cf. also *ibid.,* pp. 6–7, and Adams, *op. cit.,* pp. 127–33.

[5] Adams [Charles C.], *op. cit. [Islam and Modernism in Egypt,* London: Humphrey Milford, 1933], pp. 134–35.

fessional classes was that the rejection of authority and the assurance of the harmony between science and religion was issued by one of the highest religious authorities and not (as might have been expected) put forward by the leaders of secular education in the teeth of ecclesiastical opposition. Thus they were both liberated from, and forearmed against, the attempted control of those whom they called the "obscurantists" of al-Azhar.

But the divorce between secular and religious education carried with it the serious consequence that those liberties were interpreted in a manner very different from Muhammad Abduh's interpretation. The graduate of the religious schools was well aware of those "limits set by the Faith" to the exercise of reason; to the secularly educated they were both less substantial and more subjective; and the wider and deeper the new education goes, the greater the divergence becomes. Leaving aside altogether the growth of a pure rationalism which rejects all the claims of religious dogma (and it is noteworthy that, although such a tendency exists, it finds only a very limited expression in Muslim lands) and confining ourselves to the larger class of those who still profess allegiance to the faith of Islam, we should expect the movement of thought to be in some degree parallel to the developments of Western thought in the nineteenth century.

5 / FUNDAMENTALIST ISLAM: THE WAHHABIS

He must have spent many wakeful hours during these years of struggle in pondering ways and means of countering the vagaries of fate which had brought down his ancestors at intervals during the chequered history of the Wahhabi movement, on which the House of Saud had built up a position of dominance in Arabia. And he himself had seen and played a prominent part in the collapse of the secular State of Muhammad ibn Rashid as soon as the strong hand of a great personality had been removed from the helm by death. Even the great Arab Empire of the early days of Islam had been dissipated by incompetent leadership and the wilting of conviction in contact with the wealth and luxuries of the conquered provinces. Evidently there was some basic weakness in the constitution of desert society: capable as it was of heroic effort under the impulse of a great cause or a great personality, but temperamentally unable to maintain indefinitely the discipline necessary to develop the fruits of victory for the common good. The desert tribes and the city States were alike obsessed by a sense of local or parochial loyalty which overrode the greater patriotism

From H. St. John Philby, *Saudi Arabia* (London: Ernest Benn Ltd., 1955), pp. 260–62, 263. Reprinted by permission of Ernest Benn, Ltd., and Frederick A. Praeger, Inc.

and public spirit necessary to the maintenance of an ordered realm.

It was to this weakness that Ibn Saud now addressed himself, determined to find a cure if possible. The history of his house readily suggested religion as the principal ingredient; and there can be no doubt that both he and his father were devout Wahhabis, though in the rough and tumble of these fighting years there is little record of any special emphasis on the religious aspect of their activities. Nevertheless it can be assumed that the idea of another Wahhabi revival had for some time been germinating in Ibn Saud's mind as an important instrument of policy. He had however grafted a new conception on the normal type of such revivals, and had made a special point of concentrating the efforts of his missionaries on the Badawin tribes, with results which began to be apparent in 1912. In that year a mixed group of Harb and Mutair tribesmen, duly impressed by the warnings of everlasting retribution conveyed to them by the missionaries, gathered at Harma, near Majmaa, to seek further information on the matter from more authoritative sources. In this they received ready help from the local zealots, though their tendency to fanaticism and exclusive self-righteousness soon embroiled them with the other inhabitants.

The new fraternity, soon to become known as the Ikhwan, or Brethren, and now numbering some fifty men and their families, decided to migrate to less compromising surroundings. The wells of Artawiya, on the caravan route between Kuwait and the Qasim, were chosen as a suitable site for a hermit colony, which soon became the prototype of the militant religious cantonments, which sprang up in rapid succession all over the country, wherever suitable conditions for communal life existed. Ibn Saud, who had started the process of regeneration among the tribes through his missionaries, placed all necessary facilities at their disposal: money, seed and agricultural implements, religious teachers, and the wherewithal for building mosques, schools and dwellings: and, last but not least, arms and ammunition for the defence of the faith, the basic article of which was the renunciation of all the heathen customs and practices of the old tribal code. The brotherhood of all men who accepted the new order, regardless of their tribal affiliations and social status, canalised the warlike propensities of the Arabs in the service of God and his representative on earth. Inter-tribal raids, highway robbery, tobacco and other amenities of the old life became taboo; and all attention was concentrated in the colonies on preparation for the life hereafter.

The activities of the first fifty Ikhwan were widely canvassed in the tribes which they had abandoned; and recruits came in from near and far to swell their numbers. Artawiya rapidly became a town with a population of 10,000 souls at the peak of its development. Ghatghat soon followed suit in the Dhurma district with a nucleus of Ataiba converts, and in due course became second in zeal and importance to Artawiya alone. Villages sprang up in every suitable centre with surprising rapidity: each having a present stake in the land as well as a contingent one in eternity. And almost before the year was out Ibn Saud found himself in command of a voluntary territorial army composed entirely of Badawin turned yeomen, on whose loyalty he could count to the death, though their undisciplined courage always needed a backing of steadier troops from the towns and villages to make them an effective force, while their fanatical zeal for the destruction of the infidel (a term liberally interpreted by them to include not only non-Muslims but also all Muslims who did not share their fundamentalist conception of the true faith) had often to be kept in check in the hour of victory, and in times of peace. Henceforth the armies of Ibn Saud always included a contingent of Ikhwan levies, marching under their own banners in company with the still unregenerate Badawin and the steadier yeomen of the old citizen army. Each category had its special function to perform in the ensuing operations; but it was the Ikhwan who leavened the whole lump with that cachet of ferocity, which often stood Ibn Saud in good stead in dealing with his enemies. These Ikhwan colonies were to run into hundreds in the coming years, as the movement spread out into the uttermost recesses of the Badawin world. . . .

Such were the clans and their colonies, which formed the nucleus of a new dispensation which Ibn Saud was soon to put to the test of action in the campaigns of the second stage of his advance to the hegemony of Arabia: campaigns which seem to have passed almost imperceptibly beyond the stage of the old parochial warfare on to the loftier plane of international conflict, with higher stakes at issue than any he had played for hitherto. That he owed much of his success to these Ikhwan contingents cannot be gainsaid, though they were in the end to put his statesmanship to a troublesome test, when the international obligations of the ruler began to conflict with the religious convictions of his subjects.

6 / FUNDAMENTALIST ISLAM: THE SENUSSIS

Origin and Expansion of the Sanusiya (1837–1902)

The Sanusiya is an Order of Sufis or, as they are sometimes called, Darwishes. They are Sunni or orthodox Muslims. This means that in

---

From E. E. Evans-Pritchard, *The Sanusi of Cyrenaica* (London: Oxford University Press, 1949), pp. 1, 6–11. Reprinted by permission of the Clarendon Press, Oxford.

faith and morals they accept the teachings of the Koran and the *Sunna,* a collection of traditions about the life and habits of the Prophet, whose example in all matters should be followed by believers. Most orthodox Muslims recognize two further doctrinal sources, *ijma,* general agreement among those of the faithful capable of holding an opinion on such matters, and *qiyas,* determination of what should be believed or done by analogy with the teachings and life of the Prophet. The founder of the Sanusiya Order, like other teachers of some of the more rigidly orthodox groups, such as the Wahhabi, rejected both, though, in practice, he made use of what amounts to analogy. Of the four canonical rites of orthodox Islam the Sanusi of Cyrenaica, like the founder of their Order, follow the Maliki, the rite dominant throughout North Africa.

The Sanusiya is, therefore, a highly orthodox Order. It is not a sect, but a fraternity. The enemies of its founder were never able to convince any disinterested person that he [the founder] was guilty of heresy, though they attempted to do so; and it was only in very small matters that they were able to accuse him of departing from the Maliki rite. Even its Sufism is conventional and austere. The Wahhabi, those stern and ruthless critics of the sects and Orders of Islam, found in it no *bida,* innovation, which in the eyes of these fanatics amounts to heresy, and, alone among the Sufi Orders, they have tolerated its presence in the Hijaz. . . .

The Grand Sanusi's desire to create around him a society living the life of primitive Islam and his missionary zeal gave an impression, enhanced by the austerity of his Bedouin followers and the remoteness of the Sahara, of excessive puritanism and fanaticism; and some writers have compared the Sanusi movement to the Wahhabi movement on account of these supposed traits. Duveyrier's account,[1] used very uncritically by other writers, is largely to be blamed for the exaggerated stories of the secrecy, puritanism, fanaticism, power, and numbers of the Order that were current at the end of the last century and in the first decade of the present century and which much prejudiced it in the eyes of European Powers with interests in North Africa. With Duveyrier it was an axiom that any foolhardy European who got himself killed in North and Central Africa had been assassinated by Sanusi agents and that any setback to French interests was due to their propaganda.

It is true that the Grand Sanusi, like the founder of the Wahhabi movement, aimed at restoring what he conceived to be the original society of the Prophet. Neither was peculiar in doing so, for every

[1] H. Duveyrier, *La Confrérie Musulmane de Sidi Mohammed ben 'Ali es Senoûsi et son Domaine géographique en l'Année 1300 de l'Hégire = 1883 de notre ère* [Paris: Société de Géographie], 1884.

Muslim preacher must have the same aim. The Grand Sanusi forbade the drinking of alcohol and the taking of snuff and at first, though not absolutely, smoking. But all Muslims are forbidden alcohol and many who are neither Sanusi nor Wahhabi think that smoking is best avoided. It is untrue, as has been asserted, that the Sanusi are forbidden coffee. The Bedouin of Libya do not drink coffee, only tea, in praise of which many poems have been written by Brothers of the Order. The Grand Sanusi forbade music, dancing, and singing in the recitations of the Order, but in this he was at one with all the official spokesmen of Islam. Most reformist movements in Islam tend towards asceticism.

Far from being extreme ascetics, however, the Sanusi Brothers eat and dress well, even using scent, and are amiable and merry companions. . . .

The Grand Sanusi discouraged the trappings of poverty by his example, his exhortations, and his insistence on the Brothers being self-supporting. Although the Heads of the Sanusiya Order, like the Wahhabi leaders, encouraged settlement on the land, they can hardly have hoped to have greatly influenced the Bedouin to this end; but they insisted on the lodges of the Order supporting themselves by agriculture supplemented by stock-raising, and thereby took a stand against *ittikal,* the dependence for livelihood on alms and not on labour which some mendicant Orders have advocated. . . .

The accusation of fanaticism is not borne out by either the character of the Bedouin adherents of the Order or by its actions. The desire to establish in North Africa conditions in which Muslims might live by their own laws and under their own government, as they did in Arabia under the first four Caliphs, led the Grand Sanusi and his successors to oppose the Turkish way of life and the influences and innovations of Western Christendom, but their intransigence in these matters did not imply intolerance, far less aggressiveness. . . .

The leaders of the Order have also been tolerant towards the cult of saints, unlike the iconoclastic Wahhabi, who have destroyed even the tombs of those nearest to the Prophet himself. . . .

The resemblance often alleged between the Sanusi and the Wahhabi movements, on the grounds of like puritanism, literalism, and fanaticism, cannot be substantiated. It is obvious that there must be resemblances between new religious movements: they usually claim to be a return to primitive faith and morals and they are generally missionary and enthusiastic. There is no great significance in such common characteristics of the two movements. Nor is there any reason to suppose that the Grand Sanusi was directly influenced by Wahhabi propaganda. A more significant comparison between the two might be made by tracing their developments from religious into political movements. Both started as religious revivals among backward peoples, chiefly Bedouin, the Wahhabi movement in the Najd in the eighteenth century and the Sanusi movement first in the Hijaz and then in Cyrenaica in the middle of the nineteenth century; the *Ikhwan* organizations of the two movements have much in common; and both ended in the formation of Amirates, or small Islamic States.

Both movements have created States, the Wahhabi in Arabia and the Sanusi in Cyrenaica, based explicitly on religious particularism. In doing so they have only done what any movement of the kind is bound to do in a barbarous country if it is to continue to exist, namely, to create an administrative system which would ensure a measure of peace, security, justice, and economic stability. A religious organization cannot exist apart from a polity of a wider kind. But they did not create the sentiment of community which made the growth of governmental functions and the emergence of a State possible. . . .

[C]onditions in Cyrenaica were particularly favourable to the growth of a politico-religious movement such as the Sanusiya became. It was cut off by deserts from neighbouring countries, it had a homogeneous population, it had a tribal system which embraced common traditions and a strong feeling of community of blood, the country was not dominated by the towns, and the Turkish administration exercised very little control over the interior. It was, as will be seen, the tribal system of the Bedouin which furnished the Order with its political foundations just as it was the tribesmen of the country whose hardiness and courage enabled it to stand up to the succession of defeats it had to endure. . . .

The Bedouin of Cyrenaica had heard similar teachings before from similar teachers and had paid them the same degree of attention as they paid to the Grand Sanusi, but these earlier missionaries won only a personal and local following for themselves and their descendants, whereas the Grand Sanusi established himself and his family as leaders of a national movement, a position they have now held for three generations. Leaving aside the remarkable personality of the Grand Sanusi and without here discussing whether the time at which he taught was particularly favourable to the growth of the movement to which his teachings led, it may be said that the great difference between the Grand Sanusi and the earlier holy men whose tombs are homely landmarks all over Cyrenaica was that, while they were, all of them, in the eyes of the Bedouin, Marabouts, the Grand Sanusi was also the head of an Order which gave to him and his successors an organization. Moreover, unlike the Heads of most Islamic Orders, which have rapidly disintegrated into autonomous segments without contact and common direction, they have been able to maintain this organization intact and keep control of it. This they were able to do by co-ordinating the lodges of the Order to the tribal structure.

7 / THE MOSLEM BROTHERHOOD

An all-inclusive statement on the objectives of the Muslim Brotherhood was made public in a letter which Hasan al-Banna addressed to
the rulers of various Muslim countries in 1936.[1] Copies were also sent
to prominent Muslim leaders in the Arab world. In presenting the
program contained in his letter, Hasan al-Banna pointed out clearly
that he was merely outlining a program, giving only the major subject
headings. He recognized that each and every one of his proposals required much study by experts in the different fields. He concluded by
noting that he was well aware of the fact that his program did not offer
a solution to *all* the problems of national development and progress.
The plan which he proposed, admittedly, would require elaboration
and its initiation would call for much patience and wisdom—it would
not be an easy task. A paraphrased summary of this document, famous
in the Muslim world, now follows.

The first part of Hasan al-Banna's lengthy letter is taken up with
an indictment of Western civilization and an exposition of the excel-
lences of Islam. Its tone is pacific on the whole, particularly with respect to the foreign relations of Muslim states with the West and the
treatment of Christian and Jewish minorities—toward whom Islam
"prescribes kindness and generosity," so long as minorities and foreigners conduct themselves peaceably and loyally toward the Muslims
among whom they live. On the other hand, Hasan al-Banna makes
quite a point of military preparedness on the part of all Muslims.
The "Awakening Nation" depends upon a strong army, which in turn
draws its strength from a healthy population. According to Hasan al-
Banna, prayer and fasting are no more important in the Islamic
scheme of things than are power and military preparedness. He seems
also to have believed that Muslims were especially qualified to lay
claim to world leadership, largely because of the ethical, just, and religious basis of Islamic nationalism.[2] Thoughts and convictions such as
these naturally proved disquieting to such non-Muslims as became
aware of al-Banna's pronouncements.

This pamphlet, or letter, gives general emphasis to the importance

Reprinted from Christina Phelps Harris, *Nationalism and Revolution in Egypt:
the Role of the Muslim Brotherhood*, with the permission of The Hoover Institu-
tion on War, Revolution and Peace, Stanford University. © 1964 by the Board of
Trustees of the Leland Stanford Junior University. [Published for The Hoover
Institution on War, Revolution and Peace by Mouton & Co., The Hague, London,
Paris, 1964.]

[1] *Nahwa al-nur*. This letter was eventually published in booklet form in both
Cairo and Amman in 1950.
[2] *Nahwa al-nur* (Amman, 1950), pp. 9–11.

of education, especially religious and scientific knowledge. The author is quite precise about the sciences, listing botany, chemistry, geology, biology, entomology, and astronomy as being of primary value to Muslims. Emphasis is understandably given to ethics and good character as the prerequisite for success, and also to economics and to public health. But a caveat is included against the pitfalls of secularization, in the firm belief that true progress in an Islamic country cannot be divorced from religion.

Hasan al-Banna associates himself with certain current criticisms of the Ulema group: their weakness in recent times vis-à-vis oppressors and foreigners, and their willingness upon occasion to sacrifice the national cause to their own self-interest.[3] But he stoutly maintains that Islam cannot reasonably be discredited by the shortcomings of a small group of Ulema with "very limited" powers.

The second part of this revealing letter sketches a detailed program for the "practical steps" to be taken by Muslims for their own rehabilitation in the modern world. This is divided into three parts.

The first part of the program deals with political, judicial, and administrative reforms, under ten major headings. Hasan al-Banna calls first of all for the dissolution of all political parties and the reformation of the laws of the land in order to conform with the principles of Islamic jurisprudence. He advocates a strong army composed mainly of young men inspired by the Muslim concept of holy war (jihad); the induction of graduates of al-Azhar University into the army and the administration; the Islamization of the civil service;[4] supervision of the conduct of workers in the government, together with improvement of their working conditions; and the elimination of favoritism and bribery in all government jobs. A significant article in this political section urges the strengthening of ties between Islamic states, notably the Arab countries, as a preliminary step toward the re-establishment of the Caliphate.

The second and by far the longest part of al-Banna's proposed program is devoted to specific social and educational reforms. More than

[3] Certain critics of the Ulema had taken exception to the readiness of the Rector of al-Azhar (who held a political appointment) and the Council of Ulema as a whole to collaborate, upon occasion, with the royal government of Egypt and with the earlier Khedivial government. The still earlier cooperation of the Ulema with officials of the Napoleonic period of occupation—when they accepted representation on the council set up by Bonaparte—was held against them by these same critics. Had the Ulema refused to cooperate with the French conquerors, it was believed, they would have been better able to maintain their independence from political pressures in later years.

[4] Hasan al-Banna seems not to have intended that only Muslims should be eligible for civil appointments. His idea was that the spirit of Islam should be spread among government employees, and that Muslim civil servants should observe Islamic rites and customs.

a third of the thirty articles enumerated in this section are concerned with the maintenance of a high standard of public morality and ethics —citizens must be held accountable for their actions and should be punished if they violate Islamic laws, in accordance with prescribed penalties. Specific prohibitions include the banning of alcoholic drinks, adultery and prostitution, gambling and night clubs, dancing and dance halls. Varying degrees of censorship of plays, songs, films, lectures, broadcasts, and all publications is urgently recommended in order to maintain unsullied the principles of Islam.

Numerous articles in this part of the program relate to the desirability of a unified educational system for Muslims and to the need for basic religious education in all schools and universities. A close working relationship between the village mosques and all village schools should be required. Study of the Arabic language and of Islamic history and culture is especially emphasized. The study of national institutions, on the other hand, is not to be neglected. Memorization of the Koran, at least in part, should still be encouraged. The question of the position of women in the new order remains unclarified. Women should be allowed to achieve progress, within the framework of Islamic custom; but co-education is condemned as un-Islamic, and a special educational curriculum for girls—different from that for boys —is considered necessary. This curriculum is not, however, spelled out. All al-Banna says is that "the curriculum for girls should be reconsidered" and that "boys and girls should have separate curricula in many stages of education." [5]

The proposed social reforms stress the need for a general public-health program—more hospitals, mobile clinics, and the training of more doctors—and concentration upon raising the standard of living in the villages. Serious attention should be given to the health, education, and recreation requirements of villagers and to raising their standard of cleanliness and improving their conduct as good Muslims.

The last part of the program deals with economic problems. Hasan al-Banna is here concerned with planning for the increased productivity of the farmer and the factory worker. To this end, he advocates aiding the workers to develop their skills, encouraging new economic projects to open up new job opportunities,[6] and exploiting more fully the natural resources at hand—notably the reclamation of waste lands and the expansion of mining industries. He is likewise desirous of improving the working conditions of agricultural and urban workers and taking cognizance of their technical as well as their social needs. He is

[5] *Ibid.*, p. 31.

[6] With respect to the encouragement of new economic projects, Hasan al-Banna called attention to the importance of making sure that foreign enterprises should serve primarily the national interest of the country.

aware of the problems of unemployment and low wages, and he advocates their control by the government. But he does not appear to have given thought, at least at that time (1936), to the relation between a low standard of living and Egypt's swiftly mounting population. One of the articles in the social section of his program specifically encourages marriage, the strengthening of the family, and a high birth-rate—presumably to increase the relative number of Muslims in the population.

A few miscellaneous articles call for special reforms. Certain time-honored customs are condemned on the ground that they are morally offensive and financially depleting. Traditional and extravagant Egyptian ceremonies connected with marriage, birth, and death are notorious examples of customs that have given rise to many abuses since the simpler days of early Islam. The stern anti-westernism of Hasan al-Banna, an ominous foreshadowing of the later xenophobia of the Muslim Brothers, is evidenced in his special exhortation to Muslims to root out all foreign influences in their home lives. Foreign nurses and teachers, alien modes of dress, and family conversation in any foreign language should all be eliminated from the home. Since the upper-class, well-to-do families were habitual offenders, in the eyes of al-Banna, his injunction to Arabize home life was primarily applicable to them. Many of the reforms demanded in this program seem designed to produce not merely cultural unity but cultural uniformity as well.

Hasan al-Banna shows the standard fundamentalist reaction against profits derived from interest; he condemns "usury," and he recommends that the government should take a hand in reorganizing banks and thus ensure that the banks function without running counter to this strict Muslim prohibition. The government should also set an example in repudiating usury by renouncing interest payments in connection with its own projects.[7] Al-Banna takes the position also that the public must be protected against monopolistic companies. In the matter of the charitable tithes (al-Zakah)[8] which every Muslim is traditionally expected to contribute for the public welfare, Hasan al-Banna urges reorganization of their administration; and he recommends that the Zakah revenues should be spent, in part, on charitable enterprises—such as asylums for the care of orphans, the poor, and the aged—and in part on the upkeep of the army.

[7] *Ibid.*, p. 34.

[8] The *Zakah* is the third "Pillar of the Faith" of the religion of Islam. Kenneth Cragg, *op. cit.* [Kenneth Cragg, *The Call of the Minaret,* New York: Oxford University Press, 1956], pp. 150–54, has an illuminating statement on *Zakat* (i.e., the *Zakah*) "as the basis of an ideology of social responsibility [and] the institutional witness to the duty implicit in ownership"—since "to have is to share," and "Islam demands economic justice and social neighborliness."

This letter contains the essence of the early teachings of Hasan al-Banna, wherein his domestic and his Pan-Islamic objectives are skillfully interwoven. He proposes a charter for Muslims the world over. The emphasis of his program is on reform—on the religious, social, and economic rehabilitation of Muslims. But he also stresses Islamic power, adequately supported by military strength, and the need for dedicated Islamic leadership in the East.

The burden of Hasan al-Banna's message to the Muslim rulers is that the Awakening Nation must have hope as well as vigor, initiative as well as determination, and that Muslims are divinely equipped for world leadership. Rulers in the Islamic world should govern according to the principles he has laid down, and he promises them the full support of the Muslim Brotherhood if they accept his program. Al-Banna's statement on strengthening the ties between Muslim countries, as a step prerequisite to the re-establishment of the Caliphate, may have been intended as a feeler outside the confines of Egypt, possibly even a tentative bid for future support toward his ultimate goal.

In 1943–1944 the Muslim Brotherhood Press in Cairo published the first edition of *Dawatuna*,[9] which some scholars translate as "Our Teachings" and others as "Our Propaganda Aims." [10] This pamphlet has a more specialized focus than the one summarized above, entitled "Toward the Light." Its professed aim is to publicize the goals and program of the Muslim Brothers. During a world war it was not practicable to push any proposal for the re-establishment of the Caliphate. By implication, the supposedly temporary limitations imposed on their ideal program are accepted. In any case, the pamphlet confines itself to noting that, since no Caliph exists, Muslims need a judge to arbitrate the inevitable and permissible differences of opinion in the Islamic world. The flexibility of Islam offers Muslims a basic feeling of solidarity.

The pamphlet *Dawatuna* contains an analysis and definition of permissible loyalties within the framework of the Muslims' overriding loyalty to Islam. The varieties of loyalty—devotion to one's country, to one's heritage, to one's own people, and so on—are tabulated in their ideal interrelationship.

Of special significance, when one considers the turmoils that confronted the Muslim Brotherhood in the decade following publication of *Dawatuna,* is the fact that this pamphlet divides Muslims into four categories, according to their attitudes toward the Brotherhood. First

[9] The literal meaning of *Dawatuna* is "our call" or "our invitation."

[10] The article by Franz Rosenthal on "The 'Muslim Brethren' in Egypt"—published in *The Moslem World,* Vol. XXXVII, No. 4 (October, 1947), pp. 278–291—contains a most interesting analysis of this first edition of *Dawatuna.* I have used Dr. Rosenthal's translation and summary for my paragraphs on *Dawatuna.*

and foremost are the wholehearted believers; next, the undecided, the potential converts; thirdly, the utilitarians, who are alien to the dedicated spirit of the Muslim Brothers; and, lastly, the opponents and the skeptics, who are blind to the truth—"may God forgive them!"

The impression given by *Dawatuna* is that the Muslim Brothers seem convinced beyond the shadow of a doubt that they possess the right program, an all-inclusive one, and that they have faithful workers and resolute leaders to achieve their aims—in short, all the ingredients of success. To their minds, Islam governs all aspects of life in this world and in the hereafter, and the Brotherhood program is Islamic in every sense of the word. They call for a united Muslim front to cope with all the social and economic problems, the intellectual heresies, the psychological weaknesses, the corrupting foreign influences that endanger the substructure of Islam.

8 / THE BROTHERHOOD'S POLITICAL THEORY

Political theory in Islam rests on the basis of justice on the part of the rulers, obedience on the part of the ruled, and collaboration between ruler and ruled. These are the great fundamental features from which all the other features take their rise.

There must first be justice on the part of the rulers. "Verily Allah commands justice." [1] "And when you judge between the people, you must do so with justice." [2] "And when you speak, act justly, even though the matter concerns a relative." [3] "And be not driven by hatred of any people to unjust action; to act justly is closer to piety." [4] "Verily on the Day of Resurrection he who is dearest of all men to Allah, and he who is nearest to Him will be the just leader; but he who is most hated by Allah on that Day, and he who is most bitterly punished will be the tyrannical leader." [5]

This refers to that impartial justice which is absolute, and which cannot be swayed by affection or by hatred; the bases of this justice cannot be affected by love or by enmity. Such justice is not influenced by any relationship between individuals, or by any hatred between peoples. It is enjoyed by all the individual members of a Muslim community, without discrimination arising from descent or rank, wealth or influence. In the same way, such a justice is enjoyed by other peoples,

From Sayed Kotb, *Social Justice in Islam,* trans. John B. Hardie (Washington, D.C.: American Council of Learned Societies, 1953), pp. 93–96. Reprinted by permission of Farrar, Straus & Giroux, Inc.
[1] Sura 16:92.
[2] Sura 4:61.
[3] Sura 6:153.
[4] Sura 5:11.
[5] Traditions.

even though there may be hatred between them and the Muslims. This is a high level of equity, to which no international law has so far achieved, nor any domestic law either.

Those who reject this justice must necessarily return to that form of justice which depends on the strength or the weakness of communities, which is the mark of those who are regularly at variance one with another. That is, they must return to that form of justice which the white man administers to the red man in the United States, or which the white man administers to the colored man in South Africa. There are other similar instances from contemporary conditions with which everyone is familiar.

The principal care of Islamic justice is that it shall not be purely theoretical, but that it shall be applied in the realm of practical life. The historical development of Islam supplies a succession of illustrations of this, which we shall consider in their proper place; here we are concerned to consider only the theoretical aspect, as it is revealed to us in the ordinances of Islam.

And secondly, there must be obedience on the part of those who are ruled. "O you who have believed, obey Allah, and obey the Messenger of Allah and those who hold authority among you." [6] The fact that this verse groups together Allah, the Messenger, and those who hold authority means that it clarifies the nature and the limits of this obedience. Obedience to one who holds authority is derived from obedience to Allah and the Messenger. The ruler in Islamic law is not to be obeyed because of his own person; he is to be obeyed only by virtue of holding his position through the law of Allah and His Messenger; his right to obedience is derived from his observance of that law, and from no other thing. If he departs from the law, he is no longer entitled to obedience, and his orders need no longer be obeyed. Thus one authority says that, "There can be no obedience to any creature which involves disobedience to the Creator." Or again: "Hear and obey—even if your ruler is an Abyssianian [sic] slave with a head like a raisin, so long as he observes the Book of Allah the Exalted." It is made very clear by this tradition that to hear and obey is conditioned by the observance by the ruler of the Book of Allah the Exalted. An absolute obedience such as this is not to be accorded to the will of the ruler himself, nor can it be a binding thing if he abandons the law of Allah and of His Messenger. "If anyone sees a tyrannical power which is contrary to the will of Allah, which violates the compact of Allah, and which produces evil or enmity among the servants of Allah, and if he does not try to change it by deed or by word, then it is Allah who must supply the initiative." [7] This tradition indicates the necessity of getting rid of a

[6] Sura 4:62.
[7] Traditions.

ruler who abandons the law by deed or by word, but with the minimum use of force. This is another necessary step beyond the mere withholding of obedience which is in itself a purely negative measure.

We must make a distinction between the fact that a ruler derives his authority from his observance of the religious law and the theory that a ruler draws his authority from the faith. No ruler has any religious authority direct from Heaven, as had some rulers in ancient times; he occupies his position only by the completely and absolutely free choice of all Muslims; and they are not bound to elect him by any compact with his predecessor, nor likewise is there any necessity for the position to be hereditary in the family. Further, in addition to this, he must derive his authority from his continual enforcement of the law. When the Muslim community is no longer satisfied with him his office must lapse; and even if they are satisfied with him, any dereliction of the law on his part means that he no longer has the right to obedience.

In this we see the wisdom of the Prophet, who did not specify anyone as his successor; had he done so, such a man might have laid claim to some religious authority, as having been appointed by the Messenger.

Thirdly, there must be collaboration between ruler and ruled. "Take counsel with them in the matter." [8] "And their affair is a matter for collaboration between them." [9] Collaboration is one of the fundamentals of Islamic politics, although no specific method of administering it has even been laid down; its application has been left to the exigencies of individual situations. The Messenger used to take the advice of the Muslim community in matters which did not pertain to the spiritual; thus he would ask their opinion in worldly affairs in which they had some skill, such as positions on a field of battle. Thus he listened to their opinion at the battle of Badr, and encamped at the well of Badr, though originally he had been some distance away from it;[10] similarly he listened to them in the matter of digging the trench,[11] and also, against the advice of Umar, in the matter of prisoners, though in this case there eventually came a revelation which supported Umar's point of view.[12] So far as spiritual matters were concerned, of course, in the

[8] Sura 3:153.

[9] Sura 42:36.

[10] (Badr was the scene of the Prophet's first major victory over the Quraish. It took place in 624 A.D. [2 A.H.]—Trans.)

[11] (In 627 A.D. [5 A.H.] the Muslim forces were besieged in Medina by Quraish troops. On the advice of Salman, the Persian, the Prophet defended the city by a ditch, a novelty in Arabia.—Trans.)

[12] (After Badr there was considerable dispute about what was to be done with the prisoners. Abu Bakr is said to have counselled clemency, while Umar advocated inflexible slaughter. When the generality of the Muslims were consulted, their advice was to save the prisoners alive and hold them to ransom. The Quranic reflection of the matter will be found in Sura 8:68–72.—Trans.)

very nature of the case there was no room for collaboration, since such matters were of the substance of the faith, and were therefore the private affair of the Messenger, the Trusty One.

In the same way the Caliphs continued to collaborate with the Muslims. Abu Bakr did so in the case of those who withheld the poor-tax; he held strongly that war should be declared on them, and though Umar at first opposed him, he finally came to agree with Abu Bakr most fully, Allah having opened his mind to understand that Abu Bakr was set on such a course.[13] Again Abu Bakr took counsel with the Meccans concerning the war in Syria, against the opposition of Umar.[14] And Umar himself took advice in the matter of going into a plague-stricken country; he came to his own conclusion, and subsequently found a precedent in the custom of the Prophet which confirmed him, and thus he kept to his course.[15] Such has been the method of collaboration; it has not followed any well-marked or definite system, because the needs of the moment have never demanded more than this type of informal counsel. And the wide variety of questions which arises leaves ample room for a wide range of systems and methods; hence no system is specified by Islam, which is content rather to lay down only the general principle.

[13] (After the death of Muhammad all Arabia threw off the yoke of Islam, and the common sign of this rejection of allegiance was the refusal to pay the poor-tax. These so-called "Wars of Apostasy" lasted only through the first year of Abu Bakr's caliphate, and it was very largely owing to his firmness of spirit that the outcome was favorable to Islam.—Trans.)

[14] (In 633 A.D. [12 A.H.] Abu Bakr resolved on a campaign in Syria; the army was under the command of Khalid ibn Said, of whom Umar did not approve, and accordingly the Caliph took counsel with the people of Mecca.—Trans.)

[15] (In 639 A.D. [18 A.H.] plague broke out in Southern Syria, the so-called "Plague of Amwas or Emmaus," the village where it originated. Umar's decision was to withdraw from the affected area; though he was reproached with "fleeing from the decree of Allah," his retort was that this was merely "to flee from the decree of Allah to the decree of Allah." His argument was, as is here mentioned in the text, by a saying of Muhammad: "If plague break out in a country, go not thither; if thou art there, flee not from it."—Trans.)

III / EARLY CONSTITUTIONALISM AND NATIONALISM

INTRODUCTION

In this chapter we return to the political sphere of reform. Three early movements that embody the principles of constitutionalism and nationalism are reviewed through selections that focus on the Turkish, Persian, and Arab segments of the Middle East at the turn of the nineteenth and twentieth centuries. An account of the growth of the Young Turk movement is provided by Geoffrey L. Lewis in the excerpts from his book, *Turkey*. In the next selection (No. 10) the aims, programs, and ideological posture of the Committee of Union and Progress are discussed by Sir Harry Luke. The author presents the changes which, due to the Young Turk revolution, had taken place in the concept and practice of the *millet* institution and analyzes the conflict which arose among three conflicting ideologies of Ottomanism, Turkish nationalism, and Pan-Islamism.

Selection No. 11 is taken from Edward G. Browne, *The Persian Revolution of 1905–1909*, undoubtedly the most authoritative and comprehensive work on the subject of Persian constitutionalism. The excerpted parts give, first, the dramatic history of events as they unrolled toward their culmination in the form of a major *bast* (sit-down strike) in the gardens of the British Legation and the granting of the constitution by Shah Muzaffar al-Din; secondly, an account of the first workings of the newly elected parliament, the obstructionist efforts by Mohammed Ali Shah's ministers, and the principal aims of reform.

The remaining selections (Nos. 12, 13, and 14) are devoted to the study of the birth and growth of early Arab nationalism and struggle for independence. The "Arab Awakening" is treated in a work of the same title by George Antonius. Although more recent research has added new insights to the understanding of that period in modern

Arab history, Antonius' work still remains a classic. Portions of the book have been selected to show the interrelationship between the first political stirrings of Arab nationalism and the Young Turk revolution. The author gives us an account of the first flush of enthusiasm that followed the overthrow of the hated rule of Abdul Hamid II, and of its immediate consequence in the shaping of Arab-Turkish relations in the form of the Arab-Ottoman Brotherhood. He follows it up with a story of deterioration of Arab-Turkish friendship, creation of Arab secret societies, and description of their objectives and methods.

The theme thus introduced by Antonius is further elaborated in two more specialized works by Professor Zeine N. Zeine of the American University of Beirut (selections 13 and 14). In his *Arab-Turkish Relations and the Emergence of Arab Nationalism,* Zeine discusses the meaning of the Arab national awakening. He distinguishes between two notions which, he claims, have often been confused by writers, namely the Arab national consciousness, on the one hand, and the birth of Arab "political nationalism" on the other. The first, according to Zeine, is not new; in fact, it had existed "throughout the four centuries of Turkish rule." The second was activated during the last phase of Turkish rule in Arab lands. It is this second phenomenon, the political nationalism, which is treated subsequently by Zeine in *The Struggle for Arab Independence.* The focus of this book is on the establishment of the first Arab Kingdom in Syria following her liberation from Turkish rule at the end of World War II. This brief but dramatic episode in the history of the Arab liberation movement has seldom been treated with adequate attention to detail in the English-language literature. Professor Zeine renders a real service by filling this gap and linking the developments in Syria to those in Lebanon and Iraq.

9 / THE YOUNG TURKS

In 1889 a group of students at the Army School of Medicine formed a secret organization which they called "The Ottoman Society for Union and Progress." Some of the leaders were driven into exile, some were executed for distributing pamphlets in which the Sultan's arbitrary rule was attacked, but the ardour of the survivors was unimpaired. From the safety of London, Paris, Naples and Cairo there flowed a stream of revolutionary publications, in which all Turkey's misfortunes were laid at the Sultan's door. His efforts to persuade the Governments concerned to suppress the exiles' publications met with little success.

A sharp reminder that his view of the Caliphate was one-sided came

From G. L. Lewis, *Turkey* (London: Ernest Benn Ltd., 1955), pp. 40–44. Reprinted by permission of Ernest Benn, Ltd., and Frederick A. Praeger, Inc.

in a telegram addressed to him from Paris by one of the exiles, his own son-in-law, Mahmud Pasha:

> Your Majesty's mode of government conforms to no law, nor does it resemble the behaviour of an upright Caliph, not even the methods of European sovereigns. You are empowered by the people to give effect to justice; you are bound to respect it.

The mainstay of the opposition consisted of young army officers, whose professional training brought them into contact with European ideas and technical development, and whose professional pride made them bitterly resentful of the debilitating influence of the Sultan's autocratic rule.

In the early years of the twentieth century revolutionary societies multiplied inside the Empire, not always through any great divergence in aims but because of the difficulties of maintaining communications in face of the omnipresent spies and *agents provocateurs* of the Sultan. By 1908, however, the underground stream of revolt was running so high that the Sultan could no longer rely on the repressive activity of his secret police. It is virtually certain that some of his chief agents had been deliberately betraying his confidence in them, on the orders of their German trainers. A man of Abdulhamid's suspicious nature could not have failed to realize that German penetration of the Ottoman Army was not entirely to his own advantage; the Kaiser may well have decided that the Sultan was not the complaisant simpleton he had at first appeared. At all events, when the blow fell, Germany did not lift a finger to maintain Abdulhamid in power.

On 22 July 1908, the Salonica branch of the Society for Union and Progress sent the Sultan a telegram, demanding that the Constitution be given effect and imposing a time-limit for convening the Chamber of Deputies, failing which it threatened action "which will not meet with your Majesty's approval." This ultimatum and the simultaneous revolt in Rumelia, the strength of which was greatly exaggerated in a telegram sent to the capital by the Governor of Monastir, terrified the Sultan into accepting the Society's demands. The Constitution was proclaimed on 23 July.

The next day the Sultan's astonished subjects looked at their newspapers, to see words which had been proscribed for years: such words as "freedom," "nation," "fatherland" and "Chamber of Deputies," which formerly would have meant the ruin of any editor rash enough to print them.

Several European eye-witnesses have described the unprecedented demonstrations of popular joy which took place in the principal cities, once it was realized that the Sultan had been forced to yield. Bulgarian priests publicly shook hands with Turkish officers, Greeks embraced

Armenians. In Macedonia, bands of revolutionaries, who had for years been waging war against the Government, came down into the towns and announced the end of hostilities.

Not everybody joined in the general rejoicing. In southern Anatolia and in Tripolitania disorders broke out among the Muslim populations, who looked on the restoration of the Constitution as a betrayal of Islam, involving as it did the granting of equal rights to non-Muslims. But apart from such diehards, the majority of people regarded that day in July 1908 as the beginning of a wonderful new era.

The Constitutional Period, 1908–1918

All too soon it became apparent that the Turks and non-Turks, who had congratulated one another on the proclamation of the Constitution, had no more in common than joy at the downfall of Abdulhamid's tyranny. Their ideas about what was to succeed it were very different. Nor did the nations of Europe, who had for so many years been sadly shaking their heads over the condition of the Sick Man, rejoice with him now that he seemed to be on the road to recovery. Austria promptly annexed Bosnia and Herzegovina, the Bulgars proclaimed their independence. In 1910 there were revolts in the Yemen and in Albania. In 1911 Italy invaded Tripolitania, and in the following year Greece annexed Crete.

Nor must it be thought that there was any unity of purpose among the Turks themselves. Three distinct political creeds vied for supremacy amongst them: Ottomanism, Pan-Islamism and Pan-Turkism.

The first of these involved the vain hope that the various peoples of the Ottoman Empire could be integrated into a homogeneous modern State.

The Pan-Islamic ideal, which, as we have seen, enjoyed the Kaiser's blessing, remained in the running until the First World War revealed that the Arabs preferred to become independent rather than follow a Turkish Caliph. Indeed, even before the war, numerous societies and parties were formed whose aim was Arab independence.

Pan-Turkism, which aspired to unite all the Turks of Asia into one State, was the latest of the three creeds to emerge, and this fact is hardly surprising, because the Turks were the least united of all the peoples of the Empire; the least self-conscious, the least advanced towards nationhood. Till quite recently "Turk" had been almost a term of abuse in the Ottoman Empire, connoting something like "yokel." All the best people were *Osmanli*. The policy which seemed natural, the policy which at first dominated the Society for Union and Progress, was Ottomanism, which envisaged a modernized Ottoman Empire, so well equipped with liberal institutions that all the conflicting religious and racial groups among the Sultan's subjects would be happy to belong to it. The hopes of the Ottomanists perished for ever in the Balkan Wars of 1912–1913, in which Turkey lost the Aegean Islands and all her European possessions, except part of Thrace.

Before the general election which followed the proclamation of the Constitution of 1908, the Society decided that those of its members who won seats in the Assembly should constitute the "Party of Union and Progress," and this title was subsequently extended to the whole movement. The Party won a huge majority, not only because of its prestige as the vanquisher of Abdulhamid but also because it controlled the Army.

For some months the administration remained in the hands of politicians of the old school, but in February 1909 the Assembly dismissed the Grand Vizier Kamil Pasha, on a vote of no confidence, and the Party formed a government. Two months later a mass revolt (known as the "Thirty-first of March Incident") broke out in the capital, in which units of the Army joined, demanding the setting-up of an administration and government that would conform to the sacred law of Islam.

The newspaper *Volkan* ("Volcano") fanned the flames, inveighing against the "Epoch of Devils," against the "men of no honour who blindly imitate the West" and the "ignoramuses who are so proud of their three days' education that they think they can look down on students of the sacred law." The Sultan, over-rating the strength of the insurrection, imprudently sent a decree to the Assembly, announcing that the State was a Muslim State, that henceforth more deference would be shown to the sacred law, and that the rebels were all pardoned.

The Commander of the Third Army, Mahmud Shevket Pasha, sent troops from Salonica "to wipe out this stain on the honour of the Ottoman Army, with its six-century-long record of obedience" and "to punish the secret agents of the Sultan and the base self-seekers who instigated the revolt." The rising was speedily crushed, and on 27 April, 1909, Abdulhamid was deposed by the Assembly, with the approval of the *Sheyhul-Islam,* and banished to Salonica. During the War he was brought back to Istanbul, where he died in 1918.

Abdulhamid having been deposed, his brother Mehmed was enthroned in his place, the fifth Sultan of the name. The pledge he gave on the day of his accession marked the opening of a new era in Turkish history. "Since the nation (*millet*) wants me, I gratefully undertake this service. My chief hope is to carry on government in accordance with the sacred law and the Constitution. I shall not swerve by one iota from the will and aspirations of the nation." The will of the nation! Never before had a sovereign of the House of Osman recognized the existence of such an entity.

But the Party of Union and Progress did not share the Sultan's liberal enthusiasm; the abortive revolt, which had provided ample justification for getting rid of Abdulhamid, also furnished them with a pretext to muzzle the opposition parties, whose strength grew as the ruling party abandoned its original Ottomanist policy and came out on the side of Turkish nationalism. Dissensions also abounded within the Party, however, and in July, 1912, the Union and Progress Cabinet was forced to resign.

The succeeding Government put forward a programme which would seriously have limited the activities of Union and Progress: they proposed, *inter alia,* to look into allegations of official interference in elections, to forbid civil servants to belong to political parties, and to put an end to the Army's meddling in politics. The Party abandoned all pretence of loyalty to the Constitution: two of its most influential leaders, Enver and Talat, staged a *coup d'état,* as a result of which a new government took office, under Mahmud Shevket Pasha, who was sympathetic towards the Party. The new Cabinet had, in the words of the British Ambassador, "a distinct German colouring." In June 1913 Mahmud Shevket was assassinated and Union and Progress availed themselves of the opportunity to exile their principal opponents and to lay an iron hand on the administration.

10 / THE COMMITTEE OF UNION AND PROGRESS

What were the true aims of the Committee of Union and Progress? Its aims were set out, succinctly and accurately enough, in the Committee's designation. The new rulers of Turkey wanted progress and they wanted union. If their proceedings were often (perhaps oftener than was necessary) conspiratorial and occult; if some of their members were shady, some of their instruments ignoble and methods ruthless; if they not only combated, as it was right for reformers to combat, the ignorant fanaticism of the *molla* but in addition despised the simple faith of the old-fashioned Moslem layman—their ambitions were not wholly unworthy of respect. If they wanted to put an end to the autocracy of Abdul Hamid less on humanitarian grounds than because it was from the practical point of view a failure, they undoubtedly wanted to rehabilitate the power and prestige of the Empire. And they wanted to break down the barriers separating the *millets* to the extent to which this was necessary in order to attain these two objectives. The Committee included in its membership, in addition to the realists, men who were altruistically desirous of making things better; to some ex-

From Sir Harry Luke, *The Old Turkey and the New: From Byzantium to Ankara* (London: Geoffrey Bles, 1955), pp. 139–47. Excerpted and reprinted by permission of the executors.

tent, although not entirely, it was justified in adopting the watchwords "Liberty, Justice, Fraternity." But, if it was to abolish the watertight compartments within which the *millets* had their political and social no less than their religious being, if it was to bring the heterogeneous inhabitants of the Empire to a common level, there clearly had to be a norm, a standard of uniformity. That standard was the Ottoman.

It is not easy to define precisely the meaning which the Young Turks of the Committee attached to their ideal of Pan-Ottomanism. They did not aim at the exclusive racial Turanianism of the subsequent Nationalists, as that policy involved the elimination from the State of racial elements that were not Turkish. The Young Turks were prepared to retain, and to collaborate with, the non-Turkish Moslems such as the Arabs, the Albanians and the Kurds, as with the Christians and the Jews. But these elements must bear the hall-mark of Ottoman. This involved on the part of the non-Turkish elements an exclusive loyalty to the conception of the Ottoman Empire, with the consequential abandonment of any national or racial ambitions of their own which they might have cherished.

That was, no doubt, all very well in theory; and it is difficult to envisage what other basis the Committee could have laid down for the restoration and reconstruction of the State. But in practice it meant that the non-Turkish elements were being called upon to surrender much that was of value in return for advantages that were of doubtful benefit to them and might never even be realized. Any separatist ambitions which these elements might have pursued were inconsistent with the new conception of the State and must be abandoned; it was a poor consolation to those who had appreciated the real benefits of cultural autonomy within their *millets* to be obliged to sacrifice some of these on the altar of a new uniformity that might prove to be the shadow without the substance. No doubt it might be gratifying in theory to the *amour propre* of the *rayah* to be admitted by the Constitution to service in the Ottoman army; but there happened again what had happened in 1856. In practice the concession pleased the Christians (who promptly demanded equality of promotion, separate units and service in their own provinces) as little as it pleased the Turks. These not only resented the possibility of Moslems being placed under the orders of Christian or Jewish officers; they disliked the prospect of potentially disloyal Greeks and Armenians being trained in the use of arms and in the science of war.

As the first delirium at the lifting of the Hamidian tyranny began to cool, as the rapture of the honeymoon dissolved before the realities of the situation, it gradually became clear that the fundamental aims of the new regime—however logical, however great an improvement they promised on what had gone before—were not capable of attainment in the peculiar conditions which the Ottoman Empire presented. There was too deeply ingrained an animosity between the different *millets,* whom previous administrations had striven to keep apart; there was too well developed a cleavage in their several aspirations; there was still an invincible repugnance on the part of the Moslems to take their orders from those whom they could not yet accustom themselves to look upon as other than *rayahs* and consequently as inferiors. . . .

Equally difficult is it to analyse the Committee's attitude towards Islam, for its attitude towards Islam was anything but consistent. If a Western parallel were to be sought, it might be found in the attitude of the Third French Republic towards the Roman Catholic Church in the last two decades of the nineteenth century and the first decade of the twentieth. The anomaly presented by Gambetta's *"Le cléricalisme, voilà l'ennemi"* and the Combes-Briand measures, combined with the French right to protect Roman Catholic interests and establishments in Turkey (to which the Third Republic clung with no less tenacity than the Bourbon kings) may be likened to that of the personal irreligion of the Young Turks and their political antagonism to what may be termed the Moslem "clergy," combined with their maintenance of the preponderance of the Islamic elements in the State.

It was significant of this attitude that the deposition of Abdul Hamid was brought about in the time-honoured way by reference to the *ulema;* that it was legalized by the issue of the Sheikh ul-Islam's *fetva,* declaring the deposition to be in accord with the Sheri (Islamic) Law because the Sultan, having infringed the law of Islam, had failed to discharge his duty as Commander of the Faithful. It was no less significant of the opposite tendency in the movement that, when the Sultan was actually apprised of his deposition, one of the four delegates of the Committee who proceeded to Yildiz to announce to Abdul Hamid that he had ceased to reign was the Jewish lawyer Emmanuel Carasso Effendi, one of the leading Grand Orient Freemasons of Salonica. This person had been one of those chiefly instrumental in bringing about the close connexion between that brotherhood and the Turkish revolutionary leaders. His inclusion in the delegation was repugnant to the Old Turks, as it was meant to be, nor was it altogether acceptable to all of the Young Turks;[1] but it was a portent of the new era. . . .

As Ottoman democrats, moreover, they did not contemplate, at all events in the early years of their rule, a racially exclusive policy of a Turanian character. On the contrary, they were as eager to keep the Arabs, the Kurds and the Albanians—who, having no longer an Abdul

---

[1] *Cf.* the obituary notice on Carasso Effendi in *The Times* of the 8th June, 1934.

Hamid to pet them, were beginning to show signs of Nationalist and separatist tendencies—safely within the fold as they were eager to influence the Moslems outside Turkey. So Sultan Reshad was as much exploited as Khalif by the Young Turks as Sultan Abdul Hamid had exploited himself in that role. When, for example, a manifestation of Albanian unrest produced a dangerous situation in Macedonia, the old man was taken to Salonica and thence to the plain of Kossovo; there he was made to officiate as Khalif in religious ceremonies intended by the Young Turk Government to revive Ottoman patriotism among the Albanians on a Pan-Islamic basis. The rulers of constitutional Turkey had not abandoned the theocratic conception of the Empire. Outwardly, Islam was still entrenched firmly as the State religion; and Islam is a faith which dislikes and transcends racial distinctions.

Nevertheless, the time was approaching when the aims of the Committee were to be narrowed and were to undergo a certain deviation from their original direction. The Committee's first principles had been those of the French Revolution, within which it had sought to free and to reconcile the people of the Empire. The Committee was not, to begin with, Nationalist; its original policy was not Turkification but Ottomanization. That a change took place in the orientation of the Young Turks was not due to a change in their philosophy but to the pressure of external events. In September, 1911, the Italian Government surprised not only Turkey but the world by declaring on the Ottoman Government a war that ended in the loss of Turkey's last direct possessions in Africa and in the forcible transfer of Libya and Cyrenaica to the "full and entire sovereignty of the Kingdom of Italy." In the same month (October, 1912) that the Turco-Italian War was ended by the Treaty of Ouchy, Turkey had to face the Balkan League of Greece, Bulgaria, Serbia and Montenegro. . . .

General Damad Enver Pasha was fully conscious of himself in his capacity of Turk and conscious of the part which, he believed, should be played by the Turkish race in the Near and Middle East. At the same time, he did not on that account contemplate the abandonment of Ottomanism or of Pan-Islam. He and his colleagues envisaged the three policies being pursued simultaneously and side by side, each one being emphasized in whatever place, at whatever time, it was the most appropriate policy to apply. Ottomanism continued to be the keynote of internal politics; Turkish nationalism, the keynote of relations with the Tatars of Russia, some of whom were beginning to manifest sentiments of sympathy with their cousins in Turkey in their time of trouble; Pan-Islam, that of relations with the Arabs and other non-Turkish Moslems within the Empire and of the Moslem peoples of North Africa and elsewhere outside it.

No doubt the policies were often inconsistent, were often incompatible with one another and were actually at times in conflict; and it was inevitable that one of them must ultimately prevail over the others. It was the First World War that hastened the failure of Pan-Ottomanism, that revealed the bankruptcy of Pan-Islam and that led to the victorious emergence of Turkish Nationalism or Yeni-Turan.

11 / REVOLUTION IN PERSIA

Finally the soldiers dispersed the people, cleared the streets, and occupied the whole town, while a large number of *mullas, rawza-khwans*,[1] students, merchants, tradesmen, artisans, and people of yet humbler rank took refuge in the Masjid-i-Jamia, a Mosque situated in the centre of the city, and there buried the body of the murdered Sayyid.[2] Being besieged there by the soldiers for three or four days they asked and obtained the Shah's permission to leave the city and retire to Qum, whither they were accompanied and followed by such numbers of people that, as Taqi-zada expressed it, the road between Tihran and Qum "was like the street of a town." This event, which took place about July 21, is known amongst the Persians as "the Great Exodus" (*Hijrat-i-Kubra*).

Meanwhile *Aynud-Dawla* ordered the *bazars* and shops, which had been closed in protest, to be opened, threatening, if this were not done, to have them looted by his soldiers. Thereupon, about Thursday, July 19, a few representatives of the merchants and bankers waited upon Mr. Grant Duff, the British Chargé d'Affaires, at Qulhak, the summer quarters of the Legation, and enquired whether, if they took refuge in the British Legation in the town, they would be expelled or allowed to remain under its protection. On receiving a reassuring reply, a few of them at once proceeded to the Legation garden and encamped there. By the following Monday, July 23, their numbers had increased to 858, and three days later to 5,000. They demanded, as the conditions of their return to their homes and avocations, the dismissal of *Aynud-Dawla*, the promulgation of a Code of Laws, and the recall of the ecclesiastical leaders from Qum. The Shah, greatly vexed and perplexed, decided on July 30 so far to yield to the popular demands as

From Edward G. Browne, *The Persian Revolution of 1905–1909* (New York: Barnes & Noble, Inc., 1966), pp. 118–19, 123, 124, 133–36. Reprinted by permission of Cambridge University Press.

[1] Professional reciters of narratives in verse and prose about the sufferings and martyrdoms of the Imams.

[2] It was, however, exhumed, by order of Muhammad Ali Shah, after the *coup d'état* of June 23, 1908.

to dismiss *Aynud-Dawla,* appoint in his place the popular and liberal Mírzá Nasrullah Khan, *Mushirud-Dawla,* and invite the *mullas* to return from Qum to the capital; but the people, no longer content with these concessions, and profoundly mistrustful of the Government, now demanded a regular Constitution and a representative National Assembly, with satisfactory guarantees of the Shah's good faith. By August 1 the number of refugees at the British Legation was stated in the *Times* to amount to 13,000 souls, and, on the same authority, to have reached within the next few days the enormous total of 16,000, though this estimate appears to be excessive, 12,000 or 14,000 being probably nearer the truth. Finally on August 5 (14 Jumada ii, which happened to be the Shah's birthday) Muzaffarud-Din granted all the demands of the *bastis,* who thereupon quitted the Legation. . . .

The return of the ecclesiastical leaders from Qum to the capital, escorted by *Azudul-Mulk* and Hajji Nizamud-Dawla, which took place a day or two after the Shah had yielded and the *bastis* had left the British Legation, i.e. about August 15 or 16, was made the occasion for great rejoicings over the "National Victory" *(Fath-i-Milli),* in which, according to a St. Petersburg telegram dated Aug. 17 (published in the *Times* of Aug. 18), the Russian colony bore a conspicuous part. Some doubt is cast on their sincerity, however, by an article which appeared in the St. Petersburg *Birzheviya Viedomosti* of Sept. 13, 1906, which said that "it was becoming obvious that Persia would succeed in obtaining reforms and even a Constitution, *thanks to the benevolent co-operation of England,* and that this would be *another heavy blow to Russian prestige in Asia."* [3] On August 19 took place the solemn official opening of the new House of Parliament, in presence of the high ecclesiastical authorities, who were entertained as the Shah's guests for three days. The proclamation announcing the establishment of the "National Consultative Assembly" *(Majlis-i-Shura-yi-milli)* was issued four or five days earlier, and a translation of it was published in the *Times* for Sept. 1, 1906. . . .

On Sept. 17 the Shah had accepted the proposed ordinance as to the constitution of the *Majlis,* which was to consist of 156 members, 60 representing Tihran and 96 the provinces, elections were to take place every two years, and deputies were to be inviolable. The voting in Tihran was to be direct, but in the provinces by means of colleges of electors. The Shah was enthusiastically welcomed by the people on his return from the country to the capital, the Parliament was announced to meet in a month, and by the beginning of October the elections had begun, four deputies representing the Royal House had been chosen, the *mullas* of Tabriz and Rasht were pacified, and the *bastis* had again left the British Legation. Arbab Jamshid was elected

---

[3] *Times,* Sept. 14, 1906.

a few days later to represent the Zoroastrians: *Saniud-Dawla* was chosen President, and the *Majlis,* or National Assembly, was opened on Oct. 7 without waiting for the arrival of the provincial deputies, the Shah's Speech from the throne being read out by the *Nizamul-Mulk.* . . .

On New Year's Day, 1907, the Constitution, signed at last by the dying Shah, under the strong suasion of the clergy (who bade him remember that he was about to meet his God, and should strive to take with him into that awful Presence some deed of great merit which might counterbalance his sins of omission and commission), was taken to the National Assembly by the Prime Minister *Mushirud-Dawla.* Not only the *Baharistan,* which almost from the first inception of the Assembly had served as the House of Parliament, but all its approaches and the gardens surrounding it were thronged with an enthusiastic concourse of spectators, many of whom wept with joy as they exchanged embraces. Commemorative poems by the *Shaykhur-Rais* and others were recited, the city was illuminated for two successive nights, and joy and gratitude reigned supreme.[4]

A week later, on Jan. 8, 1907, Muzaffarud-Din Shah was gathered to his fathers, and was succeeded by his son Muhammad Ali Mirza, who was duly crowned on Jan. 19, and whose second son, Sultan Ahmad Mirza, was proclaimed *Wali-ahd* (Crown-Prince) on Jan. 25. That the new Shah should dislike the Constitution and regard the *Majlis* with suspicion and aversion was perhaps natural enough, for he had looked forward to exercising the same autocratic and irresponsible powers as his predecessors had been wont to enjoy, and it could hardly be expected that he would welcome the limitations of his authority laid down by the Constitution, which limitations, it was clear from the beginning, the National Assembly intended to enforce. He manifested this dislike by not inviting the Deputies to be present at his Coronation (of which brilliant ceremony a description is given in No. 5 of the *Nida-yi-Watan*). This omission, the first of a series of slights put upon the *Majlis* by the Shah, was greatly resented by the Deputies, and their anger was increased by the refusal of the responsible Ministers to appear in the House and answer questions. For it was provided by the Constitution that, though the Ministers were to be nominated by the Shah, they were to be responsible to the Assembly, and that without its consent no tax should be imposed, no expenditure incurred, and no foreign loan or concession allowed. Now at this juncture not only did the responsible Ministers absent themselves from the Assembly, but the raising of a fresh loan of £400,000 in equal moieties from Russia and England, on certain conditions not made public, was still

[4] See No. 2 of the *Nida-yi-Watan* ("The Country's Call"), dated Thursday, 18 Dhul-Qada, A.H. 1324 (Jan. 3, 1907).

in contemplation.[5] The project for this loan had been drafted in Russia and the draft had been approved by England, while the Shah's one object was to obtain money, regardless of Persia's future well-being. But at the last moment the Assembly, which nobody seems to have taken into account, came to the rescue and absolutely refused to sanction this transaction, which the *mullas*, with a wise and far-sighted patriotism, denounced as the final sale of Persia's independence. So convinced was the Prime Minister that the people were in earnest that he refused to go forward with the matter, understanding that if he did so his life would not be safe. And although he still refrained from appearing in the Assembly in person, he caused the other Ministers, including the *Nasirul-Mulk*, to be present at its deliberations.

Thus it became apparent from the very first that the *Majlis* had no intention of becoming a cypher. As Aqa Mirza Mahmud, one of the Deputies, said in the debate of January 19 (the day of the Coronation) in the course of the discussion which arose on the absence of any notification to the Assembly as to the important ceremony which was then taking place, "Now that the *Majlis* is at the beginning of its career, let it demand its rights if it can,[6] otherwise it will hereafter be unable to do anything." "We should have been content," added Aqa Sayyid Husayn, "to be represented by our President alone: the point is that the Assembly was disregarded."

Although it was politely assumed at this period that the Shah was the friend and supporter of the Assembly, his Ministers and governors were freely criticised. In several cases the progress of provincial elections had been hampered or even arrested by the local governor, as in Khurasan by the *Asafud-Dawla*, and at Tunkabun, where Amir Asad had actually inflicted the bastinado on Shaykh Muhammad for endeavouring to carry out the election. The punishment of these autocratic tyrants ("*istibdadis*") was demanded by several Deputies, and Hajji Sayyid Nasrullah remarked that "these matters clearly shewed that the Government did not co-operate with the Nation, and that the same autocratic and wilful conduct which had formerly existed in the ruling class still characterized their actions," and he then proceeded to criticize the irregular attendance and unsatisfactory replies of the Ministers of Finance and Education. "These Ministers," observed another Deputy, Sayyid Hashim, "do not at all like the Assembly. They are the same men who wrought all this mischief in the kingdom, who slew some of its people, drove some into exile, suffered many to be shot at Karbala, and wasted men's honour and property." "Why do ye sit here?" he concluded: "What sort of Assembly is this? What

[5] In Hazell's *Annual* for 1907 this Anglo-Russian loan is spoken of as a *fait accompli*.

[6] See No. 30 of the *Majlis*, p. 1.

work is this? We must put a stop to the depredations of these traitors and give effect to the laws." "The Shah is surrounded by persons," resumed Hajji Sayyid Nasrullah, "who are opposed to the success of the Assembly, and who do not want a law; else, if they desired reform, it would be well that they should entrust the artillery, for example, to some more capable person, and so with other departments. And though these things are not the business of the Assembly, I must observe that affairs cannot be permitted to revert to their previous condition, when such offices were merely nominal: henceforth they must be assigned in accordance with merit and capacity." And these utterances, culled from the debate of Jan. 19, 1907, fairly represent the general tone and feeling of the Assembly.

The Assembly, whatever its defects may have been, saw quite clearly where reform was most needed. Warned by the experience of other Muslim countries, such as Egypt and Tunis, which have suffered from European intervention, they clearly perceived the danger of being indebted for even so comparatively small a sum as three or four millions of pounds to one, and still more to two, of the great European Powers; and they saw that the extravagance of the Shah and his Court was the primary source of this danger. They were also thoroughly alive to the evils inherent in the abominable system of farming the revenues, whereby of ten *tumans* extorted by every species of tyranny from the peasantry, hardly one ultimately reached the State Treasury. Hence their efforts were at an early stage directed:

(1) To preventing any fresh loans from Russia or England;

(2) To fixing the Shah's Civil List, and vigorously limiting him to that amount;

(3) To the establishment of a National Bank;

(4) To the abolition of *madakhil,* or irregular and illegal profits, especially in the collection of the revenues;

(5) To getting rid of the Belgians and other foreigners who, originally introduced to organize the Customs, had latterly increased in power to a most dangerous extent, and whose object was rather to encourage than to check the extravagance of the Court. Amongst these Belgians, M. Naus and his co-adjustor M. Priem were specially obnoxious.

12 / THE BIRTH OF ARAB NATIONALISM

On the 24th of July 1908, in a panic caused by the sudden outbreak of a military revolution, Abdul-Hamid granted his subjects a constitution.

From George Antonius, *The Arab Awakening* (New York: Capricorn Books, 1965), pp. 101–5, 107–12. Copyright 1946 by G. P. Putnam's Sons. Reprinted by permission of G. P. Putnam's Sons.

On the following day, he abolished the censorship, released all political prisoners and disbanded his army of 30,000 spies. Like a carnival queen, Liberty—or at any rate a paper incarnation of her—made her entry from round the corner and bowed, scattering her favours by the armful.

The revolution was the work of the Committee of Union and Progress,[1] a secret association which the Young Turks had formed in Salonica with the object of overthrowing the Sultan's despotism. It is not necessary for our purposes to trace the rise of the Young Turk party back to its origins, for there was no inter-connexion between its aspirations and those of the Arab movement save in so far as hatred of the Hamidian despotism was common to both. Although a few Arabs, most of them army officers, had joined the party and worked hand-and-glove with its leaders, they had done so as Ottoman citizens rather than as Arab nationalists. The C.U.P. were a medley of races and creeds, in which Turks predominated and Jews came second, with Ottoman nationals of other races in tow, and political refugees and exiles abroad in the background; and while it is true that the motives which prompted the party were as mixed as its composition, its first object was to put an end to Abdul-Hamid's autocratic rule and secure good government for the empire on the basis of racial fusion as envisaged in the 1876 Constitution. The military members were influential in the councils of the party, as became a generation in which military education was held in high honour, and it was perhaps inevitable that it should have resorted, for its sudden *coup d'état,* to a revolution proclaimed by the army—the very thing that Abdul-Hamid had dreaded most.

The constitution of 1908 was none other than Midhat's project of 1876, resuscitated by a stroke of the pen, with its old imperfections rendered more incongruous by the passage of time and the growth of national sentiment. But its revival was greeted with enthusiasm, and nowhere perhaps was the jubilation greater than among the Arab nationalists who, in the first flush of deliverance, had mistaken it for real liberty. There was rejoicing all over the empire, in which Turks fraternised deliriously with Arabs, and Moslems with Christians, in the genuine belief that the constitution would meet everybody's wants. Its incompatibility with cultural aspirations seems to have passed unperceived. The fact that it provided for the fusion of the different races into a single, Ottoman democracy with Turkish for its distinctive language was in itself the very negation of the doctrine of cultural identity. But such was the intoxicating effect of the mere appearance of freedom that few were left with the power to think clearly; and

[1] Henceforth referred to as the C.U.P.

months were to elapse before those few could get a hearing for their misgivings.

It was during this Turco-Arab honeymoon that the first Arab society was founded under the name of *al-Ikha al-Arabi al-Uthmani*.[2] At a large meeting of the Arab colony in Constantinople, held on the 2nd of September, and attended by members of the C.U.P., the society was formally and enthusiastically inaugurated. Its main objects were to protect the Constitution, unite all races in loyalty to the Sultan, promote the welfare of the Arab provinces on a footing of real equality with the other races of the empire, spread education in the Arabic tongue and foster the observance of Arab customs. Its membership was open to Arabs of all creeds, and branches of it were to be founded throughout the Arab provinces, and a newspaper was actually started to promote the diffusion of its ideas which, as we have seen, rested on a confusion of thought.

Two measures were taken at the time, which deserve our notice. One was the formal inauguration in September of that year of the Hejaz Railway line which had been completed to Madina. The other was the appointment of the Sharif Husain ibn Ali to be Grand Sharif of Mecca.[3]

Husain was still living in Constantinople, in that enforced quietude to which the Sultan's guests were bound. He had been a captive for nearly sixteen years, and his captivity had restrained but not deadened his spirit. He was by nature keen and talkative; but the caution he had had to exercise, sharply driven home by an episode of confidences betrayed, had taught him a wary reserve. In public life—the Sultan had appointed him to be a member of the Council of State—he was a conspicuous and venerated figure, as a descendant of the Prophet could scarcely escape being in the capital of Islam. In addition to his descent, his piety, his exquisite manners and the irreproachable pattern of his life had earned him the reverence of a large circle of admirers. Because of that, and still more because they knew him to be unbeloved of the Sultan, the C.U.P. in power chose him to be Sharif of Mecca, in place of the ruling Sharif. Abdul-Hamid opposed the appointment, urging with canny foresight that Husain in an office of that importance would be no mere tool, but a force and possibly a danger. But his warnings went unheeded, and Husain sailed for the Hejaz. He was a man of 53 at the time.

[2] The Ottoman Arab Fraternity.
[3] The title of *Sharif* was borne by all descendants of the Prophet and carried no function with it. The post to which Husain was now appointed, of which the full designation was *Sharif and Amir of Mecca,* carried with it a definite and important function of which the main attribute lay in the custody of the Holy Places of Islam in the Hejaz, and the supervision of the pilgrimage and other observances.

Then elections were held for the first parliament under the new constitution, and it was over this question that the unnatural alliance of Turks and Arabs received its first jolt. The electoral machinery was controlled by the C.U.P., and had been so geared as to ensure the return of a great majority of their nominees. But more than that, the electoral constituencies had been demarcated in such a way as to favour the Turkish element at the expense of the other races. The Turks were by no means the largest element in the empire, and were actually outnumbered by the Arabs, roughly in a ratio of three to two.[4] Yet in the Chamber of Deputies which assembled in December, out of a total of 245 elected representatives, 150 were Turks and 60 were Arabs, a ratio of five to two to the advantage of the Turks. In the Senate which numbered forty members appointed by the Sultan, there were only three Arabs. This was the first of a series of measures which were to reveal an ever-widening gap between what the Turks professed and what they practised in the matter of racial equality. It gave the sceptics among the Arabs their chance, and this time, their misgivings met with a ready hearing.

In April of the following year, another revolution broke out with the same suddenness as in the preceding July. This time it was Abdul-Hamid trying to overthrow the C.U.P. On the 13th of April, incited by agents of the Sultan, the troops forming the garrison of Constantinople broke into mutiny, rushed the Parliament buildings and killed, besides several of their own officers, the Minister of Justice and an Arab deputy.[5] When the news of the outbreak reached Salonica, Mahmud Shaukat Pasha decided to march on the capital. He was an Arab who had risen to high rank in the Turkish army and was then in command of the army corps stationed in Salonica. He entered Constantinople, after some stiff fighting, on the 24th and restored the authority of the C.U.P. Three days later, the Senate and the Chamber sitting together pronounced the deposition of Abdul-Hamid and proclaimed his brother Prince Reshad sultan in his stead.

The new sovereign who took the name of Mehemed V, was sixty-four years of age, and a gentler, more self-effacing and ineffectual old man was never girded with the sword of Othman. He had none of the ambition or the vices of his predecessors and was willing to let others rule him as well as rule in his name. With his accession, the C.U.P. found themselves in absolute mastery, and in the five years which elapsed before the outbreak of the First World War, they held office

---

[4] No accurate statistics exist. A fair approximation would give the total population of the Ottoman Empire in 1908 (excluding Egypt) as amounting to 22 million, of whom 7½ were Turks by race, 10½ Arabs, and the remaining 4 Greeks, Albanians, Armenians, Kurds and smaller elements.

[5] The Druze Amir Muhammad Arslan, one of the deputies for Syria.

with but few breaks and established a tyranny which, albeit different in kind from that of Abdul-Hamid, was not less despotic and, so far as the Arabs were concerned, a good deal more detested. One of their first acts after they had overcome the outbreak in April was to ban the societies founded by the non-Turkish racial groups, amongst them *al-Ikha al-Arabi* which, barely eight months before, had been inaugurated with vows of everlasting fidelity, at an impassioned meeting of Arabs and Turks in the gaudy radiance of their honeymoon. . . .

By their suppression of *al-Ikha al-Arabi*, the C.U.P. drove the Arab leaders to underground methods, and a series of societies came into being, among which were some whose existence never became known to the Turks. The propagation of Arab national ideas was henceforth conducted on two planes: that of the open platform, functioning through the agency of recognised clubs and associations; and that of the subterranean channel, fed by secret, conspiratorial organisations. A number of those societies were formed and became active between 1909 and 1914; and four of them, of which two were public and two secret, deserve special mention.[6] The activities of each group were to a great extent complementary to each other, and it would perhaps make their inter-connexion clearer if, taking liberties with their chronological sequence, we were to review the two recognised societies first, and then pass on to the activities of the two secret groups.

The earliest, *al-Muntada al-Adabi* (i.e., the Literary Club), was an association founded in Constantinople in the summer of 1909 by a group of officials, deputies, men of letters and students,[7] to serve as a meeting-place for Arab visitors and residents in the capital. Its clubhouse was equipped with a library and a hostel, and it did become the busy and useful centre it was intended to be. The C.U.P. tolerated it, and for a time gave it their patronage, since its objects were not avowedly political. In actual fact, it exerted a good deal of political influence, and there came a time when its committee became the recognised intermediary in negotiations for the settlement of differences between the Arabs and the C.U.P. But its function was essentially

---

[6] I have collected from numerous written and oral sources—in most cases from the founders themselves—enough material for a fairly complete record of those societies. But since a full inventory would take too long and make for redundancy, I am confining myself here to an account of those societies whose contribution to the history of the movement formed an essential link in the chain of its development.

[7] Among whom were: *ᶜAbdul-Karim al-Khalil (Moslem from the Lebanon); *Saleh Haidar (Moslem from Baalbek); *Rafiq Sallum (Christian from Homs); Jamil Husaini (Moslem from Jerusalem); Yusuf Mukhaiber (Moslem from Baalbek); *Saifuddin al-Khatib (Moslem from Damascus).

* An asterisk denotes that he was hanged by the Turks during the War on a charge of treasonable nationalistic activities.

that of a clearing-house rather than a factory of ideas, and its contribution to the Arab movement did more to strengthen its appeal and extend its reach than to give it a new impulse. It had an enormous membership running into thousands of whom the majority were students, and it established branches in various towns of Syria and Iraq; and not the least of its uses was that it provided centres in which Arabs from all parts of the Empire felt at home and talked freely in an atmosphere in which minds relaxed and the traffic of ideas could move.

The other important public society was founded in Cairo towards the end of 1912, with the name of "The Ottoman Decentralisation Party." [8] Its objects were twofold: to impress upon the rulers of Turkey the need for decentralising the administration of the empire; to mobilise Arab opinion in support of Decentralisation. Its founders were, for the most part, men of experience and good standing, who had made their mark in public life.[9] The statutes of the society provided for an elaborate party machine. The control was vested in a powerful committee of twenty members domiciled in Egypt and a smaller executive body of six of their own number. Branches were established in every town of Syria and smaller agencies in a number of other localities; and the closest contact was maintained between its branches and other Arab political associations in Syria and Iraq, and of course with *al-Muntada al-Adabi* in Constantinople. In about a year, the committee of the Decentralisation Party had become the best-organised and most authoritative spokesman of Arab aspirations.

The importance of this society in the history of the Arab movement was that it provided its first essay in the science of organised effort. The battle between the C.U.P. with their policy of unification at the centre and the Arabs clamouring for home rule had gone on for three years in that intermittent dispersed way which is characteristic of Arab warfare; and the foundation of the society was an attempt at co-ordinating the efforts into one, concerted and continuous pressure.

Meanwhile, the two secret societies had come into being. One was *al-Qahtaniya*[10] which was established towards the end of 1909, not long after *al-Muntada al-Adabi*. Its founders were men of a bolder stamp, and its objects were to promote a new and daring project—

[8] *Hizb al-Lamarkaziya al-Idariya al-ʿUthmani.*

[9] Among them were: Rafiq al-Azm (Moslem from Damascus); Rashid Rida (Moslem from Tripoli in Syria); Iskandar ʿAmmun (Christian from the Lebanon); Fuad al-Khatib (Moslem from the Lebanon); *Salim Abdul-Hadi (Moslem from Jenin); *Hafez al-Said (Moslem from Jaffa); *Naif Tellu (Moslem from Damascus); *ʿAli Nashashibi (Moslem from Jerusalem).

* An asterisk denotes that he was hanged by the Turks during the War on a charge of treasonable nationalistic activities.

[10] Named after Qahtan, one of the legendary ancestors of the Arab race.

that of turning the Ottoman Empire into a dual monarchy. This was yet another attempt to grapple with the problem created by the C.U.P's centralising policy. The Arab provinces were to form a single kingdom with its own parliament and local government, and with Arabic as the language of its institutions; the kingdom was to be part of a Turco-Arab empire, similar in architecture to the Austro-Hungarian edifice; and the Ottoman sultan in Constantinople would wear, in addition to his own Turkish crown, the crown of the Arab kingdom, as the Hapsburg emperor in Vienna wore the crown of Hungary. Thus unity could be reached through separation, and the destinies of Turks and Arabs linked together on a more lasting, because more realistic, basis.

Here was a concrete plan with a definite idea behind it, and the authors of it were a band of practical and determined men who saw the impossibility of carrying it through by public advocacy. They were led by Aziz Ali al-Masri, an officer in the Turkish army, of whom we shall hear more hereafter. The members of al-Qahtaniya were chosen with care, only those being admitted whose patriotism was above question and who could be trusted to guard a secret.[11] Its membership included several Arab officers of high rank in the Turkish army, and two of the founders of *al-Muntada al-Adabi*. The society had a password and a signal for identification, and branches were established in five centres besides Constantinople. It derived its strength from the personalities of some of its members, and its importance in the history of the movement was that it made the first known attempt to win the Arab officers serving in the Turkish army over to active co-operation in the national movement.

The society was very active in the first year of its existence, until the founders were given cause to fear a betrayal. Despite the care with which candidates were chosen, one member—his name is not in the preceding footnote—was found to have betrayed confidences, and the rest of the company became uneasy. The society was not actually dissolved, but its leaders found it impossible to continue with a presumed traitor in their midst, and it died of wilful neglect.

The other secret society was *al-Fatat*,[12] which was founded in Paris in 1911. No other society has played as determining a part in the history of the national movement. Its founders were seven young Arabs,

[11] Among them were: *Salim Jazairi (army officer, Moslem from Damascus); the Amirs Amin and Adel Arslan (Druzes from the Lebanon); Khalil Himadeh (Moslem from Bairut); Amin Kazma (Christian from Homs); Safwat al-Awwa (army officer, Moslem from Damascus); *Ali Nashashibi (army officer, Moslem from Jerusalem; *Shukri al-Asali (Moslem from Damascus).

* An asterisk denotes that he was hanged by the Turks during the War on a charge of treasonable nationalistic activities.

[12] Its full name was *Jamiyat al-Arabiya al-Fatat;* i.e., the Young Arab Society.

all of them Moslems, who were pursuing their higher studies in the French capital,[13] and who, by reason of their youth, their keenness and the unanimity of their views, gave it unity and vigour. In that respect, its foundation recalls that of the Bairut secret society of 1875, with this difference that the initiative had passed into the hands of Moslems. The objects of the society were to work for the independence of the Arab countries and their liberation from Turkish or any other alien domination—a significant advance on those programmes which aimed at autonomy within the empire, and an unconscious return to the ideals of the Bairut secret society.

The influence of *al-Fatat* on the march of events will appear presently. Here, we are concerned with its development, which was cautious yet rapid, and which made it into the most effective of the Arab societies of the time, remarkable alike for its objects and methods as for the admirable discipline of its members. Membership was made subject to a long period of probation. Each recruit was introduced by one of the sworn members but was kept in ignorance of the identity of all the other members until he had been tried and proved, when he would be invited to take an oath to serve the ends of the society, to the point of forfeiting his life, if need be, in its service. For the first two years, its centre was Paris; and its membership remained small: then, as its founders graduated and returned to their homes, it was shifted to Bairut in 1913 and in the following year to Damascus. Its membership rose to over 200, most of whom were Moslems, with but a few Christians. The secret of its existence was guarded to the end, and the Arab countries had gained their liberation from Turkish rule before it was disclosed. During the [First World] War, when the Turks were prosecuting Arab nationalists for treason, one member of *al-Fatat* was driven by physical torture to attempt suicide, and another went to the gallows rather than betray the society's secret. The oath its members had had to take may seem a trifle melodramatic, but there is little harm in melodrama when it can inspire fidelity.

[13] They were: Auni Abdul-Hadi (Jenin); Jamil Mardam (Damascus); *Muhammad al-Mihmisani (Bairut); Rustum Haidar (Baalbek); *Taufiq al-Natur (Bairut); Rafiq Tamimi (Nablus); *Abdul-Ghani al-Urayisi (Bairut).

* An asterisk denotes that he was hanged by the Turks during the War on a charge of treasonable nationalistic activities.

13 / ARAB-TURKISH RELATIONS

It is also time for Western historians to abandon some of their long cherished misconceptions about Arab-Turkish relations. Taking the

From Zeine N. Zeine, *Arab-Turkish Relations and the Emergence of Arab Nationalism* (Beirut: Khayat's, 1958), pp. 118–25. Reprinted by permission of the author.

latter part of the nineteenth and the beginning of the twentieth centuries as their observable starting points, at a time when corruption in the Ottoman administration was reaching its nadir and Arab-Turkish relations were strained severely both because of the shortsightedness of the Turks themselves and because of the political machinations of the Western Powers, they have projected this picture into the previous 375 years of Turkish rule in Arab lands and have reached the conclusion that the Arabs "suffered" for four hundred years under the yoke of Turkish misgovernment and despotism! Nothing is further from the truth than this assertion.

It is true that the Ottoman Empire was composed of a mosaic of races, nationalities and religions which the Turks did not attempt either to unite by force or to "Turkify." But it must be remembered that during the greatest part of Turkish rule the Arabs did not consider the Turkish rule as a "foreign" rule. The word "foreign" did not have in those days the twentieth century political connotation of a *nationally* alien and, often, politically "undesirable" person. The world in which the Arabs and the Turks lived together was in the nineteenth century sense of the term, *politically* a non-national world. The vast majority of the Arabs did not consider the Turks as "foreigners"—except when the Turkish leaders themselves, after 1908, ceased to be considered in Arab eyes as good Muslims and defenders of Islam and as brothers in the Faith.

It is thus unjustifiable to regard the Turks as the oppressors of the Arabs except in the last years of Turkish rule, during which time the Turks suffered at least as much as the Arabs from Turkish misgovernment. Numerous facts and accounts support the conclusion that the Turkish government before its decline and fall was, on the whole, orderly and reasonable in the treatment of its subjects. For nearly three hundred years, the Ottoman administration in Arab lands compared favourably with that of most of the governments of Europe. . . .

It has often been said that the Arabs experienced a national *awakening* as a result of the impact of the West on them in the nineteenth century. There is no satisfactory historical evidence for this contention. If by Arab awakening be meant the awakening of Arab *national consciousness*, then the term "awakening" is a misnomer. Throughout the four centuries of Turkish rule, the Arabs remained conscious of their religion, *Islam,* and of their language, *Arabic.* They never ceased to think of themselves as *Arabs.* Indeed, the vehemence with which the Arabs opposed the Turkifying policy of the Young Turks is in itself a proof that their Arab consciousness was wide awake. Had Arab consciousness been submerged and destroyed by the Turks as is commonly asserted, the Young Turks would have had very little difficulty in "Turkifying" the Arab lands. Nationalism has undergone several changes in meaning during the course of its evolution in various States. But if we take into consideration, basically, the racial, cultural and spiritual concept of nationality, we find that Arab nationalism is one of the oldest nationalisms in the world.

The true birth of Arab nationalism took place with the rise of Islam. Even as a generalization, there is no support for the contention that Arab nationalism was born as an "intellectual movement" in literary circles and secret societies and especially through the fiery poems of Arab poets. Islam was revealed by an Arabian Prophet, in the Arabic language, in Arabia. We read in the Quran: "A Messenger has now come to you from among yourselves. . . ." [1] There is a tradition that the Prophet said one day: "I am an Arab, the Quran is in Arabic and the language of the denizens of Paradise is Arabic." And according to another tradition, he is reported to have stated: "He who loves the Arabs loves me, and he who hates them hates me." The Arabs could not help feeling that they were a "chosen race." It was the Muslim Arabs of Arabia that the Prophet glorified in these words: "Ye are the best people (*Umma* or "nation") that hath been raised up unto mankind." [2] One of the basic aims of Islam was to replace the narrow blood and tribal ties existing among the Arabs in pagan days or the "Days of Ignorance" by a broader, a wider "religious patriotism" found in Islam itself. The Arabs were to be united into one great community, the Community of the Faithful—the *Umma* or the "nation" of Islam. "Verily, you are the people of one 'nation' and I, your Lord; therefore, worship me." [3] The Arab nation was, thus, a nation originally born out of Islam. This "religious nationalism" remains an indelible part of the hearts and minds of the Arabs. . . .

Arab national consciousness survived throughout the centuries, in spite of all the vicissitudes of the Arabs during their long history, because two of the strongest ties of national unity, in the broad sense of the term, were never destroyed: the linguistic and the religious. The Arabs continued to *feel* as Arabs, because they continued to speak one language and believe in one religion. Their cultural and spiritual ties remained far stronger than either territorial unity or geographical separation. Hence the Arabs never lost or "forgot" their "nationalism" under the Turks, especially as the Turks made no attempt, except at the eleventh hour—to "Turkify" the Arabs. All that the Arab leaders wanted at first—the masses were still indifferent—was that the Arab provinces *within the Ottoman Empire* should have an independent Arab government. They believed that the best form of government for the multi-national, multi-racial Ottoman Empire was a decentralized

[1] Sura 9, *Al-Tawbah:* "Repentance," v. 128.
[2] Sura 3, Al-Imran ("The Family of Imran"), v. 106.
[3] Sura 21, Al-Anbia ("The Prophets"), v. 91.

government. Some had in mind visions of an Ottoman "Commonwealth of Nations." As to *complete separation* from the Ottoman Empire, the idea was only in the minds of few extremists among the Muslims, before the Turkish Revolution of 1908. Its exponents and real supporters were primarily the Christians of Lebanon. But after 1908, the idea was almost forced upon some Muslim Arab leaders by the short-sightedness and chauvinistic Pan-Turanian policy of the Young Turks. The despotic policy of Djemal Pasha, Commander-in-Chief of the IVth Army in Syria, during the First World War when he ordered the hanging of prominent Arabs in Beirut and Damascus, widened still further the breach between the Arabs and the Turks and greatly intensified the Arab leaders' desire to break away completely from the Ottoman Empire. Finally, the promises of the Allies, again during that War, to "liberate" the Arabs from the Turks and to give them their "independence," led to the Arab Revolt which started in Mecca on June 10, 1916, under the leadership of Sharif Husain. . . .

This "political nationalism" which marks the second stage in the development of Arab nationalism was primarily a product of political and social conditions prevailing during the last years of Turkish rule in Arab lands. But even then, religion was not divorced from Arab nationalism. Not only the vast majority of the Arabs were Muslims, but together with the goal of self-determination and self-government went the further aim of rising to the defence of Islam, restoring its past glories and raising the Arabs—"the race by means of which God had led the peoples (of the world) from darkness to light"—to their rightful place under the sun, the glorious place which God had destined for them, as His own "chosen Umma." [4]

[4] See King Abdullah's *Muthakkarati,* p. 121 and *Al-Manar,* vol. XVI, Part 10, pp. 735–754.

14 / THE STRUGGLE FOR ARAB SELF-DETERMINATION

On the 6th of March [1920], the General Syrian Congress met in Damascus. This Congress had originally been convoked by Faisal before the arrival of the American King-Crane Commission. It had already decided on the drastic step which it was going to take. Faisal addressed them briefly asking them to decide on the future course of the Arab lands in the light of the doctrine of self-determination and the freedom of nations which President Wilson and the Allies had announced. He reminded them that the Arabs had fought during the [First World] War for their freedom and national independence.

From Zeine N. Zeine, *The Struggle for Arab Independence* (Beirut: Khayat's, 1960), pp. 137–49. Reprinted by permission of the author and the publisher.

Theirs was a great responsibility and a grave duty, today. They had to decide on the form which their new country was going to take and lay down a constitution for it. He also reminded them, in conclusion, that their Iraqi brethren had fought and served well the national patrimony. For their future strength and happiness, cooperation between them all was most essential.

The following day, 7th March, the General Syrian Congress "representing the Syrian Arab nation" drew up a historic resolution. After reviewing the purpose of the Arab Revolt, the sacrifices of the Arabs during the War, the promises of the Allied leaders on the principle of self-determination, the division of Syria into three enemy-occupied zones, the resolution went on to say that the people of Syria wanted to put an end to their doubts and uncertainties and obtain their independence. Consequently, the Syrian Congress was unanimous in proclaiming the full independence of Syria with "its national boundaries," including Palestine in which they rejected the claim of the Zionists for a National Home for the Jews. "We have, accordingly," said the resolution, "chosen His Highness the Emir Faisal, the son of His Majesty King Husain . . . a constitutional King over Syria with the title of His Majesty King Faisal I, and we hereby declare the termination of the present occupying military governments in the three Zones. They will be replaced by a constitutional monarchy." The national aspirations of the Lebanese were to be respected. The Lebanon will have its autonomy within its old pre-war frontiers provided it keeps away from any foreign influence. As the purpose of the Arab Revolt was to liberate the Arab nation from Turkish rule, "We ask for the full independence of Iraq," the resolution proclaimed with the understanding that there will be a political and economic union between Syria and Iraq.

The resolution ended with an assurance that friendship with the Allies would be maintained and their interests respected, and with the hope that the Allied Governments and all the other countries would recognize the independence of Syria.

The following day, 8th March, the foregoing resolution was read to the populace at about three o'clock in the afternoon from the balcony of the town hall in Damascus, the Emir having arrived there riding through cheering crowds. Faisal was proclaimed as King of the "United Kingdom of Syria," i.e. of Syria, the Lebanon and Palestine, while one hundred and one salvoes greeted the birth of the new Kingdom and its new flag was unfurled. A few minutes later and from the same balcony another proclamation was read declaring the "complete independence of Iraq" under the sovereignty of Faisal's brother, the Emir Abdullah. This decision had been taken by an "Iraqi Congress" meeting in Damascus and working in cooperation with the General Syrian Congress.

It is to be noted that the proclamation of the United Kingdom of Syria was contrary to the original aim of Sharif Husain, which was the independence of all the Arabs and Arab countries in the Near East under his Kingship. But the Arab leaders assembled in Damascus found the former step more in line with the exigencies of the time. However, the late King Abdullah of Jordan frankly criticized the proclamation of his brother as King of Syria. It was done against the advice of his father, who wanted it postponed until after the treaty of peace with Turkey had been signed and the latter had renounced its rights in all the Arab lands. The Arab policy of recognizing and proclaiming an independent Syria and an independent Iraq was, according to King Abdullah, one of the greatest mistakes of the Arabs after the First World War. It destroyed Arab unity and led directly to the establishment of Mandates in those two countries. He believed that it was brought about by the influence of those Arab leaders who had for years served under the Turks and who were still thinking in terms of "Decentralization," which was then the principal objective of Arab independence.

On the 9th March, Rida Pasha al-Rikabi became the first Prime Minister of the New Kingdom of Syria and formed his first Ministry. He wrote immediately to the Allied Governments notifying them of the proclamation of Syrian independence, sending them a copy of the resolution taken by the General Syrian Congress, explaining the good intentions of the new Syrian Government and trusting that the Allies would recognize the new Syrian Kingdom. Faisal himself sent personal letters and cables to President Wilson, Lord Curzon, General Allenby and General Gouraud, explaining why it had become necessary to proclaim the unity and independence of Syria, emphasizing that this was not against the interests of the Allies and assuring them of the friendship and cooperation of the new State of Syria. Lord Curzon sent an immediate telegraphic reply on 9th March in the name of the British and French Governments, protesting strongly. He stated that the Arab Congress was not a legal body, that it had acted against the wishes of the British and the French Governments, and that the proclamation of independence would complicate the settling of the Turkish question at the Peace Conference. Moreover, he added that Great Britain did not recognize the right of any group of people in Damascus to speak on behalf of Palestine and Iraq. It should be stated that, on 7th March, Faisal had informed the British Government of the resolution taken on that same day by the General Arab Congress, but as he was proclaimed King the following day, there was no time for the British Government to communicate to him their views. But when Faisal cabled again to Lord Curzon, through Colonel Easton, the British Liaison Officer in Damascus, justifying the action taken by the Congress, the British Government refused to recognise Faisal as anything more than a "Hashimite Emir" and the Head of a Provisional Arab Government under the supreme authority of General Allenby as Commander-in-Chief of the Enemy Occupied Territories. Any permanent settlement had to wait the final decision of the Peace Conference. The French Government, Press and public opinion were greatly irritated, particularly at the inclusion of the Lebanon in the Faisal Kingdom, as he had no right, they said, to meddle in areas *"soumis à l'influence directe de la France."* To a telegram from the French Prime Minister, M. Millerand, to the British Government stating that if Faisal was recognized as King, it would be an unfriendly *("inamical")* act towards France, the British expressed regret at what had taken place and their readiness to protest to the Emir.

The British, French and American press showed much interest in the affairs of Syria at this time. In the [London] *Times* of 13th March, its diplomatic correspondent wrote that Faisal had always expressed readiness to accept a French Mandate over the Lebanon and a British one over Palestine, but "apparently events have proved too strong for him. The proclamation of Faisal as King of an independent and integral Syria, to include Northern Mesopotamia, the Lebanon and Palestine . . . was far from unexpected. But the rapidity with which it has been rushed to an accomplished fact is decidedly disconcerting, and is held to reinforce its character as a challenge to the upholders of the Anglo-French agreements." Mr. Ernest Smith, correspondent of the [London] *Daily News,* wrote from Cairo, on 20th March: "If the Emir Feisul had not come down on the independence side of the fence, his authority would have been entirely lost, carrying with it probably also the loss of the Hedjaz."

Faisal also accorded a number of interviews to the representatives of the foreign press. J. M. N. Jeffries (as representative of the [London] *Daily Mail*) has reported at length on his visit to Damascus and his meeting with Faisal. "It was the first opportunity he had as King," wrote Jeffries, "to speak to the British and European public, and my interview was endowed with some formality." Faisal is reported to have said on this occasion: "Our action was quite justified. Long ago, the Allies promised us an independent Arab State where we have proclaimed it. But what immediately forced Congress to take the step of proclamation was the never-ending delay of the Peace Conference in coming to a decision concerning us. . . . Men (i.e. the Arabs) have lost their confidence: they are convinced that the Allies mean to leave Syria divided into three parts as it is now, and that the promised union of the Arab people in an Arab kingdom or confederation is a myth. The result is that the most dangerous public opinion has been formed in the country and will not hear of further postponements." When

Faisal was asked what would be his attitude towards a Mandate, he smiled and said: "I've not yet arrived at a clear understanding of what a Mandate means. It may mean nothing but friendly support and relations; it may mean colonization. It is too elastic a phrase. Everything depends upon how the 'Mandate' would be exercised." Jeffries' comment on what Faisal told him was: "It disposes absolutely of any idea that he accepted the permanent division of Syria into zones, or that he stood for anything less than the independence of the whole area of Syrian soil."

On 18th March, answering a question asked by Mr. Ormsby-Gore in the House of Commons about the "recent political and military developments in Syria," the Prime Minister said:

> It appears that the Emir Feisul was proclaimed King of Syria, including Palestine and Syria, by a Congress at Damascus on March 8. . . . As it is obvious that the future of these territories which have been conquered from the Ottoman Empire can only be properly determined by the Allied Powers who are at present assembled in Conference for the purpose, the Emir Feisul has been informed by the British and the French that they cannot recognise the validity of these proceedings, and the Emir has been invited to come to Europe to state his case.

A word should be said about the reaction of the Lebanon to the proclamation of Faisal as King of United Syria. The Lebanese Delegation headed by Patriarch Huwayyik had returned to Beirut on the 10th October 1919. But soon after the arrival of Faisal in Damascus in January 1920, Maronite public opinion became greatly perplexed and apprehensive by the turn of events in Syria, particularly when it became evident that, as a result of the pressure of extremists, Faisal had abandoned the idea of signing an agreement with France. Whereupon the Patriarch sent a new Delegation to Paris headed by Bishop (*Monseigneur*) Abdullah Khuri. The delegation arrived in the French capital on the 11th February and started immediately the next day on its task of "saving the independence of Lebanon," by contacting the Ministry of Foreign Affairs. When the news of the 8th March reached Beirut, protests began to pour in at the Maronite Patriarchate from all over the Lebanon, rejecting the claim of the fifteen prominent Muslims of Beirut, who had joined the Syrian Congress as "representatives of Lebanon," and vehemently objecting to the inclusion of the Lebanon in the new Kingdom of Faisal without consulting previously the wishes of its inhabitants. On the 15th March, the Lebanese Delegation in Paris, which had already redoubled its activities, learned that the Patriarch himself had sent a telegram to the Prime Minister, M. Millerand, protesting against the Emir Faisal proclaiming himself as "King over Lebanon." A day earlier, on the 14th, Abdullah Khuri, after consultation with the Ministry of Foreign Affairs and with their approval, had sent a telegram to the Patriarch—through General Gouraud—assuring him that no modification had taken place in the intentions of France towards the Lebanon. General Gouraud incorporated that telegram in a letter which he wrote expressing his own pleasure that the French Government had renewed its intention of standing by the people of the Lebanon.

Three days later, Abdullah Khuri addressed an appeal to M. Millerand to protect the interests of the Lebanon, which were so closely tied with those of France. On the 20th, the Lebanese Delegation was received by the French Prime Minister and assured that the French Government considered the letter of M. Clemenceau to the Maronite Patriarch as a binding agreement which the Government intended to carry out. However, for the time being, the French Government did not feel free to comply with the request of the Lebanese Delegation and act unilaterally to add any new territory to the Lebanon (the plain of the Biqa and the towns of Hasbaya and Baalbek), without consulting other Powers.

Meanwhile, the situation in Mesopotamia was causing the British Government much anxiety. Intense discontent and agitation had finally led to a serious rebellion against the British authorities. The story of that rebellion does not fall within the scope of this work, but it is important to note that the revolt had not only been encouraged by the ex-Iraqi officers in the Turkish army, who had joined the Arab Revolt and were now the trusted advisers of Faisal in Damascus, but was actually organized and led by them. While Faisal himself cannot be accused of having directly participated in the events which convulsed Iraq, his indirect responsibility cannot be entirely denied. He could not resist the pressure of senior Iraqi officers for at least some help, lest he should completely lose their confidence if not altogether their support.

There were also those who strongly advised Faisal to make common cause with Mustafa Kemal Pasha and let the Arabs and the Turks fight once more side by side and thus prevent the French from establishing themselves anywhere in the Middle East. Disappointed at the lack of success which Faisal had in Paris during his second trip to obtain the full independence of Syria, this group convinced the Emir Zaid of the necessity of getting in touch with the Turks and sounding their attitude towards Arab aspirations. Two prominent Syrians did actually travel to Turkey and met secretly the representatives of Mustafa Kemal Pasha in Istanbul. A tentative agreement as a basis of cooperation was drawn up. But when the emissaries returned, in April, the situation had already changed in Syria. King Faisal refused to enter into negotiations with the Turks. When Faisal did change his mind some time in July 1920, it was then too late. Not only in Syria, but in Iraq also, the idea of joining forces with the Turks was being seriously considered by some of the Iraqi nationalists. No wonder then that when Churchill, as Minister of Colonies, spoke in the House of Commons on the situation in the Middle East, on the 22nd of March 1920, he said, referring to the causes of anxiety in Mesopotamia: "There are the Arabs who have been disturbed by the occupation of Syria, and who are inclined now, for the first time, in many ways to make common cause with the Turkish Nationalists, thus uniting two forces by whose division our policy has hitherto prospered." Concerning the recognition of the validity of Syrian independence as proclaimed in Damascus, which was brought up in the House on the same day and to which Mr. Ormsby-Gore referred as "the recent proceedings in Syria," the Prime Minister gave the following answer: "The Emir Feisal was informed that the question of Syria would shortly be examined by the Peace Conference, with a view to arriving at a settlement in accord with the declarations that have been exchanged between the British, French and Arab Governments."

The most important consequence of the 8th March was the irreparable loss of strength and standing of Faisal on the international plane. He was left with no real friends or supporters. He embarrassed his British ally to such an extent that he lost much sympathy for his cause and he confirmed the French and Lebanese fears and suspicions of his real intention. The Lebanese took matters in their own hands —with the knowledge and support of the French authorities. A great meeting composed of the Administrative Council of Lebanon, of Lebanese notables and of representatives of various Christian communities met in Beabda, the old administrative capital of Lebanon, on Monday 22nd March, and proclaimed the independence of Lebanon. At three o'clock in the afternoon and in the midst of an imposing ceremony, the first Lebanese flag was hoisted and unfurled on the Government House at Beabda, in the presence of contingents of the Lebanese army, who marched past and took the salute. The significance of this event could neither be ignored nor minimized in Damascus.

IV / MODERNIZATION AND TUTELAGE:
TURKEY AND IRAN BETWEEN TWO WARS

INTRODUCTION

In this chapter we pick up the interrupted thread of the reform movement in Turkey and Iran. Viewed in perspective, the reformist systems
that came into being between the two world wars in this Northern Tier
of the Middle East appear as the third act in the process of modernization, the first being the era of the Tanzimat (mid-nineteenth century)
and the second supplied by the Young Turk and Persian constitutional-
ist revolutions of the 1906–1909 period.

The distinguishing features of this third period are: emphasis on
nationalism as the only valid basis for loyalty to the exclusion of religious and supranational appeals, stress on external symbolism to under-
line the radical nature of the transformation (removal of veil, introduction of western dress, adoption of Latin script in Turkey), and
popularly based authoritarianism as conducive to assure the best and
speedy results. In some ways, i.e., in the abandonment or rather suspen-
sion of the parliamentary process (for which the reformers of the
previous period had fought with so much zeal), this new act represents a reversal to the patterns set by Sultan Mahmud II and Mohammed Ali of Egypt. As has been said earlier, the two latter rulers laid
stress on the strengthening of the state without being truly concerned
about the democratic process. However, their autocratic rule was content to draw its legitimacy from traditional (and largely irrational)
sources of religious and dynastic nature (even though Mohammed Ali
was only a lately-legitimized usurper). In contrast, both Mustafa Kemal
and Reza Shah, who had different degrees of articulateness, based their
authoritarianism on the actual or presumed will of their nations, and
thus introduced a new—populist—element into their search for legitimacy.

The first three selections in this chapter refer to Kemal and his reform in Turkey. The Kemalist movement was clearly not a coup d'état. It was a real revolution in the political, social, and (although not as strongly) in the economic sense. Not only in the Middle East but in non-Soviet Asia as a whole, Kemalism represented the most radical break with the past in those days. In this respect, Turkey played a role at the western extremity of Asia comparable to Japan's in the eastern extremity of Asia. But while Japan's modernization was primarily socio-economic and technological, Turkey's was primarily political and cultural.

From Lewis V. Thomas' contribution to *The United States and Turkey and Iran* we have selected those sections which speak of the two major conceptual stages of Kemalist revolution: the stage of building a national homogeneity of the Turkish state and the following stage of modernizing it. "Nationalism and Westernization" give in capsule form the essence of this revolution. To build a base for national homogeneity, Greece and Turkey exchanged their respective minority populations. Bold, symbolic acts were needed to bring about modernization. These were provided by moving the capital from effete, Levantine Constantinople to austere, Anatolian Ankara, and by the proclamation of the republic.

The essentials of Kemal's political philosophy are given in selection No. 16 in which parts of his famous eight-day speech to the Grand National Assembly are reproduced. He discusses and rejects the old theories which at one time or another were supposed to provide cohesion and strength to the defunct Ottoman Empire—the theories of Ottomanism and of Pan-Islam. He also derides—as fictitious and utopian—the concept of a universal "humanitarian" state in which the existence of national differences would be ignored. He also implicitly rejects Pan-Turkism as unrealistic. His choice leaves no doubt: "The political system which we regard as clear and fully realisable is national policy." Such a system is an "expression of science, reason, and common sense." Furthermore, Kemal argues, a clear foreign policy must have as its base internal strength which can rest only on a national foundation.

In his *Grey Wolf—An Intimate Study of a Dictator,* H. C. Armstrong gives us a "portrait" of Ataturk as a leader and a man of action. The passages selected present Kemal in the course of his earliest struggles for mobilization of the Turkish masses, civil and military, at a time when a spirit of defeat and resignation prevailed throughout Anatolia. Kemal appears here at his best: as a man devoid of formal authority and yet as fulfilling a task of destiny: struggling, persuading, cajoling, arousing the people from their torpor and despair. Armstrong's account is also valuable for its presentation of the essentially grassroots character of Kemal's early political activity. He traveled widely from village to village, exhorted the people, and encouraged them to organize local committees. No Arab dictator of the 1950s and 1960s has ever managed to establish this kind of close rapport with the popular base.

The last two selections (Nos. 18 and 19) deal with Kemal's contemporary and—in many ways—counterpart as a reformer, Reza Shah of Iran. Reza's rise from obscurity to prominence and his successful subduing of opponents—among the clergy, landowners, and liberals—is presented in Amin Banani's brief, but highly informative, narrative. This background material is followed by a selection from the autobiographical work of Reza's son and heir, Mohammed Reza Shah Pahlavi, in which he devotes considerable space to the description of his father's character and the nature of the reform carried out by him. The picture that emerges is that of a man who had extraordinary leadership qualities, was fiercely independent, and was possessed by an overwhelming urge to mold his people into a pattern that would be consonant with the demands of the twentieth century.

15 / KEMALIST REFORM

In addition to the Treaty of Lausanne, there had also been signed a separate Greek-Turkish agreement providing for the compulsory exchange of populations. The system devised was eventually extended to include more than Greece. For Turkey, it meant that her territory was finally cleared of inhabitants whose language or religion had become gauges of at least potential loyalty to some other nation-state, the Greek and Armenian populations of Istanbul alone excepted, for the people of this sort now all left. They were only partly replaced by Moslem Turks who had hitherto been subjects of Greece, Bulgaria, and so on. To the American reader, comfortably unaware of the pitch to which nationalist tensions rise in this region, the spectacle of large numbers of people painfully being sorted out and relocated in this way, in a sort of hectic international game of musical chairs, is most dismaying, especially as one appreciates the human suffering and sadness involved in plucking simple people from their traditional homes and possessions, and plumping them down in what is still a strange land, for all that it also "should be" their "own land," in habitations and at work unfamiliar and uncongenial to them. Yet, in a broader view it may be that these Draconian measures save much more misery in the long run than they cause at the time. The exchange of populations marked a near-final stage in the forcible execution in Turkey of

From Lewis V. Thomas and Richard N. Frye, *The United States and Turkey and Iran* (Cambridge, Mass.: Harvard University Press, 1951), pp. 69–74. Copyright, 1951, by the President and Fellows of Harvard College. Reprinted by permission of the publisher.

the centuries-old, and formerly largely voluntary, processes of Turkification and Moslemization; it marked an acknowledgment that the old Moslem millet system of a layered society had become unworkable; and it represented a tenable solution for problems which they had caused. Turkey emerged from this long ordeal, through which she had attained a homogeneous population, on many counts poorer. For one thing, she had suffered a sizable net loss of population—how large it is impossible to say, for it occurred before even approximately accurate statistics were available for this area, but certainly a loss to be reckoned in millions. More important, what she lost was largely a class of relatively skilled farmers (compared with the peasants she received in exchange) plus almost the whole of Anatolia's small-town artisans and craftsmen and tradesmen. Her loss was thus a severe economic and social setback in many respects. There are Turks aware of this, but they can still contend that nevertheless the net gain represented in getting the population-uniformity essential for a viable nation-state overweighs all other considerations. As for the western observer, he may properly regret that the trend of history should be such as to make such an assertion true, but he can scarcely hold that it is not true, unless for some reason he opts to argue that the Turks should not have tried to survive as a nation.

So, by 1923, the result of the First World War and of the action-packed years which followed it was, for the Ottoman Empire, death, and for the Turks, life in a new, comparatively small nation-state which they had themselves erected, by force and by diplomatic skill, in the face of heavy odds and with little sympathy or help from any effective non-Turkish power aside from such aid as was given them by Soviet Russia. *Turkey for the Turks was a reality.* The war for national sovereignty was at an astonishingly successful end.

It is at this point that the real measure of Turkey's great good fortune in possessing the leaders she did begins to emerge. Her leaders now had the energy and the vision not to relax, not to regard their success as an end in itself, but only as an essential step towards the real end. *Turkey for the Turks* as it now stood would have poor chances of survival in the turbulent twentieth century, and they knew that. What was needed was nothing less than a truly *new* Turkey, new because its inhabitants would be new-style Turks. July 24, 1923, the date of the Treaty of Lausanne, marked the attainment only of the goal *Turkey for the Turks*. Three months later, with the proclamation of the Turkish Republic, October 29, 1923, came a more important date, for this date, Turkey's independence day, marked the formal starting point of the real Turkish Revolution; the systematic attempt quickly to evoke enough New Turks to ensure New Turkey's continuing survival.

New Turks for a New Turkey

Mustafa Kemal's raw material as of October 29, 1923, is familiar to us in general outline. It included the remaining "true Ottoman" class, perhaps 15 per cent or a bit more of the total population, and the peasants. Non-Moslem minorities were of trivial significance, numerically and otherwise. Westernization had made only the most tenuous and tentative progress among the peasants. During the nineteenth century they had made general acquaintance with the coal-oil lamp, and quite ordinarily used it in their houses; some of the more prosperous of them had western style heating-stoves, but this was relatively rare; and the western-produced looking glass was in nationwide use. These, however, were mere trinkets when compared with what a total direct impact of the west upon the peasant might produce. And to date, little more than trinkets were evident. The growth of an effective self-conscious Turkish nationalism among illiterate people at this cultural level was clearly almost impossible. If such a development was to come, it could not be expected to come from the grassroots up, but would have to be evoked and imposed from the top down.

The ruling group, in contrast, was already quite extensively westernized, but a great deal of that westernization was also made up of fundamentally trivial details and trinkets. It was often more in the nature of a thin veneer laid over the living heritage from the past than it was a vigorous, self-perpetuating organism. In area after area of life, those individuals who were approaching the west were still obliged to deal only or largely with the *letter* of the west, while the *spirit* behind that letter still largely eluded them. . . .

Thus the attempt to evoke and raise up enough truly new style Turks, enough thoroughly westernized Turks, to make a truly New Turkey viable had to begin with the ruling group itself rather than with the peasants. It was not only that large-scale and deep-seated changes in the peasants were practically impossible. Quite beyond that there was the consideration that only an upper class itself united in effective westernization and determined eventually to bridge the gap with the peasantry could hope for success in what would be a nationwide Operation Bootstraps.

So, to begin, Mustafa Kemal aimed his Operation Bootstraps principally at the partially westernized ruling group inherited from the Empire, for it was the only ready material with which he had to work. His program is best described as wholesale, forced-draft, compulsory westernization-plus-nationalism, aimed in the first instance at the upper class and secondarily at the peasant, and designed to produce as quickly as possible a Turkish state and nation which would have not only the several kinds of strength necessary to survive, but which would also have the blessings of western civilization, such as this new Turkey's young leaders conceived those blessings to be.

Step one concerned the form of government . . . A show-down came on the 14th of October, 1923 when Kemal Pasha, with his indomitable personal methods, forced through the reluctant provisional assembly the measure which made Ankara the permanent capital of the Turkish state. This was a move full of implications. Ankara had been well enough for wartime headquarters, but it was nothing but a miserable Anatolian provincial town, devoid of almost all comforts of life, scorched in the summers and frozen in the winters of the plateau's severe climate, treeless, sewerless, without modern buildings, and all the rest. To stay there, deliberately forsaking the inviting comforts of metropolitan and Levantine (that is to say, non-national) Constantinople with its palaces and mosques and countless Ottoman monuments and associations, and also with its capitulations-geared economy and its millet-system-geared society, this was really to burn one's bridges with a public declaration that the nationalists' reiterated claim to stand for the Turkish people, for the nation in whom alone sovereignty and government should rest, was not a mere slogan but was the principle upon which the government now would act in most un-Ottoman fashion. And Mustafa Kemal Pasha had his way. Ankara remained the capital. Before the month was out, the sequel came. On October 29, 1923, the Turkish state was proclaimed a Republic whose power and sovereignty were theoretically vested in the entire citizenry, to be exercised by means of a unicameral legislature, the Grand National Assembly, which was to be responsible only to the electorate. From its own membership the legislature was to choose a President to serve as Chief of State for a four-year term, this being the life of the Assembly as well. . . .

Why was it that Mustafa Kemal and his associates chose a republican form of government? The assertion that they simply and more or less slavishly imitated western models, in so far as they understood them, is a facile and unjust oversimplification. Any attempt to treat any phase of westernization in any area of the Orient simply as a slavish imitation of the west is bound to produce only a lifeless caricature of reality. Of course, the factor of imitation is always present in the westernizing individual's mind, but it is seldom itself dominant. Instead the real and complex motivation is frequently so preponderantly patriotic or idealistic or crusading that the western ideas which the westernizer strives to introduce into his own milieu thereby become important to him simply as "his own," and certainly are his own in fundamental senses. So, in the cases of Turkish nationalism and of Turkey's westernization, the western critic whose principal goal is to tabulate specific western origins and specific paths of entrance of western influence, as important in themselves, is really going down a blind alley. That elements in Turkish nationalism derive from late-nineteenth-century French fiction, as has been argued, may very well be true, but it is not very important. Turkish nationalism is important in direct ratio to two sums: (1) the sum of the people who embrace it, and (2) the sum total intensity with which they embrace it. And these things depend not upon the pedigree of that nationalism, but upon living Turks themselves.

16 / FROM IMPERIAL TO NATIONAL CONCEPT

Soon after the Assembly was opened I described the position and circumstances in which we found ourselves. I also pointed out the course that I considered it would be necessary for us to follow. The most important thing being the political principles which Turkey and the Turkish Nation would have to adopt.

It is well known that under the former systems of Government various political doctrines were held. For my part, I had arrived at the conviction that none of these doctrines could be accepted by the political organisation of the New Turkey. I took care to express my views on this question clearly before the Assembly. Later on I still laboured with the same idea before me. I think I ought now to summarise the generality of the principles which I have exposed at different times concerning this.

You know that life consists of struggles and conflicts. Success in life is only possible by overcoming difficulties. All depends upon strength, upon moral and material energy. Further than that, all the questions that engage the attention of mankind, all the dangers to which they are exposed and all the successes which they achieve arise from the turmoil of the general combat which is raging throughout human society. The conflicts between the Eastern and Western races mark some of the most important pages in history. It is a generally accepted fact that among the peoples of the Orient, the Turks were the element who bore the brunt and who gave evidence of the greatest strength. In fact, both before and after the rise of Islam, the Turks penetrated into the heart of Europe and attacked and invaded in all directions. We must not omit to mention the Arabs also, for they attacked the Occident and carried their invasion as far as Spain and across the frontiers of France. But in every offensive we must always be prepared for a counter-attack. The end that awaits those who act without considering this possibility and without taking the necessary precautionary measures against it is defeat, annihilation, extinction.

From *A Speech delivered by Ghazi Mustapha Kemal, President of the Turkish Republic*, October 1927 (Leipzig: K. F. Koehler, 1929), pp. 376–79, 577–78.

The counter-attack delivered by the West which was aimed at the Arabs began in Andalusia with a heavy historical defeat which pointed a moral. But it did not stop there. The persecution extended to North Africa.

Passing over the Empire of Attila, which extended as far as France and the territory of the West-Roman Empire, we will turn our minds to the times when the Ottoman State in Stambul, founded on the ruins of the Seldchuk State, was master of the crown and the throne of the East-Roman Empire. Among the Ottoman rulers there were some who endeavoured to form a gigantic empire by seizing Germany and West–Rome. One of these rulers hoped to unite the whole Islamic world in one body, to lead it and govern it. For this purpose he obtained control of Syria and Egypt and assumed the title of Caliph. Another Sultan pursued the twofold aim, on the one hand of gaining the mastery over Europe, and on the other of subjecting the Islamic world to his authority and government. The continuous counter-attacks from the West, the discontent and insurrections in the Mohamedan world, as well as the dissensions between the various elements which this policy had artificially brought together within certain limits, had the ultimate result of burying the Ottoman Empire, in the same way as many others, under the pall of history.

What particularly interests foreign policy and upon which it is founded is the internal organisation of the State. Thus it is necessary that the foreign policy should agree with the internal organisation. In a State which extends from the East to the West and which unites in its embrace contrary elements with opposite characters, goals and culture, it is natural that the internal organisation should be defective and weak in its foundations. In these circumstances its foreign policy, having no solid foundation, cannot be strenuously carried on. In the same proportion as the internal organisation of such a State suffers specially from the defect of not being national, so also its foreign policy must lack this character. For this reason, the policy of the Ottoman State was not national but individual. It was deficient in clarity and continuity.

To unite different nations under one common name, to give these different elements equal rights, subject them to the same conditions and thus to found a mighty State is a brilliant and attractive political ideal; but it is a misleading one. It is an unrealisable aim to attempt to unite in one tribe the various races existing on the earth, thereby abolishing all boundaries. Herein lies a truth which the centuries that have gone by and the men who have lived during these centuries have clearly shown in dark and sanguinary events.

There is nothing in history to show how the policy of Pan-Islamism could have succeeded or how it could have found a basis for its realisation on this earth. As regards the result of the ambition to organise a State which should be governed by the idea of world-supremacy and include the whole of humanity without distinction of race, history does not afford examples of this. For us, there can be no question of the lust of conquest. On the other hand, the theory which aims at founding a "humanitarian" State which shall embrace all mankind in perfect equality and brotherhood and at bringing it to the point of forgetting separatist sentiments and inclinations of every kind, is subject to conditions which are peculiar to itself.

The political system which we regard as clear and fully realisable is national policy. In view of the general conditions obtaining in the world at present and the truths which in the course of centuries have rooted themselves in the minds of and have formed the characters of mankind, no greater mistake could be made than that of being a utopian. This is borne out in history and is the expression of science, reason and common sense.

In order that our nation should be able to live a happy, strenuous and permanent life, it is necessary that the State should pursue an exclusively national policy and that this policy should be in perfect agreement with our internal organisation and be based on it. When I speak of national policy, I mean it in this sense: To work within our national boundaries for the real happiness and welfare of the nation and the country by, above all, relying on our own strength in order to retain our existence. But not to lead the people to follow fictitious aims, of whatever nature, which could only bring them misfortune, and expect from the civilised world civilised human treatment, friendship based on mutuality. . . .

17 / KEMAL ATATURK—A PORTRAIT

Suddenly once more Fate gave Mustafa Kemal a full hand of cards. As Liman von Sanders had said of him, he had that essential qualification of a great commander—Luck, and again Luck. He had also the second great qualification of a great commander—the power to seize his Luck and use it.

The Sultan and the English had decided that the first movements of resistance in Anatolia must be checked at once. Someone must go as the Sultan's representative to deal with the situation on the spot, enforce the delivery of arms, the disbanding of troops and stop the meetings of the local committees of Union and Progress.

The Sultan wished to nominate Mustafa Kemal. The English mili-

From H. C. Armstrong, *Grey Wolf—An Intimate Study of a Dictator* (London: Arthur Barker, Ltd., 1933), pp. 125–26, 129–33. Reprinted by permission of Hope Leresche & Steele.

tary authorities objected; he was a dangerous and capable man; they remembered his attitude over Alexandretta. The English High Commissioner was of the same opinion.

Damad Ferid, the Grand Vizier, however, was prepared to vouch for him. . . .

For several days the decision hung in the balance between arrest and deportation or to go to Anatolia as the Sultan's representative. At last Damad Ferid persuaded the English. Mustafa Kemal was taken off the list for arrest. He was already A.D.C. to the Sultan. He was now appointed the Inspector-General of the Northern Area and Governor-General of the Eastern Provinces.

Though unaware of the danger he had been in, Mustafa Kemal, the minute he received the offer, saw his chance. His depression fell from him like scales; his vitality returned and with it his health. Keeping his own counsel, trusting no one but Arif with his ideas, agreeing heartily with the instructions that Damad Ferid outlined for him, he began to plan: as the Sultan's representative he would have an unquestionable standing in Anatolia among the Turks; he would pretend that he had been sent to save them from the English, he would organise resistance; he would yet save Turkey. . . .

The same evening he took passage on a tramp steamer and sailed up the Bosphorus for the Black Sea coast, taking with him Arif and Colonel Refet, who had been nominated to Sivas to command the 3rd Army Corps. . . .

Samsun was held by English troops. An English intelligence officer pried into all that Mustafa Kemal did. The local Greeks and Armenians reported his every move, his interviews, even his telephone calls. The Turks were half afraid to talk with him.

Making an excuse he moved his headquarters to Kavsa, and then to Amassia—a town farther inland and on the main road junction between the east and west of Turkey.

Here at last he was free of the accursed English. He opened his shoulders with a sigh of relief and put out both hands to take a grip.

For six months he had sat in Constantinople boiling with rage, forced to remain passive and to hold himself in while the city writhed under the heel of the victorious Allies. For six months he had been forced to watch the politicians and officials, led by the Sultan and Damad Ferid, cringe and crawl before the English. His high pride as a Turk had been torn down to the quick. Grinding his teeth, storing up the bile of a great hatred, he had sat powerless.

Now he could act. From the drab months of sour inaction he reacted with tremendous energy. Resistance to the enemy and the accursed English! He must organise resistance. The first thing was to establish his standing with the army. From Amassia he telephoned and telegraphed out for reports from all over the country.

The position was simple: Turkey lay prostrate in defeat; she had no active power of military resistance. There were four army corps in Anatolia and one in Europe on the other side of Constantinople. Of these, four were mere skeletons: the headquarters staff remained, but the men had been disbanded and the arms had been collected in depots and were being handed over to the English. Only in the east the army corps at Diarbekir under Kiazim Kara Bekir still existed. But in front of Smyrna the mountains were full of guerilla bands sworn to resist the invading Greeks. Rauf had resigned his post as Minister of Marine and was organising these bands.

Mustafa Kemal realised that he must get the backing of the army corps commanders. He called Refet back from Sivas. In Angora with the 20th Army Corps was Ali Fuad. He invited Ali Fuad to meet him in Amassia. Ali Fuad came bringing with him Rauf.

The meeting was secret. Arif kept notes of what was said. Mustafa Kemal put forward his views. All agreed that resistance was their only hope. They sketched out a joint plan of action. In front of Smyrna they must raise more irregular bands to harry and hold up the Greeks. Covered by these they must, on the old army framework, build up a new national army. All through the country they must create local centres for enlisting men and collecting arms. They would find it difficult. They must be cautious, or the English would crush them at the beginning. From the Sultan and the Central Government they would get no help. The people throughout the country were tired out and would not rouse easily.

All the scattered organisations for resistance must be concentrated under one control: Ali Fuad was to command all in the west; Kiazim Kara Bekir all in the east; Mustafa Kemal to be at the centre.

"Further," said Mustafa Kemal, "as the Sultan and the Central Government are in enemy hands, we must set up some temporary government here in Anatolia."

As soon as Mustafa Kemal touched politics the others hesitated and began to doubt him. They knew his revolutionary outlook. Rauf was against anything which could hurt the Sultan-Caliph or the Central Government in Constantinople. Ali Fuad was shrewd and cautious and not prepared to accept Mustafa Kemal as his senior at once. Refet suspected Mustafa Kemal. He remembered that flood of talk on the ship in which Mustafa Kemal had revealed his ambitions, his revolutionary ideas, his complete lack of respect for all traditional loyalties.

Mustafa Kemal used all his persuasive power to win them over. It was vital that he should have their support. Rauf and Ali Fuad agreed. Refet still hesitated; he saw no use in creating a separate government in Anatolia. At last, against his better judgment, he agreed.

They decided that a congress of delegates to represent all Turkey be called to Sivas as quickly as possible. From Diarbekir Kiazim Kara

Bekir, from Adrianople Jaffar Tayar, and from Konia the general in command telegraphed that they agreed with these decisions. Mustafa Kemal had won the first round of the fight. He had the army leaders with him.

At once he set out to raise the country. He toured the villages, harangued the officials, collected up the officers who had become unemployed as the army was disbanded. Always and everywhere he preached resistance to the accursed English. The enemy had decided to destroy Turkey, their Turkey, to break it up; they were planning to make a Greek State round Samsun; all the villages round were full of the agents of the Greek patriarch; the Sultan, their Padishah, was helpless—a captive in English hands; the Sultan had sent him, Mustafa Kemal, to save them: but they, the Turks, must save themselves; no good sitting down and hoping for outside help; arm, volunteer for the new national army, resist; so only could they save themselves from destruction and protect their wives and homes from dishonour.

In each village he appointed representatives to form a committee and become a centre of resistance.

It was heavy work. The people were worn out, utterly crushed. They had given up all hope; the idea of any resistance, or even protest, was gone. They had sunk into a dull lethargy after years of decimating wars and continuous defeat. All they wanted was peace and time to live their quiet lives and harvest their fields.

But as they listened to Mustafa Kemal they woke slowly. News was coming in from Smyrna that the Greeks were burning the villages and massacring Turks. Mustafa Kemal fanned on the poor dull embers of anger and they came to life. A flame of hatred ran through the villages stinging the people into a new energy. The officers, to a man, came in. Mustafa Kemal worked on their enthusiasm and sent them out to rouse more villages.

Leaving Amassia he made eastwards to Erzerum. Here his work was easier. In the Caucasus, out of the country evacuated by the Russians after their Revolution the English had created an Armenian Republic with a frontier joining that of Turkey. They had promised the new republic that when peace was imposed on Turkey the Eastern Provinces of Turkey round Erzerum should be made part of the Armenian Republic.

To the local Turks this meant annihilation. They swore to fight or be wiped out before they would be ruled by Armenians. Moreover Kiazim Kara Bekir and his regular troops were handy and gave them confidence; and the English were far away.

They listened eagerly to Mustafa Kemal. Everywhere he went he electrified the people to hope and action. The men came crowding back to the colours, a ragged riff-raff of good and bad alike. One corporal in a village outside Angora collected three hundred men, drilled them and marched them in to the commander at Angora. In many places the depots under English and French guards were raided and the arms carried away and stored in the mountains, ready for use.

From Erzerum, in the name of the Sultan, Mustafa Kemal sent out orders to the military commanders to delay the handing over of arms to the English and to call back the men to the colours. He instructed the civil authorities to form local committees in the towns and villages for enlisting volunteers, to hold meetings of protest against the occupation of Smyrna, to divert the taxes and make forced collections from the well-to-do merchants.

News of these activities went quickly to Constantinople. The English threatened reprisals. The Sultan flew into a rage: resistance was folly; it was useless and would merely force the Allies to smash Turkey completely; he had sent Mustafa Kemal to the Interior to stop resistance, and now Mustafa Kemal was even using his name to encourage resistance. He had suspected as much. He ordered Mustafa Kemal to be recalled to report.

As soon as he got the orders Mustafa Kemal went to the telegraph office and sent a long, urgent and personal telegram to the Sultan, begging him as the Padishah, the Sovereign and the Leader of his people, to come out and lead them against the foreign enemy. All through that night he waited by the machine for the reply.

At dawn came a peremptory order for his return. He refused categorically.

"I shall stay in Anatolia," he telegraphed, "until the nation has won its independence."

18 / THE RISE OF REZA SHAH

The Character of Reza Shah

Little is known of the early life of Reza Khan, and for several reasons no real biography of this forceful man has been written.[1] He never encouraged people to delve into his past, presumably because there was nothing to fit the traditional mold of the noble savior. Furthermore, during his sixteen years on the throne very little was made public about his personal life. Even the date of his birth is unknown, for there was

From Amin Banani, *The Modernization of Iran, 1921–1941* (Stanford: Stanford University Press, 1961), pp. 39–43. Reprinted with the permission of the publishers, Stanford University Press. Copyright © 1961 by The Board of Trustees of the Leland Stanford Junior University.

[1] A few purported biographies, e.g., Essad-Bey, *Resa Schah: Feldherr, Kaiser, Reformator* (Vienna, 1936), are in reality accounts of his reforms. The biographical passages they contain are inaccurate, contradictory, and sketchy.

no registration of vital statistics in Iran until 1931. His official birthday was celebrated as March 16, 1878. He was born in the Caspian Sea province of Mazanderan, a region that remained the special object of his favor until the end of his reign. Biographical accounts that appeared early in his reign described his ancestry as being from the lower strata of the military class—his father was a sergeant of the cavalry. In later accounts the social standing of his family was elevated, and his father was raised to the rank of colonel. He himself began a military career at an early age, and not much is known of his life until he attained a position of command in the Cossack Brigade. He never received an adequate formal education, and his spelling was the subject of many anecdotes.

Reza Khan was tall, broad-shouldered, and possessed a natural air of authority. He was strong-willed and impatient, quick-tempered and uncouth; but he had to perfection the politician's talent for opportunism. Most of the qualities that alienated him from the refined, Europeanized, and often effeminate sections of society were the same that won him the support of the hero-worshipping lower classes. Although in the early, uncertain days of his career he showed that he knew how to play upon the religious emotions of the people, he was basically apathetic to religion and antagonistic toward the clergy. Moreover, once his power was consolidated, he acted with less caution, and he affronted the clergy and other religious elements on many occasions. His broad social reforms, such as the removal of the veil, were, of course, the subject of deep religious controversy. In his personal life, too, he would occasionally take advantage of an opportunity to offend the sensibilities of the clergy and the zealots. At trade fairs, for example, he made a point of sampling the local beer and commenting on its year-by-year improvement, and at the wedding reception of the Crown Prince he raised a toast to his son in champagne.[2]

He possessed a keen mind, an excellent memory, and an unusual ability to absorb information and briefings even if of a highly technical nature. He seldom made public speeches, but when occasion demanded he was always brief and to the point. Upon laying the foundation stone of the University of Tehran, the first university in Iran, he made the following speech: "The establishment of a university is something that the people of Iran should have done a long time ago. Now that it has been started, all efforts must be made for its speedy completion." [3]

His personal morals were above reproach. His conduct as a public figure, however, showed some serious faults, for as he grew in power,

[2] Nematollah Mehrkhah, ed., *Ketab-e Reza Shah* [*Appreciations of Reza Shah*] (Tehran, 1946), pp. 59, 79.

[3] As quoted in Ali-Asghar Hekmat, *Parsi-ye Naghz* [*Pure Persian*] (Tehran, 1951), p. 464.

his desire to accumulate a fortune developed into a voracious greed, and he became very suspicious and ill-tempered.

The Seizure of Power

Following the *coup d'état* of February 1921, Sayed Ziya tried to pursue a drastic and independent course of action. He made sweeping arrests and resorted to violent means of repression. Fearing unpopularity, Reza Khan arrested and exiled Sayed Ziya in April of the same year. He did not consider the time ripe for a complete assumption of power, and he therefore accepted the post of Minister of War in the cabinet formed by Qavam os-Saltane. The chief accomplishments of this government were the reorganization of the armed forces and the defeat of Kuchek Khan and his Bolshevik-inspired and Bolshevik-aided movement in Gilan. For these achievements Reza Khan alone was responsible, a fact which he did not fail to impress upon the people. One of the avowed policies of Qavam os-Saltane's government was employment of foreign advisors from non-neighboring countries only, a move directed against Russia and the British Empire.[4]

The fourth session of the Majlis was elected in the summer of 1921, the last Majlis to be elected without the complete control and supervision of the central government for more than two decades. Destined to witness profound changes not of its own making, it was a heterogeneous group that symbolized the futility of Iranian politics. Its membership was made up of a minority of well-meaning liberals and a majority of selfish, jealous, reactionary, and defeatist landlords and clergy, and it was dominated by Modarres of Isfahan, an egotistical *mulla* who had no aims beyond self-aggrandizement and the acquisition of power. For no other reason than to test his personal power he pitted himself against Reza Khan in political combat.

In 1922 Reza Khan was preoccupied with the primary task of suppressing revolts and restoring law, order, and governmental authority throughout Iran. In a series of successful campaigns with his reorganized and revitalized army, he put down political and tribal revolts in Azerbaijan, Luristan, Kurdistan, Fars, and Khorasan. He did not fail to derive the maximum political advantage from these military feats. Qavam os-Saltane was replaced by Mostowfi ol-Mamalek as Premier early in 1923.[5] Reza Khan kept the post of Minister of War, but by now he was acknowledged and popularly acclaimed as the chief power in the government.

In the two years that he had acted as Minister of War, Reza Khan had developed a deep-rooted distrust of and contempt for the Majlis. By nature he was not averse to highhanded action, to disregarding

---

[4] See Q4 (1921–23), 321–28.
[5] *Ibid.*, pp. 331–33.

legal procedure and circumventing constitutional democracy. The opposition of a Modarres-led Majlis, and the intrigues of Modarres himself, served only to convince him of the soundness of his instincts. Thus in 1923, as the time for the election* of the fifth session of the Majlis approached, Reza Khan realized that if he were not once more to face a hostile Majlis, he must achieve a more complete control of the government. A plot against his life was discovered, supplying him with the necessary pretext to arrest the Prime Minister. In October 1923 Ahmad Shah appointed Reza Khan as Prime Minister and left for Europe, never to return to Iran.

Having now completed the preliminary steps to the assumption of total power, Reza Khan turned to the task of consolidating his position. He was strongly influenced by the events in neighboring Turkey, and he considered forming a republican government in Iran. The spring of 1924 accordingly witnessed a vigorous campaign for the establishment of a republic, and the enlightened segments of public opinion were prepared for its acceptance. However, the abolition of the Caliphate by the Turkish Republic coincided with this campaign and provided Modarres and other religious elements with their last potent weapon against Reza Khan. Quick and irrational arguments were advanced against a republican form of government. Ugly passions were aroused against Reza Khan by suggesting that he was a Babi and that he conspired to destroy Islam. But Reza Khan proved himself a master politician who could defeat his enemies at their own game.

On the morning of *Tasua,* the anniversary of the martyrdom of Imam Hussayn and the most elaborately commemorated event in *shiah* Islam, a strange procession appeared before the bazaar, the heart of orthodoxy and religious power in Tehran. Traditionally such processions include much flagellation, mortification of the flesh, wailing, and recitation; but this one was a comical combination of East and West. An army band, without caps, marched to a less than definitive version of Chopin's funeral march. At the head of the band marched Reza Khan Sardar Sepah, his bare head covered with straw. To convince any who needed further proof of his piety, he then made a pilgrimage to the *shiah* shrines in Najaf and Karbala. Thus once again Reza Khan triumphed. He had been obliged to abandon the republican project in order to gain this victory; but the last serious opposition was overcome.[6]

In December 1924, returning from a successful campaign against Sheikh Khazal in Khuzistan, Reza Khan received a hero's welcome in Tehran. On February 14, 1925, the fifth Majlis passed the following Act:

* Elections of the Majlis are held every two years in the summer.
[6] See Bahar [Political Parties], p. 363.

The Majlis recognizes the supreme command of the country's defense and security forces as the special domain of Reza Khan Sardar Sepah. He shall exercise his command with complete authority, within the frame of the Constitution and the laws of the land. This command may not be removed without the approval of the Majlis.[7]

The next step was taken on October 31, 1925, when the Majlis passed the following Act:

Majlis-e Showra-ye Melli, in the name of the welfare of the nation, declares the end of the Qajar Monarchy and bestows the provisional government, within the bounds of the Constitution and the laws of the land, to Reza Khan Pahlavi. The final form of the government shall be decided by a Constituent Assembly which shall convene for revision of Articles 36, 37, 38, and 40 of the Supplement to the Constitution.[8]

In December 1925 the Constituent Assembly, elected under the watchful eye of the government, met in Tehran and revised article 36 of the Supplement to the Constitution to read as follows:

The Constitutional Monarchy of Iran is vested by the Constituent Assembly, on behalf of the nation, in the person of His Majesty, the Shahanshah Reza Shah Pahlavi, and shall remain in his male progeny generation after generation.[9]

Similarly articles 37, 38, and 40 were revised to bar any member of the Qajar dynasty from the throne, from the exercise of regency, and from marriages affecting the succession to the throne.[10]

[7] Q5 (1923–25), 253.
[8] *Ibid.*, p. 254.
[9] Iran, *Constitution,* p. 29.
[10] *Ibid.*, pp. 29–30.

19 / REZA SHAH—A PORTRAIT

My father had been born in 1878 in the province of Mazanderan near the Caspian Sea. Unlike the Qajars, who as I have mentioned were of Turkic origin, my father was of genuine Persian stock. Both his father and grandfather had been officers in the old Perisan army. His grandfather had distinguished himself for gallantry in one of our wars against the Afghans, and his father had been commanding officer of a regiment usually stationed in Mazanderan province. When Reza Khan, as my father was called in his early days, was only forty days old, his father died. His mother decided to bring her infant son to Teheran, but on the way the baby almost perished in the intense cold of the mountain roads in winter.

From Mohammed Reza Shah Pahlavi, *Mission for My Country* (New York, Toronto, London: McGraw-Hill Book Company, Inc., 1961), pp. 35–39. Reprinted by permission of Curtis Brown Ltd. on behalf of the Shah of Iran.

When my father was only about fourteen, he enlisted in the Persian Cossack Brigade, which had been formed the year after his birth. At that time he was completely illiterate, for in those days education in Persia was the monopoly of the leisured classes and of the clergy, who kept this privilege to themselves, preventing it from spreading among the common people. They intended the public to remain in ignorance, so that they themselves might do whatever they wished.

When later my father was crowned, he became known, in the style of our ancient royal nomenclature, as Shahanhah (King of Kings), Shadow of the Almighty, Vice-Regent of God, and Centre of the Universe. But when as ruler he received foreign visitors or when he talked with me, he still referred to himself as a simple soldier.

By force of character and his dominant personality my father rapidly advanced. The Persian army had no noncommissioned officers in those days, so that at a certain point he had to make a great leap from private to the officer ranks. Although normally that didn't happen in the Persian army, in my father's case his personality could not be ignored. Broad-shouldered and tall, he had prominent and rugged features, but it was his piercing eyes that arrested anybody who met him. Those eyes could make a strong man shrivel up inside. I have been told that the Russian officers in command of the Persian Cossack Brigade were in awe of him, perhaps actually frightened of him.

One thing that helped my father forge ahead was his habit of study. As a grown man he felt no shame in starting from the beginning. Each day at the end of his army duties, he would sit patiently at his studies in his barracks, learning to read and write with the help of one of his friends. He prepared his lessons by the dim lamps, and when he was tired, he would come out of his tiny room and stand gazing at the twinkling lights of Teheran in the distance.

The Persian military life was not an enviable one in those days. Since the Government had no real authority in the country, it couldn't collect taxes to pay its employees. Soldiers often sold eggs or chopped wood or found other odd jobs just to get a little pocket money for themselves and their families. If and when they were paid anything, it might be in bricks or other construction materials, for the Government was regularly out of cash. My father told me how one day the Foreign Ministry was to give a dinner for a distinguished foreign visitor. Since the ministry had no funds, it had to borrow some money from the shops in the bazaar in order to be able to honour its official guest.

The army's organization was obsolete, its equipment was ancient (the entire army possessed only a handful of cannon, all out of date), and its morale was low. But much worse, as my father saw it, was the terrible knowledge that foreign officers commanded the force to which he belonged. Imagine how galling it was to him to realize that he marched under orders that were often dictated from the Russian rather than the Persian capital. I think he developed his intense feeling of patriotism and nationalism because he knew so well the meaning of foreign domination.

Both as a private and as an officer my father fought many campaigns, especially against the rebellious tribes who were playing havoc with our towns and villages in many parts of the country. Throughout our history, whenever the central government has been weak, tribesmen have pillaged, robbed, and raped as they chose. But when the central government has been strong and could control them, the tribes have played a constructive role in our society. In addition to such expeditions against the tribesmen, many of whom are fierce fighters, my father and his troops engaged other bands of marauding brigands, some of whom were organized into small armies terrorizing the countryside; and after the Russian Revolution he fought the Bolsheviks who had invaded the country.

I remember the moving story my father told me of his feelings in one engagement against brigands. Suddenly he was so consumed by disgust at the whole condition of Persia that he deliberately exposed himself to enemy fire. Mounted on a white horse at the time, he provided a stationary and conspicuous target, but none of the enemy's bullets found its mark.

Why was my father in such a state of mind? I can visualize him now as he sat astride his horse, a man whose regal bearing yet revealed the shame he felt for his country. Really it was not a country, for this once-proud land now possessed no central government worthy of the name. Much of Persia was in the grip of local chieftains paying nominal allegiance to the king, thereby allowing him to save face; actually they were doing whatever they pleased in their own regions, thus compounding the miseries of the people. There was no modern army, and none that owed true allegiance to Persia; there was no law and order; there were no Persian courts save those of the clergy and the tribes. In most of the country it was the law of the stronger that prevailed. The pillagers pillaged, and the common people suffered.

Even in the capital city of Teheran, people normally did not leave their homes after dark except for an emergency such as getting a doctor, if and when one could be found. They knew that cut-throats might set upon them at any moment. From the great days of Darius our communications had deteriorated to the point that to travel from Teheran to Meshed in North-eastern Persia, you had to go by way of Russia, to avoid the decrepit and bandit-infested roads. To go from Teheran to the south-western province of Khuzistan, you had to pass through Turkey and Iraq.

Under the system of capitulations, as I have said, foreigners (including the Bolsheviks who were now infiltrating the country in great numbers) could not have been tried by us for crimes they committed in Persia—if, indeed, we had had any effective courts in which to try them. (Our lack of proper courts was of course the persuasive reason why foreign powers insisted upon continuing the capitulations.) We had no real economic sovereignty because of all the concessions the Qajar kings had granted. Foreign armies, as well as domestic insurgents, roamed the land. The people festered with poverty, illiteracy, ignorance, and lack of hygiene. They were consumed with frustration, discontent, and misery. And in the midst of their desolation the then Shah preoccupied himself with his lavish trips to Europe and his other self-centred luxuries. How could a true patriot have felt otherwise than filled with shame?

It seems that the era, the people, and the necessities of a nation demand that at a certain time the right man be found in a particular position: such a man as will profoundly affect the fate of a country and modify the course of history. Already there had been ample signs that my father might be such a man. At the beginning of 1920, Russian officers still commanded the Persian Cossack Brigade. They were nominally all White Russian, but some of them had sold out to the Bolsheviks. When the brigade went into action against Red Russian units which had invaded northern Persia, the Bolshevik officers were guilty of outright treachery to us. My father's nationalism convinced him that he must get rid of all Russians in the brigade.

In August of 1920, my father acted as his conscience required. He engineered the dismissal of the Russians in the brigade and he himself became commander. The Iranian Government soon confirmed and endorsed his action. My father made no secret of his desire eventually to minimize all foreign influence in Persia.

From that point my father rose rapidly to supreme power. He allied himself with a crusading young journalist named Seyed Zia ed-Din Taba-Tabai. This man, who was the son of a *mullah* (as we call our Islamic clergymen), had courageously been writing about the sad state of governmental and other affairs in Persia. He was a kind of revolutionary, and was well equipped to bring political pressure to bear in the capital while my father applied military force.

Setting out from the north-western city of Ghazvin, my father now staged his famous march on Teheran. On 21 February, 1921, in a virtually bloodless coup, he overthrew the weak and tottering Government. Zia ed-Din assumed the premiership, while my father became Minister of War and Commander-in-Chief of the Persian armed forces.

Zia ed-Din, instinctively the radical reformer, was soon promoting measures that alienated the wealthy conservatives of the country. I think my father disagreed with him more as to tactics and timing than the substance of his political and economic ideas. About three months later Ahmad Shah appointed a new Prime Minister, and my father didn't oppose this move.

My father remained as Minister of War in several successive cabinets, and meanwhile it had become clear that he was the paramount influence in the Government. In 1923 he became Prime Minister. Before long the vacillating Ahmad Shah departed for an indefinite stay in Europe.

The year before my father became Premier, the Turks had abolished their archaic caliphate; and soon afterwards they established a republic under the dynamic leadership of Kemal Ataturk. Some Iranian circles, influenced by these events, leaned towards the idea of setting up a republic in Persia, too. I am sure that my father for a time preferred the concept of a republic. But the tide of opinion now shifted back towards the idea of continuing the monarchical system which after all had for thousands of years been our tradition. Most of the constitutionalists all over the country had always been firm supporters of the monarchical principle.

On 31 October, 1925, Parliament deposed the still-wandering Ahmad Shah, who later died in Europe. On 13 December of that year, Parliament proclaimed my father Shahanshah of Persia. On 25 April, 1926, the actual coronation took place, and at the same ceremony I became Crown Prince.

V / LIBERAL DEMOCRACY IN THE ARAB WORLD

INTRODUCTION

To speak of liberal democracy in the Arab world may appear to some as either grotesque or irrelevant, considering the fact that in the 1960s there was only one Arab state, Lebanon, that could lay claim to such a status. The irrelevance of such a concern may further be reinforced by the pessimistic argument of those who, claiming deeper knowledge of psychology, consider Arab mentality as incapable of accepting and practicing the basic premises of democracy—namely empathy, tolerance of dissent, obedience to the will of majority, protection of the rights of minority, respect for impersonal institutions and procedures, independent judicial process, and self-imposed restraint of those who wield power. These pessimists may ultimately prove right. Their reasoning, however, could be challenged on at least two counts: (a) has the time span during which Arabs have had an unfettered opportunity, free of foreign pressures, to experiment with their political systems been long enough to demonstrate their definite inability to practice democracy? (b) does not the adoption of this pessimistic thesis imply a sort of deterministic "racism" in the sense of denying a given ethnic group, *a priori,* the possibility of changing and reforming its ways?

Even if political democracy in the Arab world is today in a sorry state, two facts deserve to be brought out: first, that the constitutional-parliamentary system that involves the functioning of political parties had been in existence in a number of Arab states prior to the wave of coups and revolutions in the 1950s and 1960s; though imperfect and often inclined toward oligarchy, such a system differed both from its immediate predecessor, the traditional Islamic state, as well as from its immediate successor, the radical military dictatorship; secondly, that between the 1920s and 1950s, a substantial part of the Arab elite had serious and positive commitment to political democracy and gave evidence of this in their thought-provoking writings.

It is from such representative writings that selections in this chapter are presented. Khalid Mohammed Khalid in his now well-known book, *From Here We Start (Min Huna Nabda)* advances a persuasive argument for the necessity of a secular state. Such a state does not imply rejection of religion; on the contrary, he claims, clear division of the secular and the spiritual will help religion to regain its rightful place and deeper meaning in the society. Pursuing this trend of thought, Egypt's foremost intellectual leader, Taha Hussein (many times member of cabinet and internationally recognized man of letters), asks fundamental questions about the character of Egyptian culture that have implications for Arab culture as a whole (selection No. 21). He claims that Egyptian culture forms part of the general environment of the Mediterranean area and, as such, stands much closer to the culture of Europe than to the typically oriental cultures of India and the Far East. His observations regarding the alleged "spiritualism" of oriental cultures as contrasted to the "materialism" of the West are an integral part of his argument and deserve serious attention. In his book, *The Policy of Tomorrow* (selection No. 22), an Egyptian Copt, Mirrit Boutros Ghali, writing in the early 1950s, i.e., at the time of Nasser's advent to power, makes a strong plea in favor of a representative political system, political parties with well-defined programs, and a competent and tenure-guaranteed career civil service that would serve the state impartially regardless of political fluctuations.

Limitations of space do not permit inclusion of excerpts from other writers who spoke on related subjects. The three selected here were chosen because they addressed themselves to the three fundamental issues of democracy, i.e., the secular character of the state, integration of Arab culture with that of the West, and the need for representative institutions and mechanisms required to make democracy work. Even though the democratic experiment in Arab lands was short-lived and squeezed between two eras—traditional and modern—of authoritarianism, the writings reproduced here should serve as a proof that concern with democratic values was more than a passing fancy.

20 / TOWARD A SECULAR STATE

> The person who tells you: "Believe what I believe, or God will send down his curse upon you," would feign tell you: "Believe what I believe, or I will kill you."
>
> —Voltaire

National Rule

There is, today, in our community a whole group of people who demand the establishment of a religious government. They understand

From Khalid M. Khalid, *From Here We Start* (Washington, D.C.: American Council of Learned Societies, 1953), pp. 117–18, 120, 122–23, 124, 125, 129–34. Reprinted by permission of the publisher.

such a government to be one which would rule in accordance with the word of God and would enforce all the prohibitions of divine law. They believe that the application of a single one of those prohibitions is worth more than a forty days' rain in a desert land.

It is futile to ignore or underestimate this view; especially since among its advocates are to be found some of the best elements of the nation—including many of the younger generation. . . . Naturally enough, neither jail nor whip is capable of eradicating or shaking a conviction. . . . Understanding, discussion and argumentation can alone succeed in purifying convictions of whatever illusions and mistakes may lie hidden in them.

If we see in religious governments nothing but failure, and in the will to return to them nothing but an aberration to the old autocracy from which humankind liberated itself at great costs; if we see in them only a risk for religion to soil its purity and jeopardize its security —then, it becomes one of our most sacred obligations to press forward to discuss our view. Our motive in so doing is simply our sincere wish to clear the road of progress for our people and to safeguard and protect religion against all storms and dangers. . . .

In this chapter we shall attempt to answer these questions with all possible frankness. We shall analyze the psychology of religious government in order to find out the fundamental instincts upon which it lives and grows. We shall also follow its evil elements whithersoever they may lead and avail ourselves of a number of great examples which stand out as "types" of chaos and cruelty in the notorious history of religious government.

We do not think we are in need of reminding the reader that in this orientation we do not mean to underestimate, in any way, the value or dignity of religion. Rather, we are earnestly contributing towards the elevation of religion to a plane of distinctiveness and conviction beyond the reach of danger or of those who blame it for the flagrant errors and evils which so-called religious governments have committed in its name. . . .

The Nature of Religion

We do not wish to raise the old question as to whether or not government is a part of religion. We shall try to avoid it, except for occasional casual mention. Our aim here is to analyze the psychology or motivation of religious government and prove that in ninety-nine per cent of the cases, religious government implies an infernal chaos. Perhaps it is a historical institution which once served a useful purpose in the growth of civilization; but in modern times, it has neither mission nor use. . . .

In essence, religion means to liberate men from tyranny and exploitation. Has anything like this ever characterized religious government?

Before we answer this question, we must make a further clarification of the nature of religion. Nothing will better serve our purpose than to seek the high ends for which religion was instituted and the means that it has followed for the realization of those ends.

Mafruq ibn-Amr once asked the Prophet:

"What do you advocate, O brother from Quraysh?"
"The unity of God and my Prophethood."
"And what else?"

Here the Prophet recited the holy verse: "God commands us to be just and benevolent and to protect our brethren. He forbids us to do evil, to accept wickedness or to practice immorality. He exhorts us to goodness, that we may remember."

Justice in government, benevolence in action—these are also properties of religion. Has religious government ever enjoyed these characteristics during its long history?

Religion also calls for love. It glorifies the lovers in and through God. It seeks to group human beings and unify them around a single man's heart. In pursuance of this end, it declares the promoter of faction to be the enemy of God and of His Prophet.

The Prophet, furthermore, was always crystal-clear about his prophetic mission; its essence never left his mind. He knew very well that he was simply a guide and messenger, not head of a government or an emperor on earth. The people once suggested that they give him the plumage and entourage of worldly sovereigns and emperors. He was alarmed at their insolence and said: "I am neither emperor, nor like an emperor, but a blessing given unto you." . . .

Religion and the State

Let us now grant, as we indeed must, that the nature and ends of religion are what the Prophet himself has declared them to be and has so beautifully condensed in his classic statement: "Prophethood, not empery. . . . For I am but a blessing given unto you." What use, then, has religion to become a state? How may it possibly become a government or a state when it is nothing but a set of eternal, immutable verities, whereas the state and government are, by nature, subject to the law of evolution and change? Does religion stand on a lower plane of worth and import than the state, so that a change into statehood is for the better? Can religion become subject to criticism and censure, exposed to defeat, overthrow and imperialism, as the state must be? . . .

The Instincts of Religious Government

Now that we have acquainted ourselves with the nature of religion—its distinguishing and essential characteristics—it behooves us to learn something of the characteristics of religious government. Such characteristics have been so firmly established that they have become inseparable from religious governments everywhere. Granted the permission of psychologists, we shall call those characteristics, "instincts." These instincts are as far removed from religion as can be. Though it may call itself religious and presume a relation to religion, religious government draws neither its principles nor its actual conduct from the Book of God or the Sunnah of His Prophet. Instead, it draws them from the ambitions and personal interests of its leaders and from the following instincts which underlie every one of its acts:

First, utter obscurity: Religious government draws its authority from an obscure source, the sanction or extent of which can never be known. Its relation to the people it rules is one of unquestioned, blind obedience to every dictate. The clearest *raison d'être* it can give of itself is that it is "the shadow of God on earth." As to its program, it gives only an obscure notion, in order to render any discussion or scrutiny thereof impossible. Yet, it claims such notion to be "a divine idea," as if divine ideas were puzzles and perplexities. When called upon to define the nature of its constitution, it has recourse to the same obscurity without which it could not live and says: "My constitution is religion. It is the Koran."

But the Koran is, as Ali said, "susceptible of many interpretations"; and so is the Sunnah. When the companions of Ali were inciting the people to avenge the blood of Muawiyah, they used to resort to a great mass of verses and Hadiths, which were exactly the same as those used against them by their opponents, the companions of Muawiyah. The case was not different in the long war between the Umayyads and the Abbasids.

•　　•　　•

Second: Religious government has no confidence in human intelligence and is never satisfied with the findings of reason. It does not grant the mind any opportunity for self-expression because it fears every intelligent statement and knows that the human mind is the sole power which can challenge its authority. It seeks to convince the rabble of the lawfulness of doing away with all thought, with what seems to them an unanswerable claim—namely, that our ancestors have not left anything unsaid that was worthy of being said and, consequently, that our situation can be improved, not by invention and creation but by observance and imitation. Thus it prefers to admit to its ranks only those who have no talent save that of denying all talents, who are immune to any deep understanding, any intelligent insight and any creative consciousness.

• • •

Third: In order to convince the people of its necessity and desirability, religious government glorifies their poverty of spirit and their stupidity, and inculcates upon their minds the belief that the seekers of the good, the pursuers of liberty and reconstruction, the thinkers—all these are the enemies of God and His Prophet, who seek to abolish religion by abolishing the authority which stands for and safeguards it.

Man is slow to respond to the call of love; he is fast to respond to that of hatred. Religious government thus wins the crowds and instills in them the hatred of all good leaders. Accordingly, the crowds enter into a long struggle with their benevolent leaders which avails only the religious authority. The people's attention is thus oriented away from their afflictions and miseries; the power of religious government is increased and its grip upon the people is tightened.

• • •

Fourth: Consecrated "false pride" is the meanest instinct of religious government. It accepts neither advice nor guidance, nor tolerates even a mere drawing of attention to something it has failed to consider. The freedom to criticize, the freedom to oppose, the freedom to think—all these Holies are fake and counterfeit items which people are forbidden to have or to acquire.

Under religious government, a person is led to the gallows as this recitation is made: "And whosoever destroys the unity of this nation shall die by the sword."

Is not opposition a division of the nation into factions and the destruction of its unity? Thus, and only thus, does religious government understand the matter; and woe to him who does not share its tyrannical, morbid understanding.

• • •

Fifth: Absolute monocracy is the most sinister instinct of religious government. This instinct forces religious government to combat opinion however wise it may be and to "liquidate" political parties however nationally devout and useful.

• • •

Opposition to the religious ruler and criticism of his mistakes and conduct is always considered the greatest of all crimes. In order to convince the people of this and eradicate their doubt, it teaches that the Prophet of God said: "Listen to your ruler and obey him, even if he should gall your back and take away your property."

That is liberty—to free oneself of all sin. And sin means any criticism of government. Sin, for the religious government, means any question raised concerning that government.

• • •

Sixth: Another instinct of religious government is its stagnancy and its attitude of opposition towards life. Religious government cannot afford to run along with life and change when it changes; it must go counter to it. It does not look forward, but backward, for only the backward look is consistent with its immobility.

If any religious government were to give up this instinct, it would do so only as a pretense. In truth, it would lie in wait for every new development in order to destroy it and thus remain true to the people's conception of religion as being indissolubly identified with the old and immobile.

• • •

Seventh: Finally, let us not forget the instinct for beastly cruelty which commands a large share of the religious government's activities and which is the queen of all the instincts. Religious government would cut throats and shed blood without scruple. In fact, it does so with a feeling of joy and emotion and sings: "Oh, the blessed air of paradise." Apparently, human heads are bolts which fasten and lock the gates of paradise and which fling the gates open as soon as they are removed.

Religious government draws sanction for its cruelty and tyranny from the same obscure source serving to give it its *raison d'être*. All it needs to do is to attach to one's neck an accusation of ungodliness and heresy. But whence, how, and what is the evidence for such accusation—well! Have you forgotten that religious rulers are never to be questioned or disputed?

21 / ARAB CULTURE: WESTERN OR EASTERN?

At the outset we must answer this fundamental question: Is Egypt of the East or of the West? Naturally, I mean East or West in the cultural, not the geographical sense. It seems to me that there are two distinctly different and bitterly antagonistic cultures on the earth.

From Taha Hussein, *The Future of Culture in Egypt* (Washington, D.C.: American Council of Learned Societies, 1954), pp. 3–10, 12, 13, 15, 17–19, 20–23, 27. Reprinted by permission of Farrar, Straus & Giroux, Inc.

Both have existed since time immemorial, the one in Europe, the other in the Far East.

We may paraphrase the question as follows: Is the Egyptian mind Eastern or Western in its imagination, perception, comprehension, and judgment? More succinctly put—which is easier for the Egyptian mind: to understand a Chinese or Japanese, or to understand an Englishman or a Frenchman? This is the question that we must answer before we begin to think of the foundations on which we shall have to base our culture and education. . . .

The meaning of all this is very clear: the Egyptian mind had no serious contact with the Far Eastern mind; nor did it live harmoniously with the Persian mind. The Egyptian mind has had regular, peaceful, and mutually beneficial relations only with the Near East and Greece. In short, it has been influenced from earliest times by the Mediterranean Sea and the various peoples living around it.

The mutually beneficial relations between the Egyptian and Greek minds in antiquity was acknowledged and lauded by the Greeks themselves both in poetry and prose. Egypt is favorably mentioned in the works of the story-tellers and dramatists. Herodotus and later writers and philosophers give great attention to her.

The Greeks before and during their golden age used to consider themselves the pupils of the Egyptians in civilization, particularly the fine arts. History has neither denied this nor subtracted anything from it. On the contrary, the facts affirm an Egyptian influence not only on Greek architecture, sculpture, and painting, but on the applied arts and sciences as well, not to mention the various aspects of daily life, including political conduct.

We must note that Egypt was not alone in influencing Greece. Other Near Eastern nations, for instance, Chaldaea, had an abundant share in contributing to her civilization and progress.

The ancient Egyptian mind is not an Eastern mind, if we understand by the East China, Japan, India, and the adjoining regions. It developed in Egypt as a result of the conditions, natural and human, that prevailed there. It only exerted influence on and was in turn influenced by the neighboring non-Egyptian peoples, principally the Greeks.

From these clear and long since proven facts, Egyptians have deduced the weird and illogical conclusion that they are Easterners not merely in the geographical sense of the term, but in mentality and culture. They regard themselves as being closer to the Hindus, Chinese, and Japanese than to the Greeks, Italians, and Frenchmen. I have never been able to understand or accept this shocking misconception. I still recall the astonishment I felt several years ago when I became familiar with the activities of a group in Egypt that called itself the

"Eastern Link Association" and sought to promote contacts with the peoples of the Far East rather than with the peoples of the Near West. I clearly, indeed intuitively, understand our consciousness of the positive relationships existing between us and the Near East not only because of identity of language and religion, but also because of geographical propinquity as well as similarity of origin and historical evolution. When we go beyond the Near East, however, these factors no longer obtain, except for religion and temporary considerations of a political or economic nature.

History shows that religious and linguistic unity do not necessarily go hand in hand with political unity, nor are they the props on which states rely. The Muslims realized this a long time ago. They established their states on the basis of practical interests, abandoning religion, language, and race as exclusively determining factors before the end of the second century A.H. [eighth century of the Christian Era] when the Umayyad dynasty in Andalusia was in conflict with the Abbassids in Iraq. In the fourth century A.H. [tenth century of the Christian Era] the Islamic world replaced the Islamic empire. Various national blocs and states emerged everywhere. They were built on economic, geographical, and other interests and differed in strength and stability.

Egypt was one of the earliest among the Islamic states to recover her ancient, unforgotten personality. History tells us that she violently opposed the Persians and Macedonians, the latter being eventually absorbed into the local population. Egypt yielded to the Western and Eastern Roman rulers only under duress and had to be kept under continuous martial law. History further relates that she acquiesced most reluctantly even to Arab domination. The spirit of resistance and rebelliousness that followed the conquest did not subside until she regained her independent personality under Ibn Tulun[1] and the dynasties that followed him.

From earliest times Muslims have been well aware of the now universally acknowledged principle that a political system and a religion are different things, that a constitution and a state rest, above everything else, on practical foundations. This is definitely applicable to the Europeans who, when relieved of the burdens of the Middle Ages, organized their respective governments in accordance with temporal considerations, not Christian unity or linguistic or racial similarity. . . .

Islam arose and spread over the world. Egypt was receptive and hastened at top speed to adopt it as her religion and to make the Arabic of Islam her language. Did that obliterate her original mentality? Did that make her an Eastern nation in the present meaning of the term? Not at all! Europe did not become Eastern nor did the

---

[1] [Ninth century of the Christian Era.—Trans.]

nature of the European mind change because Christianity, which originated in the East, flooded Europe and absorbed the other religions. If modern European philosophers and thinkers deem Christianity to be an element of the European mind, they must explain what distinguishes Christianity from Islam; for both were born in the geographical East, both issued from one noble source and were inspired by the one God in whom Easterners and Westerners alike believe.

How is it possible for fair-minded persons to see no harm coming to the European mind from reading the Gospel, which transports this mind from the West to the East, and at the same time to regard the Koran as purely Eastern, even though it has been clearly and straightforwardly proclaimed that the Koran was sent only to complete and confirm what is in the Gospel?

If it is true that Christianity did not transform the European mind or eliminate either its inherited Hellenism or Mediterranean qualities, it must be equally true that Islam did not change the Egyptian mind or the mind of the peoples who embraced it and who were influenced by the Mediterranean Sea. . . .

We Egyptians must not assume the existence of intellectual differences, weak or strong, between the Europeans and ourselves or infer that the East mentioned by Kipling in his famous verse "East is East and West is West, and never the twain shall meet" applies to us or our country. Ismail's statement that Egypt is a part of Europe should not be regarded as some kind of boast or exaggeration, since our country has always been a part of Europe as far as intellectual and cultural life is concerned, in all its forms and branches. . . .

The noted French author Paul Valéry once identified these three elements of the European mind: Greek civilization with its literature, philosophy, and art; Roman civilization with its political institutions and jurisprudence; and Christianity with its appeal for charity and its exhortation to good works. An analysis of the Muslim mind in Egypt and elsewhere in the Near East will yield comparable results: a literary, philosophical, and artistic component essentially related to Greek civilization; a politico-juridical component very much akin to the Roman system; and a religious component, the noble Islamic faith, with its advocacy of charity and good works. Islam, no one will deny, came to complete and confirm the Old and New Testaments. . . .

The dominant and undeniable fact of our times is that day by day we are drawing closer to Europe and becoming an integral part of her, literally and figuratively. This process would be much more difficult than it is if the Egyptian mind were basically different from the European.

This is not all. Since the [First] World War we have taken such decisive steps forward that any attempt to retrace them or abrogate the rights won would, I am certain, be violently resisted by many Egyptians. Which one of [us] is willing to see Egypt retreat from the progress she had made toward democracy, or who would go back to a system that did not center about a constitutional representative government? This form of government, although adopted from Europe, became almost immediately a vital and inseparable part of our being. Anyone urging Egyptians to return to the way of life characteristic of Pharaonic, Greco-Roman, or early Islamic times would be ridiculed by the people, including the arch-conservatives and those who loathe any tampering whatsoever with our ancient heritage. . . .

Our educational system is also based on exclusively European methods, which are applied throughout our primary, secondary, and higher schools. If for the sake of argument we suppose that the mentality of our fathers and grandfathers may have been Eastern and essentially antithetic to the Europeans, we must see that our children are quite different. We have been putting into their heads modes of thought and ideas that are almost completely European. I cannot conceive of anyone seriously advocating abandonment of the European system in our schools and revival of techniques used by our ancestors. As a matter of fact, the Europeans borrowed the methods that prevailed in the Islamic world during the Middle Ages. They did then just what we are doing now. It is essentially a matter of time. They began their new life in the fifteenth century, while we were delayed by the Ottoman Turks until the nineteenth century. If God had preserved us from the Ottoman conquest, we should have remained in unbroken touch with Europe and shared in her renaissance. This would certainly have fashioned a different kind of civilization from the one in which we are now living.

However, God has bestowed on us a boon to compensate for our misfortune and calamities. The world has struggled for hundreds of years to attain the present stage of progress. It is within our power to reach it in a short time. Woe to us if we do not seize the opportunity! . . .

Europe is Christian. I do not call for the adoption of Christianity, but for the adoption of the motive-forces of European civilization. Without them Egypt cannot live, let alone progress and govern herself. The Europeans differ among themselves in many respects. Some follow various types and forms of Christianity, some are not Christian, some are irreligious. Nevertheless, they all remain in basic agreement both as to the motive-forces of their civilization and the methods of obtaining and enjoying its fruits. . . .

Europe today resembles the Umayyad and Abbasid Near East in the richness of its civilization which, like any human creation, possesses good and bad aspects. Our religious life will not suffer from contact with the European civilization any more than it suffered when we took over the Persian and Byzantine civilizations. In practice, we are confronted with the choice of either repudiating our ancestors, which I think we are not prepared to do, or emulating their attitude toward Byzantium and Persia by adopting in full measure the motive-forces of Europe. We have actually been doing this last since we became acquainted with Europe at the beginning of the past century, and the tempo, if anything, quickens from day to day. A reversal of this process would mean our end.

My plea, therefore, is for nothing new. I simply want the apprehensive to be reassured and to accept willingly rather than grudgingly the inevitable. I know some fine men of conservative bent who deprecate Western civilization and yet are literally steeped in it. Many of those who object to the unveiled face and the commingling of boys and girls send their daughters to foreign schools where they dress in typically European fashion.

It would be absurd to pretend that I am the first to recommend adopting the motive-forces of European civilization when the radio has long since penetrated al-Azhar and has been used by the Rector himself in addressing the Muslims throughout the world. Not only have the sciences and arts of this civilization come to al-Azhar, but the institution has taken the initiative in sending special missions to the capitals of Europe to learn at first hand from European professors. In passing, I should like to refer to the irony that while al-Azhar, citadel of conservatism in the East, has been frantically rushing toward this civilization, the Egyptian University, an offspring of this era, is inclining in the opposite direction owing to its belief that Egypt should progress at a measured pace using forethought and mature judgment.

In short, I want us to harmonize our words with our actions. Let us admit the truth and banish hypocrisy. Only by eagerly welcoming the modern civilization can we have true peace of mind and a wholesome attitude toward the realities of life. A sound philosophy, it seems to me, requires the frank acknowledgment of one's desires and a straight-forward attempt to satisfy them.

Some Egyptians object to Europeanization on the grounds that it threatens our national personality and glorious heritage. I who have long argued that we stoutly protect our independence naturally do not advocate rejection of the past or loss of identity in the Europeans, although occasional bewitched individuals and groups have done this very thing. The only time that we might have been absorbed by Europe was when we were extremely weak, ignorant, and possessed of the notion that the hat was superior to the turban and the fez because it always covered a more distinguished head! However, such fears are completely baseless now that we know our history and are aware of the essential similarities between ourselves and the Europeans.

Although great powers imposed their will on us for many centuries, they were unable to destroy our personality. In modern times Egypt stood up to the mightiest nation on earth lacking every weapon except faith in itself and its cause. After emerging victorious from this struggle, does anyone imagine that it is likely to lose its identity to the English? Hardly! This could happen only if Egypt were unable or unwilling to fight Europe with its own weapons.

The controlling factors in Egypt's destiny are its geographical situation, religion, artistic heritage, unbroken history, and the Arabic language. To defend our country with its geographical situation, against aggression necessitates adopting European weapons and technique. Our religion, I feel, will be best maintained by doing as our ancestors did and keeping it responsive to contemporary needs. Guarding and advancing our linguistic and artistic achievements have always been dear to my heart. We render sincere homage to the past only when we strive to make the present and future worthy of it.

I cannot be justly accused of advocating loss of Egyptian identity since I am merely asking that the preservatives of defense, religion, language, art, and history be strengthened by the adoption of Western techniques and ideas. These constitute as little danger to Egypt's personality as they do to Japan's, perhaps less so because her past cannot match ours.

Other objectors to Western civilization use two lines of argument, one dangerous, the other ridiculous. Sometimes they assert that it is ultra-materialistic and a source of misery both to Europe and to the rest of the world. At other times they insist that Europe is tired of her own civilization, as evidenced by the number of writers, scholars, and philosophers who are turning away from it and seeking nourishment in the spirituality of the East. Why then, they ask, should we abandon the good that the Europeans themselves desire for the evil that they are rejecting?

Certainly, there is a good deal of materialism in European civilization, but it is absurd to deny that it possesses spiritual content. The brilliant successes of modern science and the inventions that have changed the face of the earth spring from imaginative and creative minds. European history is replete with men like Descartes and Pasteur, who cheerfully devoted their time and effort to ideas alone. Besides scientists and scholars, there are such men as airplane test-pilots who expose themselves to horrible injury and even death in order to extend man's mastery over nature.

Yes, we know of writers, poets, and philosophers who are tired of

European civilization; yet they will sacrifice their lives for it. Some of them look toward the East, or appear to do so, but you can be sure that they would flatly refuse to live like Easterners. Dissatisfaction with modern life is a characteristic of men who are alive and progressing. Submissive contentment is a characteristic of lazy, decadent people. When Europeans tell us that their civilization is materialistic and hateful, they are either truthful—in which case we know that they seek its improvement—or lying, their purpose being to induce us to shun this civilization so that they may retain all its benefits for themselves, while we remain stationary, clinging to our spiritual civilization which makes us their slaves.

Moreover, what is this spiritual East? It is assuredly not our Near East which, as previously noted, is the cradle of the mind that I have been lauding. This area was also the source of divine religions adopted both by Europeans and Easterners—Christians, Jews, and Muslims alike. Can these religions be spirit in the East and matter in the West?

No, the spiritual East by which some Europeans are fascinated is clearly not the Near East but the Far East. It is the East of India, China, and Japan with religions and philosophies that scarcely resemble our own. In all seriousness, do we want to embrace the religion, philosophy, and motive-forces of the Chinese just when they are rapidly Westernizing themselves? . . .

This talk of a spiritual East is sheer nonsense. Egyptians who deride European civilization and praise the spiritualism of the East are joking, and they realize it. They would be the last to choose to live like the Chinese or Hindus. Nevertheless, their arguments are dangerous and demoralizing, particularly to the youth, who are thereby led away from the European civilization which they know toward the Eastern civilization they do not know. . . .

State supervision of al-Azhar's primary and secondary schools is vital at this stage of Egyptian history since the traditions and religious obligations of the venerable institution have made it a focus of conservatism and antiquated practices. Those students who are given an exclusively Azharite education remain temporarily isolated from the modern world of which they are a part. Consequently, adjustment after graduation to the complexities of daily life is harder for them than for other youths.

We must also bear in mind the fact that al-Azhar's outmoded thinking probably makes it difficult for its students to grasp the concepts of patriotism and nationalism in the modern European sense of the terms. Some time ago the Rector of the University in a radio address to the Muslims commemorating a religious holiday proclaimed the holy "qiblah" [the direction to which Muslims turn in praying] as the pivot of Islamic nationalism. This traditional view is valid when a Muslim sheikh is talking to his co-religionists. However, the young Azharites must learn early in life that the narrow geographical borders of their native soil also form a pivot of nationalism that in no wise conflicts with the pivot mentioned by the Rector. Nationalism came to Egypt along with other products of contemporary civilization and now forms the basis of our internal and external relations. Al-Azhar must realize this and revise its primary and secondary school programs accordingly.

22 / REPRESENTATIVE SYSTEM

In this country this long evolutionary process, which led to the establishment of representative government in many European countries, has not taken place. Egypt had remained subjected to other states superior to it in power and resources for long centuries, and for that reason the Egyptians have not been able to lay the foundations of a political public opinion or give themselves a true social and political education. It was only after the foreign power had weakened through international events, and after our struggle and fight for self-liberation had brought about our independence as a national state that we got around to organizing our national life on the model of those countries that preceded us to liberty and independence. Since the historical development which transformed absolute rule into a democratic system has not completely taken place in Egypt, democracy is a strange system with us, a system transplanted to a milieu unprepared for it and lacking the elements necessary for its maintenance and growth. Democracy is a weak system among us, incapable of realizing all that is expected of it, for the representative system has not yet met with our national spirit, and its new procedures do not accord with the mentality of the people. The most important aspect of political life in Egypt is the weakness of the political parties, their disorganization, and their inexperience in matters of state and democratic procedure.

The politics of personalities and of personal ulterior motives have been an important factor in disuniting the people and in preventing the execution of many a great scheme, ever since Egypt achieved its partial and, after the treaty with Great Britain, its full independence. During that period of national struggle the only real party in existence was the *Wafd,* because it distinguished itself from other political associations through its strong spirit and its will to a definite end, namely, the unconditional liberation of Egypt from all foreign powers. This

From Mirrit Boutros Ghali, *The Policy of Tomorrow* (Washington, D.C.: American Council of Learned Societies, 1953), pp. 5–7, 10–13. Reprinted by permission of Farrar, Straus & Giroux, Inc.

aim was a whole, real political program in itself. As Egypt became an independent state and the period of foreign concessions was over, that end was consummated, and the party's program was completed. The Wafd should have then immediately veered its attention towards the interior and set up economic reconstruction as a basis for its program and governmental policy. Unfortunately, however, the Wafd had no ready-made plans, no known internal policy for the new regime of complete independence, although it had had plenty of time and opportunity for drawing such political, social and economic national reconstruction programs. After its goal was reached, the party seemed to have no more work to do, and its *raison d'être* was lost. The weakness that befell the party in those days was then an expected, natural outcome. The dissolution that shook the ranks of its members was perhaps the result of diversion of opinion on this very matter. But if we want to persist in demanding the revocation of our foreign rights, is it then not our duty to guard against the mismanagement of our domestic affairs? Other than the Wafd, there are no real Egyptian parties that we may speak of; for those so-called political parties have no proclaimed exact policy regarding national life, no constant idea regarding the forms and methods of government, and no outlined schemes for economic or social reconstruction. True, they have newspapers and organized administrations and all the other externals belonging to political parties; but they lack, in most cases, the essence and the kernel.

Today, the nation is at the crossroads: No advance can be hoped for unless it be under the light of fully elaborated cultural, economic and social programs, which can only be the work of political parties. For, *only a political party, confident of its strength, firmly believing in its convictions, prepared to execute its programs and to assume for them full responsibility, can prepare a reasonable, practical program and present it to the nation. Such suggestions of the political party should not be mere theories or opinions, but, such that they may, one day, become real and active in national life and be studied and debated by everyone.*

We do not find reason, after all this, to go into the details of the other factors which guarantee the natural running of the democratic and representative system of government. For everything we see is open to criticism, whether it concerns election, parliamentary procedures, the continual change of cabinets, or, generally, every aspect of our political life which points to instability and change. All this is well-known to us all, and so are the ways in which it can be solved. But it should be said that no solution will be forthcoming unless the men who are responsible for our national affairs are convinced of it. The spirit is more important than the letter of the law, and no advantage should be expected to accrue from a literal application of our constitution when such application is far removed from its spirit. . . .

The Administration

In Egypt the administration enjoys the greatest prestige and influence in national life. The fact that there is no social aristocracy to which the public may look for example leaves to our administrators, through their conduct, the opportunity to influence public traditions and customs. It is indubitable that the conduct of governmental officials provides the looked-for standard in towns and villages. The growing need of the people and the scarcity of those who assume public responsibilities or are even interested in them have, on the other hand, increased the responsibilities and duties of the administration. It is regrettable that, this being the situation, no firm system has yet been developed for the selection and appointment of public officials. Hence, it is natural to expect that public interest is scarcely regarded in their appointments, transfers, and other movements. There are two fundamental conditions which are imperative for any normal, efficient running of the administration: (1) that the officials be completely assured of their rights and, (2) that it should be made impossible for them to violate the rights of the public. Only when these conditions are satisfied will administrative officials discharge their duties in perfect harmony with their social responsibility.

During the whole of the last fifteen years we have not, unfortunately, given due regard to these two principles. We have punished officials and held grudges against them following our personal prejudices, or we have given them full scope to do that which runs counter to their responsibilities. Often, appointments, transfers, promotions have been used by the government for the enslavement of its officials. Often, appointments have been subject to no clear rule. Or, if such rules were available, so many exceptions were made that the rules were no more valid. It was as if the administration was a property of the parties, as if these parties were free to dispose of it as they came to power and distribute it in gifts to their own favorites and supporters. Administrative officials have so often been discharged or transferred from their posts at the opening of election terms that they have lost all feeling of security. . . .

Because of its permanence, it is to be expected that the administration should remain immune to all changes of cabinets so that the continuity of the affairs of state may not be interrupted. In the big democratic countries like France and Great Britain we notice that the administration preserves this continuity in spite of the changes of cabinets and the many ministerial crises which, for instance, characterize French political life. This is possible in those countries because of the aloofness of administrative officials from the strife, disputes and prejudices of the political parties. It is not by accident that the administration in France is called "the Public Service" and in England, "the Civil Service." It is our opinion that this is due to a real fact which the French and the English have well understood. But in Egypt, at the time of change of power, the administration provides no service, as is the case in the European countries. All its services become, in fact, paralyzed on such occasion. Thus, public affairs and administrative services have become annexed to the action of parties and follow in their trail. They move only when these move and they stop when these slumber. To separate them from one another and set them in independent motion is our first obligation.

The relation between the administration and the people has thus become more and more tyrannical in character. Often very strong and extraordinary measures are taken to influence the opinion and political conviction of certain individuals. Properties have been expropriated and lands have been denied irrigation; public contracts and agreements have been revoked though they were in the nation's interest. Blind partisanship insists upon warring against its enemies though this may be to its own disadvantage. License-issues of all kinds have been one of the important means by which the party in power achieved its own ends. Moreover, the public was at all times devoid of legal means to defend itself against such scandalous abuse. The only means open to the people, therefore, was either the recourse to personal intervention for avoiding whatever injustice they could avoid, or to some other dishonest means which we may well omit to discuss in detail. These circumstances have made current among the public the opinion that, in the view of the administration, no weight attaches to any right as such. Only personal intervention and great influence could avail in such matters. However, we do not mean to assert that in every administrative matter this has been the case. But it is a fact that this is a general feeling. It is not impossible for anyone to trace our social evolution during the last ten years, to follow the continuous line of our ever degenerating public standards and to note that it runs parallel to the increasingly great role of political parties in the administration.

Tyranny and instability in administrative affairs prevent, therefore, the political, social and economic growth of the nation. There is a dire need for setting up a special commission which would regulate the affairs of government personnel and their relations with the people. Such a commission would be very much like the State Commissions in France. Many of us have begun to see the advantage of the French State Commissions and realize their capacity to solve the difficulties and correct the mistakes against which we complain in our system. *If such a commission could be guaranteed practical independence and perfectly free choice, it would certainly prove to be of great advantage for the settlement of the relations between government and officials and between administration and public upon firm legal grounds. Such a commission would equally insure the stability of the administration and its freedom from party influences. . . .*

INTRODUCTION

Beginning with the Egyptian revolution of 1952, the Arab world entered a new phase of its political development—the phase of radical nationalism. While nationalism as a basic political orientation had been in evidence for at least forty years prior to 1952, its new version differed from the old one in that it put emphasis on the radical social transformation of society. Defeats in the external sector—such as the loss of a good part of Palestine to the newly created Jewish state—and underdevelopment in the internal sector were ascribed by the revolutionaries to the antiquated structure of Arab society. According to the new revolutionary leadership, the three main enemies of the Arab people were identified as imperialism, Zionism, and feudalism. The latter term embraced more than big landowners whose wealth contrasted with the subsistence level of peasant masses; it embraced also all those privileged strata in the state whose hold on economy was viewed as leading to undue political power, hence constituting an obstacle to social reform. By 1955, the Egyptian revolutionary regime coined a slogan almost identical to that previously launched by the Syrian-based Baath Party: freedom, socialism, unity. It took another seven years to define more precisely the meaning of these terms: the definition was contained in the National Charter of the United Arab Republic, its basic ideological document, that was adopted in the spring of 1962. Freedom was defined in socio-economic categories, somewhat borrowed from the Soviet vocabulary, rather than in political-democratic terms accepted in the West. Socialism was described as the only proper means to assure freedom. But this was to be an "Arab Socialism" differing both from the West European variety and from the Soviet version. It rejected Western socialist internationalism and anti-clericalism inasmuch as it acknowledged the supreme value of the national principle and loyalty; it admitted the coexist-

119

ence of the public and private sectors of economy; and it refused to adopt the inhuman methods of forced industrialization that, under Stalinism, caused Russia and her satellites to sacrifice one or two generations for the benefit of future ones.

The third appeal was that to Arab unity. The Arab world was defined as embracing one Arab nation, the latter divided artificially into separate sovereign states, partly as a result of imperialist machinations and partly due to the traitorous domestic reaction.

This was, broadly, the Egyptian way to clarify the meaning of the slogan of freedom, socialism, unity. By and large, other Arab revolutionary regimes accepted this interpretation. However, within its broad framework, there existed a possibility of different definitions of detail. Thus local variations came into existence.

For this chapter we have selected a number of readings that throw light on the ideological foundations of the new Arab nationalism and that also take account of the above-mentioned local variations. Actually, three main variations have developed in the Arab East: the Egyptian, the Syrian, and the Iraqi. In selection 23, Nasser's early statement of principles and objectives is presented as indicative of the broad foundation of the radical nationalist thought. Selection 24 contains a much more elaborate ideological statement excerpted from Egypt's National Charter of 1962, with special emphasis on the definitions of socialism and unity.

Selections 25, 26, and 27 contain expressions of the second version of Arab nationalism, that espoused by the Baath Party. Prominent and influential in Syria's politics since 1954, the Baath has been in power in Damascus since 1963. A Pan-Arab party, with branches beyond Syria, and with—at one time or another—a Pan-Arab supreme command, the Baath has been holding regional and national congresses at irregular intervals. Excerpts from resolutions of two such congresses are presented in selections Nos. 25 and 27. In between (No. 26) is given the speech on Yemen by the Party's co-founder, Michel Aflak. The speech clearly indicates that while a broad unity of objectives exists among Arab radical nationalists, local variants are strong enough to warrant the name of "Arab revolutionary polycentrism" as a term descriptive of the lack of cohesion in the revolutionary camp.

The *de facto* polycentrism goes hand in hand with repeated official attempts to achieve some sort of formal unity. Documents contained in selections Nos. 28 and 29 reflect two such attempts: one is aimed at the tripartite union of Egypt, Syria, and Iraq, and the other at the phased bilateral unification of Iraq and Egypt.

The third variant of Arab revolutions is shown by Iraq's experiences since 1958. Iraq's political history after that date may be divided into four periods: (a) the Kassem rule (1958–63); (b) the Baath rule (spring to fall, 1963); (c) the Aref era (1963–68); and (d) the second Baath rule (beginning July, 1968). From these four periods we have selected three documents (Nos. 31, 32, and 33) that are illustrative of the Kassem era and one of which contains a speech by President Abdul Salam Aref. The two sets of documents contrast the two basic orientations that have been present in Iraqi politics since the revolution, namely the Iraq-first tendency espoused by Kassem and the Pan-Arab policy followed by Aref.

The Kassem era constituted, in many ways, an experiment in brutal frankness alternating with hypocrisy. Whenever Kassem or his official propagandists referred to the preceding (royalist) regime, they used the adjective "exterminated," rather aptly chosen because of the physical suppression of both the royal family and the regime's leading figures. Similar frankness could be observed in those passages of Kassem's official literature that spoke of the so-called People's Court, a revolutionary tribunal described as a "political school and a political seminar." On the other hand, Kassem's approach to political parties and Arab unity was ambivalent and insincere. While he pretended to recognize the freedom of political association, Kassem suppressed it; at the same time he favored only certain groups he considered compatible with his objectives. As for Arab unity, he paid lip service to it, but no more. In reality, he opposed it by launching a contrasting slogan for an "eternal Iraqi Republic."

After a brief interlude of the Baath rule (nine months in 1963), Iraq entered a new phase under the consecutive leadership of the Aref brothers (Abdul Salam Aref, 1963–66, and Abdur Rahman Aref, 1966–68). This was a phase of military dictatorship that in spite of some similarities to the by-gone Kassem era differed from it in two respects: (a) it was less repressive, and allowed a measure of tolerance toward various dissenting elements; (b) it was oriented toward a close relationship with Cairo, whose ideological and organizational patterns it tried to emulate. The earlier mentioned selection No. 29 (the U.A.R.-Iraq Unity Agreement of 1964) and the last selection of this chapter (No. 34), that reproduces Abdul Salam Aref's speech on the first anniversary of his advent to power, serve to illustrate this pro-Egyptian orientation that—though Pan-Arab in its general concept—did not result in a complete merger of the two countries.

23 / NASSER'S PHILOSOPHY OF THE REVOLUTION

Geographical Limits

There is one thing we should agree upon at the beginning, and before we proceed with the discussion, and that is the definition of the limits of place as far as we are concerned. If anybody tells me that place for us means this capital where we live, I differ with him. And if anyone tells me that place for us means the political boundaries of our country, I also differ.

If the whole matter were limited to our capital, or our political boundaries, it would be much simpler. We would shut ourselves in, and live in an ivory tower, and we would try to our utmost to get away from the world, its problems, wars and crises, which all burst in on us through the doors of our country and influence us, though we have nothing to do with them.

The age of isolation is gone.

And gone are the days in which barbed wire served as demarcation lines, separating and isolating countries from one another. No country can escape looking beyond its boundaries to find the source of the currents which influence it, how it can live with others, how . . . and how. . . .

And no state can escape trying to determine its status within its living space and trying to see what it can do in that space, and what is its field of activities and its positive role in this troubled world.

Sometimes I sit in my study reflecting on the subject, asking myself: What is our positive role in this troubled world, and where is the place in which we should fulfill that role?

I review our circumstances and discover a number of circles within which our activities inescapably must be confined and in which we must try to move.

Fate does not jest and events are not a matter of chance—there is no existence out of nothing. We cannot look at the map of the world without seeing our own place upon it, and that our role is dictated by that place.

Can we fail to see that there is an Arab circle surrounding us— that this circle is a part of us, and we are a part of it, our history being inextricably part of its history?

These are facts and no mere idle talk. Can we possibly ignore the fact that there is an African continent which Fate decreed us to be a part of, and that it is also decreed that a terrible struggle exists for its future—a struggle whose results will be either for us or against us, with or without our will? Can we further ignore the existence of an Islamic world, with which we are united by bonds created not only by religious belief, but also reinforced by historic realities? As I have said once, Fate is no jester.

From Gamal Abdul Nasser, *Egypt's Liberation* (Washington, D.C.: The Public Affairs Press, 1955), pp. 83–90, 109–10, 111–12. Permission of The Public Affairs Press, Washington, D.C. Copyright 1955 by The Public Affairs Press. Reprinted by permission of the publisher.

It is not without significance that our country is situated west of Asia, in contiguity with the Arab states with whose existence our own is interwoven. It is not without significance, too, that our country lies in northeast Africa, overlooking the Dark Continent, wherein rages a most tumultuous struggle between white colonizers and black inhabitants for control of its unlimited resources. Nor is it without significance that, when the Mongols swept away the ancient capitals of Islam, Islamic civilization and the Islamic heritage fell back on Egypt and took shelter there. Egypt protected them and saved them, while checking the onslaught of the Mongols at Ain Jalut. All these are fundamental realities with deep roots in our lives which we cannot—even if we try—escape or forget.

A Role in Search of a Hero

I do not know why I recall, whenever I reach this point in my recollections as I meditate alone in my room, a famous tale by a great Italian poet, Luigi Pirandello—"Six Characters in Search of an Author." The pages of history are full of heroes who created for themselves roles of glorious valor which they played at decisive moments. Likewise the pages of history are also full of heroic and glorious roles which never found heroes to perform them. For some reason it seems to me that within the Arab circle there is a role, wandering aimlessly in search of a hero. And I do not know why it seems to me that this role, exhausted by its wanderings, has at last settled down, tired and weary, near the borders of our country and is beckoning to us to move, to take up its lines, to put on its costume, since no one else is qualified to play it. . . .

The First Circle

There can be no doubt that the Arab circle is the most important, and the one with which we are most closely linked. For its peoples are intertwined with us by history. We have suffered together, we have gone through the same crises, and when we fell beneath the hooves of the invaders' steeds, they were with us under the same hooves. . . .

So far as I can recall, the first glimmers of Arab awareness began to steal into my consciousness when I was a student in secondary school. I used to go out on a general strike with my comrades every year on the second of December to protest the Balfour Declaration which Britain had made on behalf of the Jews, giving them a national home in Palestine, thus tyrannously wresting it from its rightful owners. And at that time, when I asked myself why I went out on strike with such zeal, and why I was angry about this act by a country I had never seen, I could find no answer except in the echoes of sympathetic emotion.

Then a kind of understanding began to develop when I became a student in the Military Academy, where I studied in particular the history of all past military campaigns in Palestine and in general the history of the area and its conditions which have made of it during the past hundred years an easy prey for the fangs of hungry beasts. Things grew still clearer and the underlying realities became apparent when, in the General Staff College, I began to study the late Palestine campaign and the problems of the Mediterranean in detail.

The result was that when the Palestine crisis began, I was utterly convinced that the fighting there was not taking place on foreign soil, nor was our part in it a matter of sentiment. It was a duty necessitated by self-defense. . . .

The Interior of the Dark Continent

If we consider next the second circle—the continent of Africa—I may say without exaggeration that we cannot, under any circumstances, however much we might desire it, remain aloof from the terrible and sanguinary conflict going on there today between five million whites and 200 million Africans. We cannot do so for an important and obvious reason: we are *in* Africa. The peoples of Africa will continue to look to us, who guard their northern gate, and who constitute their link with the outside world. We will never in any circumstances be able to relinquish our responsibility to support, with all our might, the spread of enlightenment and civilization to the remotest depths of the jungle.

There remains another important reason. It is that the Nile is the life artery of our country, bringing water from the heart of the continent. . . .

Islamic Parliament

There remains the third circle, which circumscribes continents and oceans, and which is the domain of our brothers in faith, who, wherever under the sun they may be, turn as we do, in the direction of Mecca, and whose devout lips speak the same prayers.

When I went with the Egyptian delegation to the Kingdom of Saudi Arabia to offer condolences on the death of its great sovereign, my belief in the possibility of extending the effectiveness of the Pilgrimage, building upon the strength of the Islamic tie that binds all Muslims, grew very strong. I stood before the Kaaba, and in my mind's eye I saw all the regions of the world which Islam has reached. Then I found myself saying that our view of the Pilgrimage must change. It should not be regarded as only a ticket of admission into Paradise after a long life, or as a means of buying forgiveness after a merry one. It should become an institution of great political power and significance. Journalists of the world should hasten to cover the Pilgrimage, not because it is a traditional ritual affording interesting reports for the reading public, but because of its function as a periodic political conference in which the envoys of the Islamic states, their leaders of thought, their men learned in every branch of knowledge, their writers, their captains of industry, their merchants and their youth can meet, in order to lay down in this Islamic-world-parliament the broad lines of their national policies and their pledges of mutual cooperation from one year to another.

24 / SOCIALISM AND UNITY:
THE U.A.R. CHARTER

The Necessity of the Revolution

Experience has shown, and ever confirms the fact that revolution is the only course which the Arab struggle can take to head for a better future.

Revolution is the only means, by which the Arab Nation can free itself of its shackles, and rid itself of the dark heritage which burdened it. For, the elements of suppression and exploitation which long dominated the Arab Nation and seized its wealth will never willingly submit.

The National forces must crush them and win a decisive victory over them.

Revolution is the only way to overcome under-development, forced on the Arab Nation through suppression and exploitation. For, the conventional methods of work are no longer capable of bridging the gap of development which has long existed between the Arab Nation and advanced countries.

It is therefore imperative to deal radically with matters and ensure the mobilisation of all the nation's material and the spiritual potentialities to undertake this responsibility.

Moreover, revolution is the only way to face the big challenge awaiting the Arab and other undeveloped countries, namely, the challenge offered by the astounding scientific discoveries, which help widen the gap of development between one country and another. With the knowledge they reveal, those discoveries add to the progress of advanced countries and, in so doing, widen the gap further between them and others, despite all the good efforts the latter may exert to narrow it.

The revolutionary path is the only bridge which the Arab Nation can cross to reach the future it aspires to.

From United Arab Republic, *Draft of the Charter* (Cairo: Information Department, May 21, 1962), pp. 11–15, 43–45, 77–78.

• • •

The Arab Revolution which is, at present, both the implement and reflection of the Arab struggle needs to equip itself with three powers, by means of which it can face and win the battle of destiny it is now fighting.

Thus the Arab Revolution would realise its objectives and destroy all its enemies.

These powers are:

First—Consciousness based on scientific conviction arising from enlightened thought and free discussion, unaffected by the forces of fanaticism and terrorism.

Second—Free movement that adapts itself to the changing circumstances of the Arab struggle, provided that this movement observes the objectives and the moral ideals of the struggle.

Third—Clarity of perception of the objectives, which never loses sight of them, and which avoids being swept away by emotion and diverted from the high road of the national struggle [thus] wasting a considerable part of its energy.

The great need for these three powers arises from the particular circumstances of the Arab revolutionary experiment, those circumstances under the influence of which it assumes its role in directing the course of Arab history.

Today, the Arab Revolution is called upon to strike a new path before the objectives of the Arab struggle.

Ages of suffering and hope finally gave shape to the objectives of the Arab struggle. These objectives which are a true expression of Arab national conscience are:

* Freedom
* Socialism
* Unity

The long suffering for the achievement of these objectives helped the nation define and analyse them.

Today, freedom has come to mean: freedom of the country and freedom of the citizen.

Socialism has become both a means and an end, namely sufficiency and justice.

The road to unity has come to be the popular call for the restoration of the natural order of a nation, torn apart by its enemies against its own will and interests and the peaceful endeavour to promote this unity and finally its unanimous acceptance as a crowning achievement.

• • •

These objectives have always been the slogans of the Arab struggle; but, the Arab Revolution now faces the responsibility of striking a new path before these objectives.

The need for a new road is not prompted by a mere desire for innovation or mere considerations of national dignity, but it arises from the fact that the Arab Revolution is now facing new circumstances, therefore, demanding more suitable solutions.

The Arab revolutionary experiment, therefore, cannot afford to copy what others have achieved.

Though the characteristics of peoples and the ingredients forming the national character of each impose the adoption of different methods for the solution of their problems, the greatest difference in method is that imposed by the changing circumstances, prevailing and governing the whole world, particularly those far-reaching changes which occurred in the world after the Second World War (1939 to 1945).

These circumstances bring about radical changes in the atmosphere of national struggle in the world.

This, however, does not mean that the national struggle of peoples and nations is to-day required to create new conceptions for its great objectives, but rather, to find the methods suited to the trend of general evolution and the changing nature of the world.

The outstanding changes that took place in the world after the Second World War may be summed up as follows:

First—The spectacular strengthening of the force of nationalist movements in Asia, Africa and Latin America to the extent that they were able to lead many a victorious battle against the forces of imperialism. Such nationalist movements, therefore, have now become an internationally effective force.

Second—The emergence of the communist camp as an enormous force, with steadily increasing material and moral weight and effectiveness in facing the capitalist camp.

Third—The great scientific and technological advance suddenly achieved in methods of production, opening up unlimited horizons before efforts for development.

The same advance was also achieved in the development of arms which are now potentially so destructive to all parties involved that they themselves have become a deterrent against war.

This, apart from the astounding and radical change brought about by the same scientific and technological progress in means of transport, as a result of which distances and barriers both physical and intellectual between one country and another have now virtually disappeared.

Fourth—the result of all this in the field of international relations, the most notable of which being the increasing weight of moral forces in the world, such as those provided by the United Nations Organisation, the Non-Aligned States and world opinion.

Side by side with these, however, is the need of imperialism under these circumstances to resort to indirect methods such as the conquest and domination of peoples from within, the formation of economic blocks and monopolies, the waging of cold wars which include, among their methods the attempt to undermine the confidence of the smaller nations in their capacity to develop themselves and to provide an equal and positive contribution to the service of human society.

Such far reaching changes in the world are accompanied by new circumstances which have an indisputable effect on the struggles of all nations, including the Arab Nation, and on their endeavour to attain their national aims.

While the aims of the Arab national struggle remain freedom, socialism, and unity, world changes have influenced the means of achievement.

As a result of the interaction between world changes and the will of the national Revolution, it was no longer believed that freedom could be attained by placating the imperialists or bargaining with them. In 1956 the Arab people in Egypt were able to take up arms and defend their freedom, achieving a decisive victory in Port Said, not to be forgotten. In the same way in their determination to secure freedom, the Arab people were able to carry on a war in Algeria, lasting more than seven years.

Moreover, socialist action is no longer compelled to observe literally laws formulated in the 19th century.

The progress in means of production, the development of nationalist and labour movements in the face of domination of imperialism and monopolies, the increasing chances of world peace, as a result of the influence of moral forces and, at the same time of the effect of the balance of atomic terror—all these factors combined of necessity created, and should create, a new situation for socialist experiments, entirey different from what existed in the past.

The same can be said of the experiments to achieve unity in the 19th century, most notable of which are those made by Germany, and Italy and which can no longer be repeated. The need for a peaceful appeal and for the unanimous approval of the whole people is not merely an expression of the desire to cling to an idealistic method in nationalist action, but it is also, and above all an absolute necessity at present if the national unity of all Arabs is to be safeguarded. In our present endeavour to achieve the national unity of the entire Arab nation, we are struggling against enemies who still retain bases on the Arab soil itself, whether in the form of reactionary palaces collaborating with imperialism to protect their own interests, or in the form of "colonies" belonging to the racial Zionist movement used by imperialism as focal points of military threat.

In facing this world the Arab Revolution must have a new approach, that does not shut itself up within the confines of theories, which are at once limited and limiting, although it must by no means deny itself access to the rich storehouse of experience gained by other striving peoples in their similar struggles.

Social experiences cannot live in isolation from one another. As part of human civilization, they only remain alive through enriching movement and creative interaction.

The torch of civilization has passed from one land to another, but in each land it crossed, it acquired a fresh supply of oil to make its flame brighter across the ages.

Such are social experiences. They are capable of passing from one place to another but not of being blindly copied, they are capable of useful study and examination, but not of being learnt heartly parrot-fashion by mere repetition.

This is then the first duty of the popular revolutionary leadership in the Arab Nation. It means that the great part of the responsibility for this pioneer revolutionary action devolves upon the popular revolutionary leadership in the United Arab Republic, since natural and historical factors have laid upon the United Arab Republic the responsibility of being the nucleus state in this endeavour to secure liberty, socialism and unity for the Arab Nation.

Such popular leaderships are now called upon to study their own history, to examine their present reality and then proceed to build their future while standing on firmer grounds. . . .

On the Inevitability of the Socialist Solution

Socialism is the way to social freedom.

Social freedom cannot be realised except through an equal opportunity for every citizen to obtain a fair share of the national wealth.

This is not confined to the mere re-distribution of the national wealth among the citizens but foremost and above all it requires expanding the base of this national wealth, to accede to the lawful rights of the working masses.

This means that socialism, with its two supports, sufficiency and justice, is the way to social freedom.

The socialist solution to the problem of economic and social underdevelopment in Egypt—with a view to achieving progress in a revolutionary way—was never a question of free choice. The socialist solution was a historical inevitability imposed by reality, the broad aspirations of the masses and the changing nature of the world in the second part of the 20th century.

The capitalist experiments to achieve progress correlated with imperialism. The countries of the capitalist world reached the period of economic drive, on the basis of investments they made in their colonies. The wealth of India, of which British imperialism seized the largest share, was the beginning of the formation of the British savings which were used in the development of agriculture and industry in Britain.

If Britain has reached its period of drive depending on the Lancashire textile industry, the transformation of Egypt into a large field for cotton growing pumped the blood through the artery of British economy leaving the Egyptian peasant starved.

Gone are the ages of imperialist piracy, when the people's wealth was looted to serve the interests of others with neither legal nor moral control. We should stamp out the remaining traces of those ages, especially in Africa.

Moreover, other experiments of progress realised their objectives at the expense of increasing the misery of the working people, either to serve the interests of the capital or under pressure of ideological applications which went to the extent of sacrificing whole living generations for the sake of others still unborn.

The nature of the age no longer allows such things.

Progress through looting or through the corvée system is no longer tolerable under the new humane values.

These humane values put an end to colonialism and an end to the corvée system. Not only did they achieve this but they also expressed positively the spirit and the ideals of the age when through science, those values introduced other methods of work to attain progress.

Scientific socialism is the suitable style for finding the right method leading to progress.

No other method can definitely achieve the desired progress.

Those who call for freedom of capital imagining that to be the road to progress are gravely mistaken.

In the countries forced to remain underdeveloped, capital in its natural development is no longer able to lead the economic drive at a time when the great capitalist monopolies in the advanced countries developed relying on the exploitation of the sources of wealth in the colonies.

The huge development of world monopolies leaves only two ways for local capitalism in the countries aspiring to progress:

First—Local capitalism is no longer capable of competition without the customs protection paid for by the masses.

Second—The only hope left for local capitalism to develop is to relate itself to the movements of world monopolies, following in their footsteps, thus turning into a mere appendage and dragging the country to doom.

On the other hand, the wide gap of underdevelopment which separates the advanced states and those trying to catch up no longer allows the method of progress to be left to desultory individual efforts motivated by mere selfish profit.

These individual efforts are no longer capable of facing the challenge.

Facing the challenge calls for three conditions:

1. Assembling the national savings.
2. Putting all the experiences of modern science at the disposal of the exploitation of national savings.
3. Drafting a complete plan for production.

These are concerned with increasing the product. On the other hand, fair distribution calls for planning programmes for social action, programmes that enable the popular working masses to reap the benefits of economic action and create the welfare society to which they aspire and struggle to promote.

Work aimed at expanding the base of national wealth can never be left to the haphazard ways of the exploiting private capital with its unruly tendencies.

The redistribution of the surplus national work on the basis of justice can never be accomplished through voluntary efforts based on good intentions however sincere they may be.

This places a definite conclusion before the will of the national Revolution, without the acceptance of which it cannot realise its objectives. This conclusion is the necessity for the people's control over all the tools of production and over directing the surplus according to a definite plan.

This socialist solution is the only way out to economic and social progress. It is the way to democracy in all its social and political forms.

The people's control over all the tools of production does not necessitate the nationalisation of all means of production, or the abolition of private ownership, or the mere touching of the legitimate right of inheritance following therefrom. Such control can be achieved in two ways:

First—The creation of a capable public sector that would lead progress in all domains, and bear the main responsibility of the development plan.

Second—The existence of a private sector that would, without exploitation, participate in the development within the framework of the overall plan—provided that the people's control is exercised over both sectors.

This socialist solution is the only path where all elements participating in the process of production can meet, according to scientific rules, capable of supplying society with all the energies enabling it to rebuild its life on the basis of a carefully studied and comprehensive plan.

Efficient socialist planning is the sole method which guarantees the use of all national resources, be they material, natural or human in a practical, scientific and humane way aimed at realising the common good of the masses, and ensuring a life of prosperity for them. . . .

Arab Unity

The responsibility of the United Arab Republic, in effecting, consolidating and safeguarding evolution embraces the Arab Nation as a whole.

The Arab Nation is no more in need of giving evidence of the unity binding its peoples.

Unity has passed this stage and is identified with the Arab existence itself. Suffice it that the Arab Nation has a unity of language, forming the unity of mind and thought.

Suffice it that the Arab Nation is characterised by the unity of history creating unity of conscience and sentiments.

Suffice it that the Arab Nation enjoys a unity of hope, the basis of the unity of future and fate.

Those who are attempting to undermine the concept of Arab unity in its foundation, giving as proof the differences among the Arab governments, are looking at the matter in a superficial way.

The mere existence of those differences is in itself an indication of the existence of this unity.

These differences stem from the struggle in the Arab world.

The rallying of the popular, progressive elements in every part of the Arab Nation, and the rallying of the elements of reaction and opportunism in the Arab world are indications that the same social currents are sweeping over in the Arab Nation, guiding and coordinating its steps across the artificial barriers.

The rallying of the popular progressive elements, having one and the same hope in every part of the Arab territory and the rallying of the forces of reaction, having interests in every part of the Arab world are actually more indicative of unity than dissension.

The concept of Arab unity no longer requires a meeting of the rulers of the Arab Nation and portrays solidarity among the governments.

The phase of the social revolution has developed through that superficial concept of Arab unity and led that concept to a stage where unity of objective was a symbol of unity.

The unity of objective is a substantial fact for the popular base in the entire Arab Nation.

The disparity in the objectives of the rulers is an aspect of the inevitable revolutionary progress and the diversity of the stages of development attained by the Arab peoples.

Yet, the unity of objectives of the popular bases will be capable of bridging the gap between various stages of development.

The unity of the Arab Nation has attained a stage of solidarity enabling it to cope with the stage of the social revolution.

The methods of military coup d'état; the methods of individual opportunism and the methods adopted by the ruling reaction can only indicate that the old regime in the Arab World is madly in despair and is gradually losing its nerves, while bearing at a distance from its isolated palaces the steps of the masses advancing towards their objectives.

The unity of objective must be a slogan of Arab unity in its progress from the phase of political revolution to that of social revolution.

The slogan that was useful at earlier stages of the national struggle, namely that of the political revolution against imperialism, must be rejected.

Imperialism has now changed its attitude and has become incapable of directly confronting the people. Its natural hideout was within the palaces of reaction.

Imperialism itself has unwittingly helped advance the date of the social revolution, when it took cover behind the exploiting elements which it directs.

As a matter of fact, genuine revolutions have benefited from action of their adversaries, thereby obtaining a new impetus.

Imperialism has unmasked itself, and so has reaction by being too eager to cooperate with it.

It, therefore, became incumbent upon the people to strike at them and defeat them at one and the same time to assert the triumph of the political revolution in the remaining parts of the Arab Nation, and to consolidate the Arab man's right to a better social life that he could not attain except by revolutionary means.

25 / THE BAATH: RESOLUTIONS OF
THE SIXTH CONGRESS

"One Arab Nation with an eternal message."

The National Command of the Socialist Arab Baath.

The Sixth National Congress of the Arab Baath Socialist Party was held at a time when the Party had come to power in two Arab states after nearly twenty years of difficult struggle during which the masses, under the leadership of the Party, offered up many martyrs on the altar of the struggle for the sake of the Unity, Freedom, and Socialism of the Arab Nation.

The Arab Baath Socialist Party has been able to plan the course of the Arab struggle with judgment and clearsightedness. It has been able to achieve a true crystallization of aims of the masses' goals at both national and socialist levels, and to embody—during the period of negative struggle—the Arab people's revolutionary aspirations to remedy the Arab predicament of backwardness, exploitation, and enforced disunity.

The Party that has been able—during twenty years of struggle— to achieve a synthesis with the struggle of the Arab masses and, especially in Iraq and Syria, to lead it towards the consolidation of its national entity and its Arab character; the Party that has been able to take over the national cause from aristocracy, reaction, and the bourgeoisie and to transform the Arab national movement into an inspiration for millions in their struggle, this Party pledges itself, through the resolutions taken at this Congress, to advance unhesitatingly and indefatigably, side by side with the masses, in their national battle for Arab Unity.

The Party that has been able to bring the spirit of modern times to the Arab National movement by committing itself to the interests of the toiling masses and by linking the nationalist revolution with the socialist revolution, this party promises the toiling masses that it will continue to advance with strength and resolution along the road towards the achievement of the socialist revolution and to embody the slogans it has carried and struggled for ever since it was formed.

The Party that assisted in achieving the first Arab national revolutionary victory in contemporary history by laying the foundations

Resolutions of the Sixth National Congress of the National Command of the Arab Baath Socialist Party, Damascus, October 27, 1963 (*Al-Baath*, October 28, 1963). From *Arab Political Documents 1963*, ed. Walid Khalidi and Yusuf Ibish (Beirut, Lebanon: Political Studies and Public Administration Department of the American University of Beirut, n.d.), pp. 438–40.

of the 1958 Union and by sacrificing itself on the altar of this Union; this Party was able, after the collapse of the Union, to restore order to its ranks, recover its strength, and mobilize the masses to defy reaction and regional secession.

The first battle was in Baghdad on the 14th of Ramadan when the Party overthrew an autocratic isolationist regime inimical to Arab nationalism and unity. This paved the way for the downfall of the secessionist reactionary regime in Syria, which was already exhausted by its struggles with the masses and the Party.

At dawn on March 8, the Arab Baath Socialist vanguards led the columns that marched to destroy the baleful secessionist regime.

Thus, once more, objective circumstances paved the way for mighty victories in the nationalist and socialist fields. The Cairo Charter of April 17 was a result of the new objective circumstances achieved by the popular masses under the leadership of the Party.

However, Cairo was unable to recognize the new objective circumstances of Arab struggle, so it refused to co-operate and interact with the Party within the framework of unity and announced its withdrawal from the Charter.

The Sixth National Congress of the Arab Baath Socialist Party was held under these new conditions which now attend the Arab struggle.

On the threshold of the phase of positive struggle, this Sixth National Congress has been convened by the Party which is full of hope and determination to lead in this new battle with undiminished strength and determination and with absolute faith in the power and common destiny of the Arab nation. Fully aware of the historic responsibilities it is facing, the Party held its Sixth National Congress in Damascus on October 5, 1963. It lasted until October 23, 1963.

The Congress discussed certain issues connected with the organization of the Party in view of the fact that it is in power in the two regions, then studied certain theoretical problems that confront the Arab struggle and passed the necessary resolutions with regard to them. The Congress also discussed political union between Iraq and Syria and socialist developments in the two countries and passed the necessary resolutions in this connection. The Congress then discussed Arab and international political problems and made the necessary recommendations concerning them. The following is a summary of the major resolutions passed at the Congress which will be issued with detailed explanations:

I. Party organization matters and the relations of the Party with the masses and the authorities.

1. *The Principle of Collective Leadership.* The Congress studied issues connected with Party organization in general. It reaffirmed the importance of maintaining the principle of collective leadership in all

Party activity since it is a perfect illustration of Party democracy. The Congress concluded that the Party's experience has proved the soundness of the principle of democratic centralization which is being applied. The establishment of a proper equilibrium between centralization on the one hand, and democracy on the other, was considered to be the only way of ensuring that both the masses and the Party are given the opportunity of exercising practical responsibility; it will safeguard the unity of the Party on the one hand and, on the other, will prove how genuinely democratic and flexible it is.

2. *The Social Structure of the Party.* In the course of a thorough study of the Party's present situation in Syria and Iraq, the Congress gave special attention to the circumstances of the socialist revolution initiated by the masses. The Congress affirmed that the social structure of the Party must affect the revolution itself and therefore decided that the Party's socialist objectives must be embodied in its social structure. Total socialist revolution and the party must fundamentally depend both on the workers and the peasants.

3. *The Right of the Masses to Criticize the Party.* Because the Party is in power the Congress warned against the dangers of opportunist elements infiltrating into it. The Congress also mentioned the dangers of Party elements succumbing to the temptations of power and of their having their heads turned, adopting an arrogant attitude towards the non-Party masses. The Congress passed resolutions on methods to be adopted to prevent the emergence of an ideological elite at the expense of the Party's principles and morality and at the expense of the non-Party masses. The Congress declared that membership in the Party has no other significance than the great responsibility that a party member must bear. The Congress asked members of the Party to think only of their responsibilities; their rights are exactly the same as those enjoyed by any citizen. The Congress affirmed that the non-Party masses have the right to criticize the Party and supervise the activities of its members.

In addition to its being the natural right of the masses, this supervision will guarantee mutual interaction and criticism between the masses, on the one hand, and the Party and the authorities, on the other. It is also a means for protecting members from the temptations of power and for preventing the emergence of bourgeois tendencies. The Congress stressed the importance of paying attention to the character of Party members, being firm in accepting applications for membership, and lengthening the probation period of candidates for membership so as to make sure of their character and their fitness to take part in the struggle.

4. *The Relationship of the Party with the Authorities.* With regard to the Party's relations with the Government, the Congress stressed the necessity of distinguishing between the two. It warned against the dangers of the Government's swallowing up the Party and the Party becoming submerged in every-day Government routine. The Party is the leader and director of the Government's general policy. The Congress em-

phasized the importance of the majority of the Party Command's concentrating on Party activity.

5. *Resolutions on Certain Theoretical Problems Connected With Party Ideology and the Arab Struggle.* The Congress discussed several issues connected with the Arab struggle and certain theoretical problems connected with Arab unity, socialism, the exercise of popular democracy, and the Party's attitude towards international socialist ideas. The Congress explained that the two epithets essentially applicable to the Party's ideology are "scientific" and "revolutionary," within a national framework. The Congress then reviewed certain ideas and opinions that have resulted from the Party's profound and creative intellectual development which has enabled it to anticipate the future clearly, without breaking away from the legacy of its past, thus ensuring its intellectual unity, its ideological clarity, the solidity of its organization, and the scientific and revolutionary confrontation of the problems of the Arab struggle.

6. *The Democracy of Socialist Change.* The Congress discussed the problems of socialist change in Syria and Iraq and decided to continue on the path of socialist change on a democratic basis and with the participation of the masses. After a scientific analysis of the social, political, and class situations in both states, the Congress declared that the Party's solidarity with the masses prepares the way for a radical democratic revolutionary experiment in both countries which will make itself felt not only in these two countries, but also in all parts of the Arab homeland. It will prepare the objective circumstances which will facilitate mutual criticism and interaction in the exchange of experiences between the different parts of the Arab homeland.

7. *The Socialist Forces of the Revolution.* On the basis of a scientific analysis of the political and economic situations in the two states, the Congress made important deductions with regard to the bourgeois middle class. This class is no longer capable of playing any positive role in the economic field and its opportunism has made it a new ally of imperialism. The Congress considered that the workers, peasants, educated revolutionaries (military and civilian), and the petty bourgeoisie are the forces which will make—if united—the socialist revolution in its first phase.

26 / REVOLUTIONARY POLYCENTRISM

I know Aden, that remote part of our Arab homeland, the region occupied by British Imperialism; I know that there is in Aden an organized popular movement that embodies some of the richest Arab

Address by Mr. Aflak, Secretary-General of the Baath Party, at the mass rally held in support of the revolution in occupied Yemen, Damascus, December 26, 1963 (*Syrian News Bulletin,* December 27, 1963). From *Arab Political Documents 1963,* ed. Walid Khalidi and Yusuf Ibish (Beirut, Lebanon: Political Studies and Public Administration Department of the American University of Beirut, n.d.), pp. 513–14.

revolutionary experiences of the age. A workers' movement was formed in Aden that soon incorporated the whole national movement, combining the people's national objectives with socialist objectives in harmony with the Arab revolutionary slogans adopted in the other Arab regions. This popular movement in Aden has upheld these slogans of Unity, Freedom and Socialism since 1956. This remote struggling part of our homeland has passed through the same problems as the other Arab regions. There are people who have distorted the nationalist movement in Aden and the South and tried to make of it a means of encouraging secession, and of strengthening the present divisions, instead of an integral part of the campaign for Unity and Freedom. But the movement's connection with the revolutionary slogans in the other parts of the Arab homeland has protected it against deviation and thwarted the imperialists' desires to entangle this great movement in the perpetuation of partition behind the thin disguise of local independence. The true revolutionary slogan that links the liberation movement in the South with the socialist and unionist movement (that is, the re-union of Southern with Northern Yemen) has overcome the imperialists' designs. Lately Aden has suffered more cruel suppression than ever before during the whole of its history under British imperialism. This was the result of a retrogression that encouraged the reactionaries, the imperialists and the racialists to raise their heads high throughout the whole Arab area. We must analyze the causes of this retrogression in order to comprehend the new situation in the Arab world and to make preparations for remedying it. The first signs of the retrogression appeared in Jordan when King Husain dared to make mass arrests of members of the Arab Baath Socialist Party. He was encouraged by the fact that the other nationalist elements had concluded a truce with him. The arrest of Baathists was accompanied by the release of those who had formerly joined ranks with the Arab Baath Socialist Party. I mean, for example, members of the Arab Nationalist Movement and National Socialists. This is how Husain of Jordan divided the Arab revolutionary ranks. This was followed by King Hasan of Morocco's attack on the National Federation of Popular Forces which alone (in the midst of reactionary, regionalist and racialist tendencies) represents in Morocco the idea of revolutionary Arabism and constitutes a link between the struggle of the Arab people in the West and that in the East, as well as embodying the great nationalist objectives of Unity, Freedom and Socialism. Reaction, supported by imperialism, exploited the rifts that had appeared in the unity of the Arab revolutionary ranks and continued the frontier-war with Algeria in an area where the imperialists' monopoly companies were concentrated. Shortly after that the rightist elements and their supporters, the national and foreign capitalists, with

Cairo's aid and encouragement, attacked the Socialist Unionist Regime in Iraq, which was represented by the Arab Socialist Party, exploiting the mistakes and deviations of certain party leaders who had become arrogant after the historic victory achieved by the Party on the 14th of Ramadan. These arrogant Baathist leaders were reckless in their actions and kept silent about the reckless actions of others. They allowed the dictatorial and rightist elements to entangle them without realizing their danger. This is how the retrogression affected Iraq, which had been on the threshold of a sound Arab Union that would have protected its Arabism from the dangers of racialism, reaction, and the tragedies of autocratic dictatorships. Many have compared the events of November 18, 1963, to the Secession of September 28, 1961. The authorities have tried to wash their hands of the collapse of the Union and put all the blame on those who conspired for Secession. But because the Baath Party feels that it belongs to all the Arab people and to the rising generation of Arabs, because it does not represent the interests of one region only or the leadership of certain individuals only, because it is above considerations that prevent other parties from being frank with the people and from stating the facts, the Baath Party courageously admits to the Arab people the mistakes and the weak points of the Party Command in Iraq. It was difficult to prevent these mistakes from leading to the retrogression because of the arrogance of the Baathist leaders and the fact that they had concealed matters both from the rank and file and from the leaders of the Party. The Party condemns them and their actions, which were not in conformity with its ideology. This condemnation is essential for the safeguarding of the entity of the Party so that it may always be worthy to carry out its historic mission.

27 / THE BAATH PHASED PROGRAM

Foreign Relations

The foreign relations of the Syrian Arab Republic are based on two fundamental principles: The achievement of the goals of the Arab nation: unity, freedom and socialism, and support for the struggle of humanity for the sake of liberation and progress.

The Baath Party, together with the popular organisations, is committed in its foreign relations to continue the struggle on the popular and governmental levels, to achieve the long-term objectives of the

The Programme approved by the Extraordinary Regional Congress of the Baath Party in Damascus (excerpts), Damascus, July 22, 1965 (*Al-Baath,* July 23, 1965). From *Arab Political Documents 1965,* ed. Walid Khalid and Yusuf Ibish (Beirut, Lebanon: Political Studies and Public Administration Department of the American University of Beirut, n.d.), pp. 256–58, 259, 260.

Arabs, to create Arab unity, develop Arab economy on the basis of socialism and to free the Arab nation from all external or internal factors which may adversely affect national sovereignty or human freedom. The revolutionary regime strives to make all its policies serve a humanistic end which is to support national liberation movements and to cooperate sincerely with all countries for this purpose. Day to day policy must be determined by these principles. In its international relations, the Syrian Arab Republic struggles for the objectives of the Arab nation as a whole and so its policies are national rather than regional. Syria fights for progress and liberation. Its policy is humanistic, not narrow, and expresses its national and humanitarian mission and its great responsibilities in the Arab and international spheres.

Arab Relations

In the Arab sphere, the policy of the Syrian Arab Republic is based upon firm faith in the unity of the Arab nation and its right to build a new and progressive society which would accomplish its objectives. The right of the Arab masses to struggle for these objectives in the various political, social and economic spheres must also be recognised. For this reason:

1. Our Arab policy aims at accomplishing proper unionist measures based upon actual conditions of Arab society and stemming from the experience gained from previous unions. Serious endeavour for the purpose of accomplishing these measures is the primary objective of our Arab policy . . .

5. The Syrian Arab Republic considers that the liberation of Palestine, which is a fundamental national objective, can only be accomplished in a revolutionary manner which makes full use of the total Arab potential in all the political, economic and military spheres. Arab power must be mobilised to accomplish this aim and the Arabs of Palestine must be given the chance to freely organise themselves and to mobilise their total revolutionary potential to this end. Syria is committed to offer support and aid of all kinds to the Palestinians and strives to provide maximum help for this cause from other Arab countries.

6. Syria believes that the Palestine Problem is a national one and all other considerations must be transcended, including narrow regional interests and political and ideological conflicts among Arab states. Syria strives to suspend all regional conflicts and meet with any Arab country, irrespective of all differences, if such a meeting should serve the interests of liberation and of the fight against Zionism . . .

8. The policy of Syria is directed towards nationalisation of Arab oil as the final objective of Arab oil policy. This aim must also be included as part of the revolutionary Arab strategy to liberate Palestine and

achieve economic development. The oil of the Arab world is not a regional issue which has to do with regional sovereignty but is a national question since it is directly related to the freedom of the Arab world and to the foremost Arab cause, Palestine, as well as to economic development. Until this is accomplished, certain basic practical measures must be adopted which would achieve results in this sphere as, for example, using part of the income from oil to set up a joint Arab fund for development and armament . . .

International Relations

The international relations of the revolutionary regime are based upon the humanitarian roots of the revolutionary movement which directs the government. Our Party, which has always fought for man's dignity in the Arab world, has prized and valued human dignity everywhere, since it believes that the struggle of humanity for progress, freedom and economic prosperity is a common one. Arising from all this, the international policy of the Syrian Arab Republic is based upon the following principles:

1. Non-alignment and the rejection of world blocs and military treaties. Syria is in favour of independent foreign policies for all states. Non-alignment serves the interests of world peace and of lessening tension. It also suits our conditions as a nation fighting against imperialism and for an independent future . . .

4. Syria pays particular attention to its relations with Socialist countries. It strives to strengthen cooperation and friendship with these states on both the official and popular levels. It seeks to gain a deep knowledge of their experiences in the various fields, especially the field of socialist reconstruction . . .

6. Syria deals with other foreign countries, including countries of the Western camp, on the basis of national interest and mutual respect of sovereignty and freedom of action. We befriend all who are willing to support us in our national problems of liberation and economic development. Accordingly, Syria deals with all countries of the world on the basis of mutual interests and unconditional economic cooperation.

7. Syria believes in the necessity of linking its foreign policy to the question of the liberation of Palestine. It will therefore constantly re-examine its relations with foreign countries on the basis of the policy of these countries to the Palestine question. It affirms the necessity for the formulation of practical plans to attain liberation and struggles with the Arab masses to make this an official policy of all Arab states. This may entail a re-examination of our political, economic and military relations with Western countries . . .

Popular Democracy

The foundation of the state's home policy is the building of a popular democracy. . . .

Popular Organisation

There can be no popular democracy if there is no Party which leads the people towards their objectives. The Party in a popular democracy is merely the vanguard of the fighting people, where all the conscious elements gather together and are bound by a well defined theory for revolutionary action. The Party leads the people and is the spearhead of its fight. Although the Party precedes the people it is nevertheless connected with it. The Party both leads the people and interacts with it. The Party rises from the ranks of the people when the latter comes to recognise its corrupt state of affairs and is determined to put an end to it. The Party therefore is an organisation that precedes the revolutionary regime. Representing the general will and the ambitions and needs of the people, the Party rules the country. The regime on the other hand may be defined as the instrument by means of which the people, represented by its vanguard, can achieve the objectives for which it is struggling.

The Party works through a popular organisation directed by certain regulatory principles which in turn are based upon a centralised democratic basis. . . . The people also struggle alongside the Party through other popular organisations like professional and trade unions and educational and economic establishments as well as various other popular organisations. Under popular democracy, these organisations play a special role different from their role under bourgeois democracies or dictatorships. These popular organisations are not merely professional unions whose job is to protect the narrow interests of their members as in bourgeois democracies. Nor are they merely a façade for the regime, willing tools wielded for the sake of propaganda as is the case under dictatorships. On the contrary, these are living institutions ordering in their ranks certain conscious and struggling groups of the people with the purpose of contributing to national development. They are well organised elements from among the population which defend the legitimate interests of the groups they represent through their defence of the higher interests of the nation and not in isolation from these interests. . . . In other words, these popular organisations have, under a popular democracy, a political function in addition to their well-known professional one. . . .

Socialist Transformation

The publication of the Socialist Decrees during the last period of the Revolution led to the creation of a large and relatively vigorous public sector in the economy. Our national economy thus began the stage of socialist transformation in a serious manner. The public sector has come to dominate the exploitation of important natural resources, public services, the important segment of industry and of the import-export trade. The Government of the Revolution also took important socialist measures in the field of agrarian reform. These measures were accompanied by other steps taken to create the cadres necessary for the implementation of these measures, whether in the organisation or training spheres.

The aim behind these socialist measures was to create a public sector capable of leading the national economy where before the private sector had dominated, with its own interests and its exploitation of workers. Socialist transformation, then, aims to change this situation by making the public sector the back-bone of the national economy and the state an instrument serving the working masses and the interests of the public rather than of feudalism and capitalism.

28 / ARAB UNITY: TRIPARTITE DECLARATION, 1963

In the name of God, the Merciful, the Compassionate;

In the name of the Arab people;

Delegations representing the United Arab Republic, Syria and Iraq have met in Cairo. In response to the will of the Arab people in the three countries and in the greater Arab Nation, fraternal talks between the three delegations began on Saturday, 6th April and ended on Wednesday, 17th April 1963.

Throughout their talks, the delegations were inspired by their belief that Arab unity is an inevitable objective which derives from a common language which is the carrier of culture and thought, a common history which is the maker of sentiment and conscience, a common popular struggle which determines and shapes destiny, common spiritual and human values emanating from divine revelation, and common social and economic concepts based on freedom and socialism.

The delegations were guided by the popular will of the Arab people which demands unity, struggles to achieve it, and makes great sacrifices to protect and safeguard it, realizing that the nucleus of a strong unity consists in the unification of those parts of the homeland, which have achieved their liberty and independence, and in which there have been established nationalist progressive governments, determined to destroy the alliance between feudalism, capitalism, re-

Declaration of the Tripartite Union Announcement of the Creation of the Federal State of the United Arab Republic. From *Arab Political Documents 1963*, ed. Walid Khalidi and Yusuf Ibish (Beirut, Lebanon: Political Studies and Public Administration Department of the American University of Beirut, n.d.), pp. 227–28.

action and imperialism, and to liberate the active forces of the people to assert their solidarity and express their true will.

The Revolution of July 23 was a historic turning point in which the Arab people of Egypt discovered themselves, recovered their will and thus pursued the road to Liberty, Arabism and Unity. The revolution of Ramadan 14 revealed the true Arab features of Iraq and lighted its way towards the horizons of unity which had been sought by such members of the Revolution of July 14 as were sincere. The Revolution of March 8 restored Syria to its place in the caravan of unity which had been destroyed by the reactionary secession, after this revolution had removed all the obstacles which the secessionists and imperialists had deployed on the road of unity.

The three revolutions converged on this point: the reaffirmation of the fact that unity is a revolutionary act which derives its concepts from the faith of the masses, its strength from their will and its aims from their aspirations to freedom and socialism.

Unity is a revolution—a revolution because it is popular and progressive and because it is a strong surge forward with the tide of civilization.

Unity is a revolution particularly because it is deeply connected with the cause of Palestine and the national duty to liberate it. It was the Palestine disaster which exposed the conspiracies of the reactionary classes and the treacheries of the subservient, anti-Arab parties and their betrayal of the people's aims and aspirations. It was this disaster which laid bare the weakness and backwardness of existing economic and social systems. It was this disaster which exploded the revolutionary energies of the masses of our people and sparked off the spirit of rebellion against imperialism, injustice, poverty and backwardness. It was this disaster which pointed the way to the road of salvation, the road of unity, freedom and socialism. The delegations had all this in mind during their talks. While unity is a sacred objective, it is also the instrument of the popular struggle and the means for the realization of its major aims which are: freedom, security, the liberation of all parts of the Arab Nation, the establishment of a society in which all enjoy an adequate standard of living, based on justice and socialism, the continued and undiverted flow of the revolutionary current with undiminished force and its extension to embrace the greater Arab Nation, and contribution to the progress of human civilization and the consolidation of world peace.

It has been agreed that unity between the three regions be established in accordance with the desires of the Arab people, on the basis of democracy and socialism, and that it be a real and solid unity which takes into consideration regional conditions and so strengthens the bonds of unity on a foundation of realistic understanding, rather than perpetuating factors conducive of division and separatism. Thus the strength of each region will be turned into a strength for the federal state and the Arab Nation as a whole, and the strength of the federal state as a whole into a strength for each state within it, and for the whole Arab Nation.

29 / ARAB UNITY: U.A.R.-IRAQ AGREEMENT, 1964

Believing in this unity of the Arab nation, a unity born of a common language, history, struggle and destiny, and taking into account the artificial divisions reflected in the present political fragmentation imposed on the Arab lands by imperialism [in order] to serve its aims of exploitation and domination, the Arab nation finds itself adhering to its unity, both historically and by experience.

The aspirations of the Arab nation were realized in a pioneer experience: the creation of the United Arab Republic of Syria and Egypt, which proved to the whole world that unity was no impossible ideal but a real fact.

The forces of evil, backed by imperialism and reaction, banded together and perpetrated secession. But the moral of the Secession was very valuable in that unity of the future would be more closely protected and better care would be taken to preserve it.

The experience of the Union proved that the slogans of unity were not sufficient to create it. The formation and unification of popular organizations is essential to protect union. Clearly enunciated and common nationalist principles must be formulated. Unity of thought leads to a real unity of action which would be implemented in a revolutionary manner so as to achieve total unity.

The revolutionary conception of unity is based on the unity of the working peoples to whom belong the advantages and rights of the revolution. It also entails the unity of Arab socialist society, based on economic self-sufficiency and justice, which is the goal of Arab social struggle so as to secure a social as well as a political content for Arab unity. The socialist society represents the determination of the Arab peoples to forge a new future for the free Arab individual.

With all the foregoing principles serving as a foundation, and representing the governments and peoples of Iraq and the U.A.R., Presidents Aref of Iraq and Nasser of the U.A.R. have agreed to the following:

The Agreement for political coordination concluded between the U.A.R. and Iraq, Cairo, May 26, 1964 (*Al-Ahram*, May 27, 1964). From *Arab Political Documents 1964*, ed. Walid Khalidi and Yusuf Ibish (Beirut, Lebanon: Political Studies and Public Administration Department of the American University of Beirut, n.d.), pp. 217–19.

Article 1. A Joint Presidential Council of the U.A.R. and Iraq shall be formed, with the two presidents and others acting as members.

Article 2.

A) The Council shall meet once every three months. It shall also meet in emergencies, with the consent of the two presidents.

B) The seat of this council shall be Cairo. It may be called to meet elsewhere, with the consent of the two presidents.

Article 3. Decisions of the Council shall be binding and operative as soon as the Council ratifies them. Other decisions requiring legislation shall be ratified in accordance with constitutional provisions in force in each country.

Article 4. The business of the Council shall be conducted according to its own by-laws, which shall become operative as soon as they are ratified by the Council.

Article 5. The Council shall be concerned to:

A) Study and coordinate the necessary measures for creating a union of the countries.

B) Plan and coordinate their economic, military, political, social, cultural and information policies.

C) Achieve a unity of thought among the peoples of Iraq and the U.A.R. through the organization and unification of popular activity in the two countries.

Article 6.

A) Each government shall appoint its members in the Council according to the following formula:

1) Three specialized members with the rank of minister.

2) Three non-specialized members drawn from members of the Government.

B) The specialized members shall supervise the implementation of the Council's decisions, coordinate the activities of joint committees and present studies and recommendations at the meetings of the Council.

C) The Council or its committees shall call upon the experts and technicians of either country to attend their meetings if necessary.

Article 7. The following committees shall be formed:

A) The Political Committee;

B) The Military Command;

C) The Economic Committee;

D) The Cultural and Information Committee;

E) The Arab Socialist Thought Committee;

F) The Popular Organization Committee;

G) Any other committees that may be required.

These committees shall study and prepare various topics with a view to implementing this Agreement. They shall also deal with any questions referred to them by the Joint Presidential Council.

Article 8.

A) The Joint Military Command shall have the task of coordinating the armament, training and equipment of the armed forces of the two countries. It shall plan the operations and movement of these forces and command them in wartime.

B) The Military Command shall take all necessary measures to counter war or the threat of war. Any aggression or threat of aggression against either country is considered to be against both.

Article 9. The Council has a Secretariat established at Cairo. It shall be headed by a Secretary-General, with the rank of Minister, and its tasks shall be:

A) To call for meetings of the Joint Presidential Council;

B) To prepare the agenda of these meetings;

C) To keep the minutes of the Council's [sic] and of the meetings of its organs, and to publish such decisions as have been ratified according to the constitutional practice of each country.

D) To prepare the budgets of the Council, the Secretariat and the other common agencies outlined in Article 7.

Article 10.

A) The budget of the Council and the other common agencies is to be shared equally between the two contracting governments.

B) Each country is to pay the salaries and compensation of officials delegated by itself, in accordance with its own fiscal regulations.

Article 11. The provisions of this Agreement do not affect the rights and obligations, present or future, which either of the two countries incur or shall incur according to the U.N. Charter. These provisions do not also affect the terms of any agreement contracted by either country within the framework of the Arab League.

Article 12. This Agreement shall remain in force until the necessary measures have been taken to establish a union.

Article 13. This Agreement shall be considered operative as soon as it is ratified according to the constitutional practices of each country.

This Agreement was signed on May 26, 1964, on two original copies, each country retaining one copy. A duplicate of this Agreement is deposited at the Secretariat of the Arab League.

For the U.A.R.	For the Iraqi Republic
Gamal Abdul Nasser	Abdul Salam Aref

30 / ARAB UNITY: NASSER'S VIEW

President Aref,
Gentlemen.

As we sign this Agreement which is a first step towards full union, we pray that God may help us to achieve the goal we, and all Arabs,

Speech of President Nasser on the agreement for political coordination between the U.A.R. and Iraq, Cairo, May 26, 1964 (*Al-Ahram*, May 27, 1964). From *Arab Political Documents 1964*, ed. Walid Khalidi and Yusuf Ibish (Beirut, Lebanon: Political Studies and Public Administration Department of the American University of Beirut, n.d.), pp. 215–16.

have striven for, namely the nationalist and popular goal of complete union.

In reality, the union of Iraq and Egypt has existed since the Revolution of November 18. We believe that the unity of objectives is the real unity, and this unity has existed since that date. We have all been working for Unity, Freedom and Socialism.

Today, as we sign this Agreement as the first step to union, we intend to forge a union on strong and solid foundations. We have designed this union to take place in stages so that it can meet and overcome its enemies.

The Arab nation knows that the enemies of unity are legion. When the Union of Syria and Egypt was forged in 1958, the whole Arab world welcomed and supported it. But I also felt then that we were up against the hatred of the enemies of the Arabs and of union namely, Zionism and imperialism and all others who wished the Arab nation to remain fragmented, weak and vulnerable to attack.

The forces of reaction, in league with imperialism, were able to strike the Union on September 28. But the Syrian people proved that union was possible and that secession was impossible. Hence, it fought reaction, imperialism, opportunism, etc. who had deceived it concerning the Union. The reactionaries aimed only to lord it over Syria. They called for Unity, Freedom, and Socialism, but were themselves far removed from these ideals.

Throughout these difficult circumstances, the people of Syria demonstrated to the whole world that they have been and shall always be at the very core of Arab sentiment for unity.

Today, as we sign this Agreement with our Iraqi brethren, we salute the brave Syrian people who strove for and laid the foundations for unity. We believe that this Agreement of ours is equally a triumph for the Syrians.

At this historical moment, we pray to God for the prosperity of the Syrians and that of all Arab peoples in order that they may achieve all their goals and aspirations.

The people of Iraq, likewise, have a long history of struggle before and after 1958. Before that date, and during the regime of Nuri Said when we fought the Baghdad Pact, the people of Iraq also struggled against it. When we faced the Tripartite Aggression, the people of Iraq marched out to demonstrate in the streets of Baghdad, then ruled by Nuri Said. As some of us died at Port Said, so some Iraqis also fell in the streets of Baghdad.

The peoples of Iraq and Egypt have always been bound together by ties of blood, brotherhood and amity.

Following July 14, 1958, the people of Iraq also fought for unity, and shed their blood for that idea. Again, after the Ramadan 14

Revolution, the people fought for union until, finally, the November 18 Revolution, led by President Aref and his noble companions, dedicated themselves in all sincerity to the cause of Arab unity.

The document we sign this day is a triumph for the people of Iraq, who fought Nuri Said, Abdul Karim Kassem, the Baathist deviation and triumphed over them all. May God always crown their efforts with victory.

As for the people of Egypt, they also have always worked for unity. The Revolution of July 23, 1952, was only an Arab revolt which aimed to restore the people to their natural place, to restore Arabism.

This Agreement is, likewise, a triumph for the ideals of the Arab people of Egypt. As the first step towards union, it is a triumph for the whole Arab world which calls for unity. May God help, guide and prosper us, that we may build this union on solid foundations.

31 / IRAQ: OBJECTIVES OF THE REVOLUTION

In the Name of God the Beneficent, the Merciful.

By the help of God and the assistance of the sincere people of Iraq and members of the National Armed Forces, we have undertaken to liberate our dear Country from the domination of the corrupt clique installed by imperialism to rule over the people and to play with its destiny for the rulers' personal interests and advantages.

Brothers:

The army is from you and for you. It has achieved what you desire and eliminated the tyrants who played with the rights of the people. You need only support the army, and know that victory cannot be achieved without consolidating it and protecting it from the conspiracies of imperialism and its agents. We therefore ask you to inform the authorities of every corrupt, harmful and traitorous element, so that they may be eliminated. We require you to stand united in uprooting these elements and overcoming their evils.

Citizens:

Whilst we appreciate your patriotic spirit and wonderful achievements, we ask you to be calm and orderly, and to co-operate in productive work for the benefit of the country.

People:

We have sworn to sacrifice our blood and everything we hold dear for your sake. Be sure and confident, therefore, that we shall continue working for you. The rule must be entrusted to a government emanating from the people and inspired by them. This cannot be achieved

Notification No. 1, issued by the Commander-in-Chief, National Armed Forces. From 14th July Celebrations Committee, *The Iraqi Revolution—One Year of Progress and Achievement, 1958–1959* (Baghdad: The Times Press, n.d.), pp. 7–10.

except by the formation of a popular republic adhering to complete Iraqi unity, and linked by brotherly ties with the Arab and Moslem states. The Republic will act in accordance with the United Nations Charter, and the principles of the Bandung Conference, and will abide by all pledges and pacts consistent with the interests of the country. As from now, the National Government will be called the Republic of Iraq. In accordance with the wishes of the people we have temporarily entrusted its presidency to a Sovereignty Council enjoying all the powers of the President of the Republic, until a plebiscite is carried out for the election of a President.

We pray to God, the omnipotent and omniscient, that He may grant us success in our work for the service of our dear country.

Baghdad, on the 26th day of Dhe Al-Hijjah, 1377 H, corresponding to July 14th 1958.

Commander-in-Chief
National Armed Forces

Official Commentary

This historic document was written by the leader of the Revolution himself. It marks clearly the ideals and objectives of the Revolution, and outlines the internal and external policies of the Republic. The outstanding points of the Notification are:

1. The army is an integral part of the people.

2. The people are called on to fight actively against imperialism through unity and co-operation.

3. It called for calm, constructive work.

4. Rule emanates from the people and according to the will of the people without discrimination.

5. The Republic of Iraq is a popular republic, which upholds Arab unity and co-operates with Moslem states and all the states of the world on the basis of equality.

One of the first actions of the revolutionary Government was to release political prisoners, and restore the full rights of those exiled. The Government granted full freedom to meetings, publishing, expression and organisation, without waiting for new laws to be passed or for the old laws to be rectified. It thus practically recognised all the legal constitutional rights which the old regime had wiped out.

The personality of the leader of the Revolution appeared closely linked with all events. Despite his modesty and his refusal to indicate, even indirectly, that he is the sole leader, organiser and planner of the Revolution, people immediately discovered that Abdul Karim Qassim possessed unique characteristics, and a deep understanding of history and of contemporary international policy and that he was a skilful organiser of extensive reform plans.

A man accomplishing a hazardous task such as this and carrying it through successfully without claiming credit for himself, and without attempting to acquire absolute power, is a man worthy of attention, respect, love and admiration. It is noteworthy that these characteristics are not assumed, but are genuine and original. Abdul Karim Qassim is quiet and reticent, and has a far-reaching foresight and excellent judgment. He is employing all these qualities for the service of his country.

Above all, he realises the desire of the Iraqi people for advancement and rapid development, and he therefore started his programme of "a revolution of a month," which produced such magnificent achievements as the declaration of the Interim Constitution; the declaration of the Republic of Iraq; the returning of all powers to the people; confiscation of the property of the royal family; the withdrawal from the Hashimite Federation with Jordan; the declaration of a law for the compensation of the persecuted; the declaration of a firm policy in oil affairs; the resumption of relations with the U.S.S.R. and the Socialist Republics; the cancellation of the Tribal Law; the purging of government machinery; the promulgation of the Popular Resistance Law; the reduction of house rentals; the improvement of salaries; the declaration of the law concerning Illegal Earnings at the Expense of the People; the withdrawal from the Baghdad Pact, from the Eisenhower Doctrine and from the Sterling Area; and the participation of women in the government.

The trial of certain of the old regime personalities by one of the greatest and most unusual courts in history was begun. The people began to exercise the authority of judgment, side by side with the military judges of the court, of those who had played with its destiny for over a century.

The path of the Revolution was not free from trouble, however, and the Al-Baath Party began to call for an immediate merger with the United Arab Republic. This call was adopted by Abdul Salam Arif, and he began to tour Iraq propagating the idea. Abdul Karim Qassim realised that such a merger was not the wish of the people and that they preferred instead a decentralised federation based on free cooperation, and abhorred the idea of being dominated by anybody. At the end, Abdul Karim Qassim was forced to detain those calling for an unqualified merger, after it was evident that the people were about to explode against them. Some troublemakers wanted to provoke the Kurds against the Revolution and its leader, but the recognition by Abdul Karim Qassim of all the rights of the Kurds caused this attempt to fail.

In actual fact, the Revolution did not have to spend too much effort in overcoming the hurdles placed in its way, as the initial momentum of the movement and the wise guidance of its leader were enough to pave the way and overcome the difficulties and avoid the traps. The Revolution forged ahead, and some of the achievements during the first year of its life are detailed in this book.

These achievements are but a minute fraction of the potentialities of the Iraqi people. The wealth of the country is immense. It possesses two of the greatest rivers in the world, and the fertile land floats on a sea of oil, the "black gold" of modern times, and the most valuable commodity of today's civilisation. There is mineral wealth everywhere, and a wealth of history in every hill, testifying to the most ancient and advanced civilisation in the world.

So long as Iraq is safeguarded from outside aggression through a wise peaceful policy and a strong defence force, and so long as justice and a fair distribution of industrial and agricultural wealth prevail, there can be no doubt that the Republic will attain a very advanced degree of development and prosperity. This will be of the greatest assistance to the Arab world in realising its ambition of independence and unity. The requirements for such achievements are included in the programme of Abdul Karim Qassim.

Iraq will not build its greatness on the misery of its people or of its brothers in race or humanity. Iraq is essentially a peace-loving country, and by peace it will realise its dreams.

The leader was quick to realise the attempts being made inside and outside the country to sow disunity through party political strife and dissension. He therefore called on all parties to restrict their activities to those which could serve the defence of the Republic and the strengthening of its foundations until the end of the transitional period. The parties themselves realised the danger and promptly responded to the Prime Minister's call.

The leadership of Abdul Karim Qassim has proved to be unique and unmatched, and the next few years will see phenomenal development and advancement in Iraq. This book is but a guide to indicate the road of the Revolution.

32 / OFFICIAL VIEW OF ORGANIZATIONS
UNDER KASSEM'S REGIME

The Freedom of Organisation:

The rulers of the old regime were much frightened by organisation. They kept watch not only over political parties and unions, but also over cultural and educational societies, and considered all these a

From 14th July Celebrations Committee, *The Iraqi Revolution—One Year of Progress and Achievement, 1958–1959* (Baghdad: The Times Press, n.d.), pp. 96–100.

major danger threatening their rule. Political parties were often banned and students were barred from forming a union. The Peace Partisans Movement was prohibited, together with all democratic youth organisations and women's organisations. In 1954, Nuri as-Said issued an ordinance banning 465 parties, societies and clubs of all types, political, scientific, economic, social, vocational and labour unions. A few camouflage unions, patronised by the government, were allowed to operate. Despite all this, patriotic organisations continued their struggle secretly, withstanding persecution and hardship.

After the Revolution, organisations flourished, and below is a summary of their activities:

1. Unions:

Over fifty labour unions, with a membership of over 250,000, were licensed—all being affiliated to the General Federation of Labour Unions in the Republic of Iraq.

Unions are endeavouring to raise the cultural and social standard of their workers, and during the various conferences, [recommendations] were made to increase and develop national production. The Unions succeeded in securing various privileges and advantages for their members, and were able to reinstate in employment over five hundred workers discharged for political reasons during the old regime.

2. Peasant Societies:

The peasants played a heroic part during the 1920 Revolution, and continued their struggle after that revolution, against feudalists and their crimes and exploitations. Even before the Revolution, various secret peasant societies were formed in the north and south.

The peasant movement gained momentum after the Revolution, and the General Federation of Peasant Societies was licensed on May 21st 1959. Within two months, the Federation licensed 734 peasant societies in all parts of the country. On the 15th April, 1959, the first conference was opened by the Prime Minister, who greatly evaluated the role played by peasants in the success of the Revolution.

Peasant societies are now actively engaged in increasing production and the application of the Agrarian Reform Law.

3. Parties:

Although not officially licensed, political parties were allowed to function freely, and played an important role in public mobilisation for the service and defence of the Republic.

During the old regime, patriotic parties met with much persecution, and in 1956 a National Front was formed of four parties—the National Democratic Party; the Communist Party; the Al-Istiqlal (Independence) Party; and the Al-Baath (Renaissance) Party—to co-ordinate efforts in their joint fight against imperialism and feudalism. During that time, the officers of the Revolution were in close touch with the National Front, and when the first revolutionary cabinet was formed, three of these parties: The National Democratic; the Al-Istiqlal and the Al-Baath, were represented. On December 23rd 1958, the Unified Democratic Party of Kurdistan joined the Front.

However, after the Shawaf Mutiny, Al-Istiqlal and Al-Baath Parties collapsed and the National Front was disbanded despite the attempts of some parties to reorganise it.

Leader Abdul Karim Qassim expressed his support for parties and announced that a free political and parliamentary life will come into being on January 6th, 1960, after a brief transitional period.

It should be mentioned that the collapse of the Al-Istiqlal and Baath Parties was not due to their ideas and belief, but due to their actual participation in conspiring against the Revolution.

4. Peace Partisans:

The movement started in Iraq during the old regime, and was met with persecution and suppression. In spite of this, however, the Peace Partisans were able to hold a conference in Baghdad in 1954 and to participate in the international conference of the movement. During the Republican era, the movement spread to all parts of the country and on April 14th 1959 the Peace Partisans Conference was opened by the Prime Minister, followed the next day by a gigantic procession attended by representations from all parts of the world.

Peace Partisans played a major role in suppressing the Mosul Mutiny.

5. The Iraqi Democratic Youths:

This organisation operated under cover during the old regime, and was subjected to persecution and hardship. The movement, which is now operating with full freedom, played its role in guarding important installations in conjunction with the official authorities during the plots against the Republic.

On June 11th 1959, the first conference of the Iraqi Democratic Youth Organisation was opened by the Prime Minister. The conference was attended by delegates from all over the world, representing over eighty-five million youths.

The membership of the organisation is, at present, over 85,000 youths of both sexes. They have all co-operated in various patriotic schemes, including the anti-illiteracy campaign.

6. Student Movements:

Student movements operated secretly during the old regime and were subjected to various suppressive measures, including prisons and expulsions.

After the Revolution all expelled students were reinstated and allowed to return to their schools and colleges, student organisations were legalised and student unions affiliated to the Iraqi Students Federation, were freely elected in all schools and colleges. On February 2nd 1959, the first conference of the Federation was held under the patronage of Leader Abdul Karim Qassim.

7. The Popular Resistance Forces:

On August 1st 1958, the Law of the Popular Resistance Forces came into being, and during the first two days of enlisting, there were over 7,000 applications to join the force, coming from people from all walks of life, including students, workers, peasants, lawyers, doctors, engineers, teachers, etc.

The Popular Resistance Force played a major part in crushing the Shawaf Mutiny and the Lolan Mutiny, and co-operated with security authorities in guarding important installations in Baghdad and other parts of the country, and watching over the security and possessions of citizens.

8. Women's Movements:

The League for the Defence of the Rights of Women was licensed by the Government of the Revolution and played its role in consolidating the Republic and participating in various projects such as the anti-illiteracy campaign and clarifying the aim of the Revolution through delegations and missions sent to other countries.

The first conference of the league was opened by the Leader of the Revolution on March 8th 1959.

9. The People's Court:

The Special High Military Court formed on July 26th 1958, occupies a distinguished place in the political life of the country. The court is more than a court, it is a political school and a political seminar, in which hall many a fine poem and an expressive speech were delivered by members of the public, who lovingly gave the court its popular name "The Peoples Court."

The President of the Court, Colonel Fadhil Abbas Al-Mahdawi and the Military Prosecutor General, Staff Colonel Majid Mohammed Amin, enjoyed wide popularity and gained the admiration and respect of such eminent lawyers as Mr. D. N. Britt, who visited the court and followed its proceedings.

Almost all the sittings of the court were in public and were broadcast and televised. In addition to trying the traitors of the old regime, the Court tried Abdul-Salam Arif and Rashid Ali Al-Gailani. In all these trials, the court gave ample chance to all the accused to defend themselves before passing its judgment.

33 / "THE ETERNAL IRAQI REPUBLIC": IRAQ VS. ITS ENEMIES

As to our policy towards our sister Arab countries, this policy is based on brotherhood and love. The Arab countries are brothers among themselves. Between them there is the elder brother and the younger one but there is no difference between them. In our Notification No. I we referred to our relations with the Arab countries when we spoke of the formation of a popular Republic adhering to complete Iraqi unity and [its ties] with the Arab and Moslem countries by bonds of brotherhood.

This is our policy with the sister Arab countries. We are prepared to co-operate with them whenever there is a call for help. We co-operate with them on the basis of solidarity in prosperity as well as in adversity.

Henceforth we will pay no attention to any attack made against us by any of these countries. Praise be to God, there is only one source attacking us. All the Arab countries support us. This applies to Syria, Lebanon, Jordan, Libya, Tunisia, Morocco and Algeria—the latter being on the road to complete liberation. . . .

The End of Traitors and Plotters

As to the existence in Syria or in Lebanon—mostly in Syria and in Egypt—of some traitors and plotters who plotted against this country, these traitors will be chased and eliminated by the Syrian people and the Egyptian people. The Syrian people and the Egyptian people can never agree to sheltering traitors assailing Iraq and working against its liberated structure. The Syrian people and the Egyptian people can never consent to provide shelter to such traitors [who] work against the immortal Iraqi Republic which is free from all ties and obligations, and which has become an independent and a fully sovereign country defending herself and defending her brethren. The end of these

From Abdul Karim Qassim, *Objectives of Iraq's Revolution*, Iraq Ministry of Guidance (Baghdad: The Times Press, n.d.), pp. 7–16.

traitors is imminent. If they remain alive, they will be haunted by disgrace and dishonour. If they are eliminated, that will be the fate of all traitors. . . .

The Duties of Patriotic Newspapers

Many newspapers during the exterminated regime displayed vigour in publishing political commentaries for Nuri as-Said for instance. It may be that those newspapers were prompted to do so. However, the owners of those papers know themselves. But we do not propose to recall the past. We appreciate the newspaper proprietors who are working sincerely under the republican regime. We forget the past and we deal with them on the basis of their sincerity to the homeland. If any of the newspaper proprietors reckons that he was guilty under the exterminated regime or under the regime of the immortal Iraqi Republic, it is always possible to abandon the erroneous course and come into conformity with the Revolution's line. We will not be able to protect the Revolution's line and to preserve our structure as long as some newspapers inadvertently or deliberately persist in a line instigated by the influences of the enemy who covets our country. . . .

Our Students are the Support of the Republic

I wish to inform you that a covetous country as well as imperialist countries are inciting and reinforcing the agents in this country from behind the screen to plot against the security of the Republic. They have for instance wanted to delude our students who are all, without exception, sincere people whose hearts are beating in faith and sincerity for this homeland. But the covetous who pay no attention to prospects of disunity and dissention wanted to avail themselves of the opportunity to divide the people, especially the students. They have therefore sent groups from the Baath party in Syria to Iraq to organise the students and create dissention among their ranks. We have come to know the names of these agents and these names will be announced to the world. They wanted to split the students' ranks. Outwardly, their duties were to organise the students to fight anarchy as well as other elements detrimental to the students. But genuinely their purpose is to fight the immortal Iraqi Republic and to undermine her system. They have sent those persons and made them agents and groups to play the students the one against the other on the basis of the United Students Front. The United Students' Front is outwardly to fight anarchy and to serve the Republic. But genuinely it reflects the intentions of the covetous people in neighbouring countries as well as the intentions of imperialism, namely to undermine the structure of the immortal Iraqi Republic and create dissention among the students' ranks. Had these students known that they were being used by foreign elements to undermine the Republic's structure they would have revolted against those who deluded them. . . .

Who Was Behind the Kirkuk Incidents?

Do you know who was behind the Kirkuk incidents? We have strong evidences confirming that behind the Kirkuk incidents were those who were behind the incidents of Mosul and those who were behind the incidents and troubles that took place in various parts of Iraq. In this, they were employing their agents. It has been confirmed to us that five cells were operating in Kirkuk despatched by the Baath Party. They were organised by those who claim for themselves authority in Syria. They have been sent to Iraq to organise these cells in Kirkuk. Do you know what were the duties of those cells? Their duty was to disseminate dissatisfaction and splits and create a permanent gulf between the ranks of the people. Their task was to add fuel to fire. In one of their letters and in one of their reports they say "we have benefited and must continue to benefit from the Prime Minister's sympathy with the People by which he has set detainees free. We must continue with this line as this is a favourable opportunity to create dissention and dissatisfaction." That is how they are showing gratitude! They are among the people. Behind the incidents of Kirkuk too were the extremist groups both from the left and from the right who are in the grip of blind fanaticism. Extremism is always abhorrent. It is like a tree whose dry branches always hurt. That group exploited the extremism of this one and widened the gap of differences. Behind the Kirkuk incidents is also imperialism which was aware of the existence of such elements. Imperialism was at work in darkness and behind the screens to promote dissension and dissatisfaction among the people of Kirkuk. Behind the Kirkuk incidents were also some old racial feuds and rivalries. All these were behind the incidents of Kirkuk. This is all in addition to the spiteful people who were living in that area. Those circumstances combined and conspired to create the Kirkuk incidents at the time of the great joy. Had it not been for the corrupt cells, which added fuel to fire, no incident disturbing peace and order would have taken place in Kirkuk. Those were the people behind the Kirkuk incidents. They were availing themselves of every joyous opportunity and of every move made by the people originally with good intention. But they always sought to exploit anything to add fuel to the fire and to widen the gap of differences between the people. Those who were behind the Kirkuk incidents were those who were guilty of aggression against us and who plotted against the security of our Republic in Mosul, who plotted against us in the Rashid Ali movement, and who plotted against us in other plots of which we are keeping record. Beware, brothers of all agents. I am addressing a counsel to all my dear brother students all over the immortal Iraqi Republic asking them to be vigilant and cautious lest they are again deluded. They must stand [as] one bloc struggling in the way of God and for the sake of the homeland. We stand above leanings and trends. We are liberated people. Our freedom is spacious. We are pursuing the healthy democratic line.

34 / IRAQ: THE POST-KASSEM ERA

I am delighted to offer you in my name and in the name of the Armed Forces our warmest congratulations and best wishes on the occasion of the first anniversary of the Revolution of November 18. It gives me added pleasure on this occasion to welcome a delegation from the United Arab Republic led by Mr. Kamaluddin Rifat, representing President Nasser and the people of the U.A.R. I say to you, my Egyptian brothers, that you are most welcome. You are in your own country and amongst your own people who share with you the spirit of Arabism and Islam.

A whole year has passed since the Revolution of November 18. This Revolution aimed simply to restore peace and prosperity and to check tyranny.

We revolted for the sake of economic self-sufficiency, justice and equality. We revolted also in order to restore the July 14 Revolution to its original path, which it had abandoned as a result of the efforts of certain deviationists.

You all know that the July 14 Revolution was no accidental occurrence but followed in the wake of a closely knit series of Arab revolutions spreading from the Nile to Algeria, then to Sana, Oman, the Occupied Arab South with more to follow. These are the revolutions of good causes, of freedom, of progress and of unity. You all know how corrupt our own country was and how imperialists stationed their forces among us while the lackeys of imperialism conspired against our freedom and enriched themselves from the resources of the country.

Our country had for a long time been the scene of imperialist designs and schemes, even before the First World War. When imperialism finally established itself in our midst, it created a small class of feudal lords, enriched them with generous gifts, and left the vast majority of the population to eke out a miserable existence. The people were

Speech by President Aref at the celebrations held by the Arab Socialist Union in Baghdad marking the first anniversary of the November 18 revolution, Baghdad, November 18, 1964 (*Al-Jumhuriyah,* November 20–21, 1964). From *Arab Political Documents 1964,* ed. Walid Khalidi and Yusuf Ibish (Beirut, Lebanon: Political Studies and Public Administration Department of the American University of Beirut, n.d.), pp. 495–97, 502, 506–507.

divided into sects, groups, parties and individuals and the political parties competed with each other for the favour of imperialism and for the control of the government, even when such governments worked against the national interest. These parties harboured many foreign and anti-Arab elements who did not care for national prestige but worked solely in order to bind the land more closely to imperialism and to sever all its ties with its own glorious past. Their only concern was to spread confusion and doubts among the people so as to convince them that they could not rule themselves but always needed foreign patronage. This state of affairs suited imperialist plans admirably and hence was born the myth of the "political vacuum." To add to this corrupt situation, our society was riddled with hypocrisy and spying activities. The feudalists and capitalists enjoyed great wealth while bitterness, jealousy and hunger grew apace. The ruling class wanted to perpetuate this state of corruption so that they could rule and lord it over the country. The forces of imperialism supported them and protected their domination over Iraq. Considerations of public or national interest were of no importance and the ruling classes placed their faith in pacts and agreements with imperialism. The imperialists, in turn, were able to consolidate their interests, sometimes by threats and at other times by dividing up the land. Thus, for instance, the imperialists linked the question of oil to the fate of Mosul and threatened to sever Mosul from Iraq if the oil deal was not clinched. The conscious elements of the population stood and watched this conflict between a powerful imperialism and a weak Iraq which has just been freed from a debilitated Ottoman Empire. Iraq was thus left only with its faith in its natural right to enjoy freedom. The people often complained and even revolted but the power-hungry always stood between them and the imperialists.

As events followed their course, so Iraq joined one pact after another, consumed all the while by poverty, disease and ignorance. In 1930, an agreement was signed which provided for the establishment of foreign troops and airfields in Basrah and to the West of the Euphrates. The rights and dignity of Iraq were compromised. That treaty was exploited by the imperialists who interpreted it to suit their own private ends and made of Iraq a battle field for their army and an important military junction in the Second World War. Your Army then rose up in revolt in 1941 but, due to the power of imperialism, Iraq was again placed firmly under imperialist domination until the end of the war. Anti-Arab and opportunistic elements then proceeded to take their revenge upon the Iraqis and some of our best men lost their lives. Imperialism worked to weaken our Army and even to destroy it, but it could not. Meanwhile, arrangements were made for the creation of a Zionist state and the Arab armies were prevented from advancing on Palestine. Treachery played its role and Palestine was lost. Had only one Arab army been allowed to operate in freedom, Palestine would have been saved in a few days. But this was not to be. Your Army returned full of bitterness, but nothing could be done as long as traitors were in power. At that time, one could advocate any cause except that of Arab unity and preach any doctrine except the doctrine of Arabism and Islam. Anti-Arabism was in full control, constantly retarding the people's progress. My brothers, it was not possible for us to acquiesce in this state of affairs, to tolerate exploitation and monopoly and to witness the corruption of the ruling class. These men, seeking to protect themselves, made Iraq join pacts and agreements of no interest to her whatsoever. We the people wanted only to live in the shadow of world peace. Finally, our patience having been exhausted, the Revolution of July 14, 1958, broke out, destroyed the corrupt monarchy, eradicated imperialism, instituted a republic and prepared for the gradual assumption of powers by the people in their own land and the enjoyment of their own riches in peace and stability. But, once more, groups of foreigners and anti-Arab elements infiltrated the Revolution and suffocated it. The freedom fighters were relentlessly persecuted and a buffoon was made a leader, and surrounded by a group of bitter, malicious and anti-Arab elements. Slogans of annihilation and murder became common. The most common of these was the slogan: Kill, Execute, Rob. This wave of violence spread to Mosul where, for three days, a frightful massacre was carried out. Kirkuk was the next target. You all know the horrible tales of savagery enacted in these two places: of people buried alive and of shops burnt and looted. The aim of these murderers was to stamp out the Arab and Islamic elements in Iraq.

Finally, on the Ramadan 14, 1963, we placed our faith in God and destroyed that regime of deviation. There was joy everywhere and the nation offered thanks to God. A few days later, however, anti-Arabism again showed its ugly head. The so-called "National Guard" again threatened the land with violence and destruction. The climax of their madness came on November 13. Once again, our patience was exhausted and your brave Army took the field to rid the country of these unethical, foreign, malicious anti-Arab and anti-Moslem elements. God granted us victory over them and we were able to rid the country of them.

Every victory, every progress, every stability and every strength gained by Iraq is a blow to our enemies, to imperialism and to Zionism. Thus we find that Israel, the imperialists and the anti-Arabs who do not want Arabism, Islam and Iraq to flourish and prosper, are the first to raise their voices against us. But I say that the unhappy past is ended, that tyranny, monopoly and exploitation are all things of the past. Today we have peace, prosperity, justice and economic self-sufficiency. We have chosen the path of Arab and Islamic socialism which is not a mere copy of a foreign socialism but is rooted in our own traditions, customs and religion. . . .

Among the most outstanding achievements of the November 18 Revolution was the promulgation of the Interim Constitution which clarified the nature of government in the country and laid down that Iraq is a democratic and socialist republic deriving its democracy and socialism from Arab traditions and the Islamic spirit and that Iraq is a fully sovereign republic no part of which can be severed from it. The Constitution guaranteed equality before the law, personal liberty, the liberty of opinion, of academic research and of creed. We are a nation that respects divine revelation, and our Koran says, "You shall find that the closest to you are those who believe and say, we are Christians." Religion belongs to God and our country belongs to all of us. . . .

The presence of Israel in our midst is unnatural and a cause for anxiety to both the Arab world and the entire Middle East. Israel is an imperialist outpost and a centre for espionage against the Arabs. It has cut off a part of the Arab world and divided our one nation. No unnatural thing can ever remain forever. Thus the presence of Israel will not be acceptable either according to Divine Justice or to human justice nor will the conscience of mankind continue to tolerate this state of affairs.

I am proud to inform you that we have taken effective steps to establish a union with the U.A.R. with the signing of the May 26 Agreement. A Joint Presidential Council has been formed for both the U.A.R. and Iraq, composed of the presidents of the two countries and a number of members. A Political Committee, a Military Command, an Economic Committee, a Culture and Information Committee, an Arab Socialist Thought Committee and a Popular Organization Committee have all come into existence.

The Joint Presidential Council has been active in the period between May 26 and October 16, 1964. On October 16, the Unified Political Command for both republics came into being and is the highest political authority of both countries. The task of this Command is to take all practical steps to achieve constitutional unity between the two countries within, at most two years. We shall never forsake this union. Unity has in fact been established between us and we shall achieve it despite the conspiracies of imperialism.

I declare that all the people are equal before the law, as mentioned in the Interim Constitution. Social justice is the foundation of our Arab and Islamic socialism. No political parties will be allowed in Iraq and I congratulate you on the birth of our Arab Socialist Union.

This Union is a new institution and may not please all people. But we must all help, organize and strengthen it since the people do not want parties and hate party politics. The Union is for every one and the time for lobbying and behind-the-scene politics is gone forever. We are trying out this Union as the U.A.R. also tried the National Union and finally developed the Arab Socialist Union. If you want unity, seek it through the Socialist Union. We are one nation and our country is for us all. Of course, the forces of imperialism, Zionism and anti-Arabism cannot rest content. But let no one think that any part of Iraq can be severed from the rest. We are responsible before God, our conscience and Arab and Islamic history for the unity of this country. . . .

We are sons of Mohammad and his Law shall rule supreme in Iraq. I ask those juvenile delinquents in Damascus why they devoted this week to Iraq. Should they not have concerned themselves with Israel or our enemies? Or were they simply placating their American masters from whom they obtained 19 million dollars last week? Why were the murderers of Adnan Malki, that Moslem martyr, released? Why did they bomb and destroy mosques? If they are really Arabs as they claim, let them come here and argue the matter with me. I do not wish to mention any names, but I tell you that in the recent meeting in Cairo they proved themselves to be atheists.

President Nasser has asked me to stop all radio campaigns against the Baathist regime. Naturally, I cannot refuse him. These campaigns have now stopped. The radio broadcasts from Damascus have obviously been used by imperialism and Zionism . . . [The Baathists'] own conspiracies shall destroy them for they have already exposed their secret and treacherous ties with imperialism, and their ideological poverty and confusion. They have no principles, no faith, no ideology, no policy and no leadership. Everyone who has left their work now accuses them of treachery and subservience.

Turning to those Iraqis whom the Baath Party was able to deceive, I say that your national Government will work to guide your steps. I speak to you as a father who cares only for the good of his children. Come back to your nation and join the ranks again. Although the people are furious about the acts of barbarism committed by the Baath, we shall forgive and forget. We are called upon to show mercy to all men and to close our ranks. We work day and night to prosper our country and while the weapon of imperialism is to divide and rule, our policy is one of love and brotherhood.

Your national Government enjoys the people's love and esteem although it was created by the Armed Forces. These Forces shall always be the main-stay of the nation. The Government is proud to have originated from among the Armed Forces and shall continue to equip and organize these forces with the latest weapons. Our Army shall remain aloof from all party activity and politics and shall be this country's great pillar of strength.

In the name of the Army, I congratulate the people for the three revolutions, especially the November 18 Revolution.

[Addressing the Army]:

You who smashed the Baghdad Pact, swept dictatorship away on Ramadan 14th and destroyed the anti-nationalist and anti-Arab Baathists on November 18: the people love you and hope that, having rid Iraq of gangsters, you will next turn to Palestine and liberate it, together with other occupied regions of the Arab world.

VII / THE WHITE REVOLUTIONS

INTRODUCTION

The last chapter contains selections from articles and documents descriptive of the White Revolutions of Iran and Saudi Arabia. A conceptual and practical alternative to revolutionary nationalism, the White Revolutions call for a controlled process of modernization and development, usually within the framework of authoritarian, tradition-based legitimacy. Primary emphasis in such programs is on economic, technical, and cultural modernization, but political development, though slower, is not altogether ignored.

Our selections present two variants of White Revolutions. The best known, and the one from which the generic name originated, is the Iranian. Carried out under the auspices of Shah Mohammed Reza Pahlavi (1941–), Iran's program of reform has been bold primarily in the sector of agriculture, where it brought about a truly revolutionary change in the land-tenure patterns. Another notable measure has been the creation of the Literacy Corps. Selection No. 35 contains significant statements by the initiator of the revolution, the Shah of Iran.

The two following selections (Nos. 36 and 37) illustrate another variant, that of Saudi Arabia. Crown Prince (later King) Faisal's ten-point program of reform is first described and analyzed; then, in the concluding section, it is followed by documents that demonstrate the mechanics of change in the highest office of the state that were carried out in accordance with the Saudi concepts of legitimacy.

35 / IRAN'S WHITE REVOLUTION

In 1960 I wrote a book entitled "Mission for My Country." In it I aimed at analysing the present situation and giving the reader a general

From Mohammed Reza Pahlavi Aryamehr, *The White Revolution* (Tehran: The Imperial Pahlavi Library, 1967), pp. 1–24 *passim*.

outline of Iran's past. I believed an understanding of Iran's position to be necessary both for Iranians and others—particularly in the present era of closer international ties. Since then, a great social revolution has taken place, radically changing the face of our society. It is the importance of this revolution and its possible impact on the future of Iran that have prompted me to write the present book.

Today, the principles of this revolution form our political, social and economic policies. Our present and future course of action is based on these principles, which have been overwhelmingly sanctioned by the people of Iran. . . .

This "White Revolution" became a reality by legal and democratic means early in 1963. On the ninth of January at the National Congress of Rural Co-operatives held in Tehran I outlined the principles of this Revolution in a six-point plan. On the 26th of January, 1963, equivalent to the sixth of Bahman, 1341, in the Persian calendar, which must be considered as the starting point of Iran's modern history, a general referendum was held. The result was a resounding and irrevocable approval of the revolutionary charter. A majority of over 99% voted in favour of the plan.

Three more points were later added to bring the total points in the Charter to nine. Each of these is separately examined in the following chapters. . . .

When I came to the throne, on September 16th, 1941, the machinery of the government had, as a result of foreign aggression, completely broken down. As I have said, corruption, reaction, and fifth-column forces—the evils of anarchy, which had temporarily been subdued during my father's reign—recovered their lost ground. For a period of more than twenty-one years, until January, 1963, my country and I were subject to frequent vicissitudes of fortune and witnessed artificial scenes played for our benefit by actors who, like puppets, were manipulated from the outside. These hypocrites chose to deceive their people, and sought to avenge themselves on me and my family by secretly serving the cause of foreigners. . . .

These agents of foreign influence in Iran formed several distinct groups. There were the so-called politicians whose aims were in some cases clearly apparent. Then there were other politicians who played a double game, and betrayed their country in the guise of nationalists and liberals. A third category were the feudal lords who had created autonomous local governments, and in order to protect their own interests competed among themselves to serve foreign designs. These were mainly active in the south of Iran. Finally there were some self-styled religious leaders, who, ever since the establishment of constitutional monarchy in Iran, were generally known to be at the beck and call of one foreign power in particular. All these groups acted as a deterrent to Iran's progress, for foreign interests depended on a permanent state of anarchy in the country to benefit fully. . . .

I was not the ruler only of a powerful class of corrupt reactionaries, feudal khans, and deluded or treacherous people who acted as a fifth column in the service of foreigners. First and foremost I was the sovereign of over twenty million hard-working, noble citizens who had placed all their hopes in me. I watched them toil, and saw the rewards of their ceaseless efforts slip through their fingers into the outstretched hands of a group of parasites, whose only abilities were in concluding illegal deals and serving foreign powers. Although perhaps many people thought my personal interests lay in co-operating with this influential class which controlled the government, I myself had no such inclination, still less the right to accept such a situation. . . .

In 1950 I issued the decree for the distribution and sale of my personal estates. I not only hoped in this way to make free men of the peasants, but I expected my example to be followed by other landowners in the performance of their moral, social, and patriotic duties.

Unfortunately my hopes were not realized, and soon afterwards the prime minister of the time, who had gained eminence by declaring anti-British sentiments (whilst he himself had been appointed Governor of Fars on the recommendation of the British Ambassador, and in my own time had made his acceptance of the premiership conditional on British approval), opposed the distribution of my estates with all his might, and in fact prevented the execution of my plans. While he was in power this state of affairs prevailed and distribution was only begun after he had been deposed.

Since land-owners made no move to follow my example, the government, in 1959, upon my orders, presented a bill to parliament restricting landed estates. According to this bill, a person or group could only possess a limited area of farming land. Land-owners were obliged to sell their excess land to the government, so that the government in turn could divide it and sell it to small farmers on easy terms. However, most of the members of parliament belonged to the ruling class of land-owners and capitalists, and through the intervention of these irresponsible individuals, who were unaware of the social advances going on in the world, the bill was rendered ineffective and meaningless.

After this episode, it became quite clear to me that setting an example, giving advice and guidance, and recourse to ordinary parliamentary methods were not enough. In particular, the two opposing poles, black reaction and the red forces of destruction, whose aims were to prevent any real progress in the country, combined to paralyse my actions. . . .

Leon Walras, the nineteenth-century Swiss economist, of Lausanne

University, observed that "as long as wealth is not justly distributed amongst the people, its abundance is meaningless." Thus, in Iran the nation's wealth had no real meaning, the public gained no benefits, and our efforts were wasted.

All the progressive countries of the world, in spite of their conflicting ideologies, seemed to have solved this problem. Although the means differed, increase of production and greater distribution of income were the common goal. Some countries managed to reach this goal without sacrificing social freedom; in other countries democratic forms of government were replaced by totalitarian regimes; but all the same, measures were taken for national welfare and higher standards of living. . . .

I looked at Iranian society, recognizing its weaknesses, needs and potentialities; I studied the structure of other societies and saw how they had progressed; I analysed the various philosophies and programmes which had been advocated or implemented. The realization came to me that Iran needed a deep and fundamental revolution that could, at the same time, put an end to all the social inequalities and all the factors which caused injustice, tyranny and exploitation, and all aspects of reaction which impeded progress and kept our society backward. . . .

In all these designs two principles must remain constant and holy for us. One is the reliance on spiritual principles and religious beliefs, which in our case is the religion of Islam. Our people and our society are devoutly attached to their religion and beliefs, and the sublime truth of religion is the governing power and the consistent factor of our moral and spiritual order. The second is the preservation of individual and social freedoms, and the strengthening of these freedoms so that they become stronger than ever before in our history. . . .

When, after deep study, I reached the conclusion that such an all-round social revolution was imperative to save the country and to elevate it to the ranks of the most progressive contemporary nations and societies, I felt very keenly where my duty lay.

When I remembered the various episodes when I had had miraculous escapes from death, and noted the fact that during my reign my country had also miraculously been saved from ruin, I became aware that my mission to my country was not completed yet. I will frankly confess that I was convinced that God had ordained me to do certain things for the service of my nation, things that perhaps could not be done by anyone else. In whatever I have done, and in whatever I do in the future, I consider myself merely as an agent of the will of God, and I pray that He may guide me in the fulfilment of his will, and keep me from error. . . .

Since I relied on this complete trust and confidence of my people, and my goal in bringing about the revolution was simply to increase their prosperity and welfare, and since I was sure the intelligent people of Iran realized this, I presented to public opinion the sum total of my studies in a revolutionary programme and offered it to the nation for approval.

On January 26, 1963, the people of Iran, with a resounding majority, gave decisive approval to this programme, and in this way the great social revolution of Iran came into existence in a completely democratic fashion. . . .

To realize these goals it was essential that land reform should take place and the feudal landlord and peasant system be abolished; that the relationship between workers and employers should be regularized so that labour should not feel exploited; that women—who after all make up half the population—should no longer be included with lunatics and criminals and deprived of their social rights; that the scourge of illiteracy should be removed so that illiterates who do not know how to defend themselves should know their rights; that nobody should die of disease nor spend their lives in misery and wretchedness through lack of treatment or care; that backwardness in the villages should be ended, and the undeveloped country districts should be connected with the rest of the country; and in general that conditions in harmony with today's civilized world should prevail. . . .

We thus recognized that industries and resources vital to the interests of all citizens had to be nationalized. Railways, posts and telegraphs, airlines, the oil and steel industries, and the like, must be put at the service of all the people, and remain in their control. We also recognized that the forests and pastures of Iran, the fisheries, dams and rivers, belonged to the people, and that no one had the right of personal possession of them.

In the case of dams and rivers, and in fact all our water resources, it must be noted that these have a direct bearing on our national life and destiny. The significance of these resources is so great that their nationalization will form the tenth article of our revolution. I will discuss this point more fully in the chapter on Land Reform.

While we declare that these resources, as well as heavy industry, are national property, the philosophy of our revolution underlines individual and social freedom, and it is our wish to encourage individual initiative and enterprise in various social and industrial fields. . . .

None of the ideologies based on enmity and antagonism or on crushing a class or classes for the benefit of other classes, or on the exploitation of individuals or classes by others is acceptable to us, because these ideologies are essentially contrary to our national spirit, culture and way of thinking.

One of the outstanding prerequisites and characteristics of such a revolution as ours is the realization of the principle of economic democracy. In point of fact, political democracy has no meaning unless it is complemented by economic democracy under which no agent of exploitation, either private or governmental, or a group which defends a minority or class, must be allowed to operate. . . .

The revolutionary aim which I have presented to my people, and to which my people have responded with decisiveness and clarity, is that, God willing, I should utilize the present opportunity to construct a modern and progressive Iran on sound and strong foundations, so that my presence should no longer affect the destiny of the country. For inevitably I will go sooner or later, while Iran and its society will remain. It is therefore my duty to try to ensure during my lifetime that this society will become as prosperous and secure as possible.

36 / SAUDI ARABIA: TRADITION AND REFORM

In 1961–1962, King Saud made an attempt to reserve the whole power to himself. This attempt failed and in response to a strong clamour from many dissatisfied quarters at home, the King was obliged to reappoint Faisal as prime minister on October 17, 1962. His reappointment closely followed the outbreak of the revolution and civil war in Yemen. Before resuming his duties, Faisal (then undergoing medical treatment in the United States) held conversations with United States President John F. Kennedy to ascertain American policies toward the events in the Arabian Peninsula and whether, in particular, Saudi Arabia could count on United States support in case of a crisis that might threaten its security.

The outcome of these talks was a letter to Prince Faisal, dated October 25 (but released only on January 8, 1963), in which President Kennedy (a) welcomed the intention of Faisal's government to embark upon a course of energetic reform and development; and (b) in consideration of the above, pledged American support to "the maintenance of Saudi Arabia's integrity." The latter point had its internal and external implications. It signified Washington's willingness both to lend Faisal a helping hand in his reform program and to protect the kingdom from external aggression should the war in Yemen degenerate into an inter-Arab armed conflict.

Faisal's return to Saudi Arabia looked like a triumphal procession. Massive expressions of welcome from many quarters were genuine. The Saudi public looked eagerly toward his leadership after years of financial mismanagement, extravagance of the palace-pampered

From George Lenczowski, "Tradition and Reform in Saudi Arabia," *Current History* (February, 1967), pp. 100–102. Reprinted by permission of *Current History*, *Inc.*

princes, and an inconsistent foreign policy which swayed from all-out support of Nasser and the Syrian leftists in 1955–1956 to a suspected embroilment in an assassination plot against the Egyptian president in 1958.

The Ten-Point Reform Program

Encouraged by domestic and American support, on November 6, 1962, Faisal issued a ten-point program of reform which could be summed up as follows:

1. While reconfirming the state's adherence to Islamic law, it promised to issue a basic law (a constitution) and set up a consultative council.

2. It pledged enactment of provincial regulations that would establish local governments.

3. It proclaimed independence of the judiciary and promised to establish a supreme judicial council and a ministry of justice.

4. It announced that the above-mentioned judicial council would be composed of 20 members chosen from both the lay jurists and the *ulema*.

5. It promised to strengthen Islamic propaganda.

6. It proclaimed the reform of the committees of public morality.

7. It proclaimed the government's solicitude for social matters and education and pledged control of retail prices, establishment of scholarships for students, social security regulations, a law protecting laborers from unemployment, and provision of innocent means of recreation for all citizens.

8. It announced the intention to regulate economic and commercial activities through appropriate legislation which would assure progress, economic expansion, and encouragement of capital investment.

9. It pledged sustained endeavor to develop the country's resources and economy, in particular, roads, water resources, heavy and light industry, self-sufficient agriculture.

10. It abolished slavery in the kingdom.

The program in question signified a major advance conceptually and in practice. While carefully reaffirming the state's devotion to the basic principles of Islam, it introduced important innovations, foremost among which stood the pledge to issue a basic law (together with the consultative assembly) and to set up a semi-secular judicial council which would put an end to religious monopoly of the administration of justice. Second in importance was the pledge to reform (i.e., to curb) the ubiquitous committees of public morality, coupled with a promise to provide "innocent means of recreation" for the masses, thus foreshadowing the abandonment of the irksome official ban on the much-demanded movies, music and television.

On the pragmatic side—i.e., in the sectors where there was no incompatibility with the traditional practices of Islam—Faisal's pledge to concentrate on problems of social and economic development was welcomed as a portent of a more consistent and determined policy to utilize the growing income of the state for constructive tasks which would result in increased prosperity and greater social justice.

How did the program of reform fare? It appears that more progress was achieved in the "pragmatic" than in the "conceptual" sector. With impressive speed, Faisal brought order into the disorganized Saudi finances, paid off all state debts, stabilized the currency, and balanced the annual budgets, while setting aside special funds for development. Development itself began emerging from the stage of planning into the stage of execution. Numerous foreign firms were engaged to carry out more complex engineering tasks. An ambitious road-building program was launched and serious efforts were exerted toward the establishment of a water desalinization plant in Jidda. New airports were built and the Saudi Arabian Airlines were modernized and entrusted to a management benefiting from expert foreign advice.

The Petromin entered into contracts aiming at the development of petrochemical industries. A geophysical survey of the country was undertaken. A petroleum college was inaugurated in Dammam. Telephone service was expanded and modernized and other utilities were extended in the rapidly growing cities. Increasing numbers of government scholarships were given to young men for study abroad. All in all, not only government-sponsored projects, but also—with the general restoration of confidence—private business experienced expansion up to the point of a veritable boom by 1966.

Somewhat in contrast, those points of the 1962 program that spoke of the basic law, the consultative assembly, and other modern institutions and regulations still (at the end of 1966) awaited fulfillment. The main reason for Faisal's reluctance to hasten their implementation was to be sought in the political sphere, partly domestic and largely foreign. In the domestic sector, Faisal's return to premiership—with an obvious new mandate from the people—brought forth the inevitable final showdown between him and the king. This came about in two successive steps: on March 28, 1964, King Saud was stripped of all powers by decision of the council of ministers backed by a *fatwa* and the resolution of the leading princes. These powers were transferred to Faisal. The king retained only nominal authority. In spite of this, he yielded to advice urging him to regain initiative and influence in public affairs, thus preventing Faisal from full enjoyment of his newly acquired rights. Ultimately, on November 2, Saud was deposed by joint resolutions of the royal family, the council of ministers, and the *ulema*. These same bodies proclaimed Faisal as king. Promptly afterward, numerous princes, tribal leaders, notables, and high government dignitaries began declaring obedience to the new sovereign.

37 / SAUDI ARABIA: FAISAL ASCENDS TO THE THRONE

At 4:30 A.M. on the morning of Monday, November 2, 1964, the Council of Ministers and the Advisory Council held a meeting under the chairmanship of Prince Khalid ibn Abdul Aziz, the Deputy Prime Minister. They examined the letter dated October 28, 1964, addressed by the entire family of al Saud to their Excellencies the ulema, and in which they announced their deposition of Saud bin Abdul Aziz bin Abdul Rahman bin Faisal al Saud from the throne and their investiture of Crown Prince Faisal bin Abdul Aziz bin Abdul Rahman bin Faisal al Saud as King of the land and Imam of the Moslems. They asked the ulema to examine that action from the canonical point of view and to issue a suitable *fatwa*. The members of the two councils also took note of the *fatwa* issued by their Excellencies the ulema who met under the chairmanship of H. E. Shaikh Muhammad bin Ibrahim, Chief Religious Magistrate and Mufti of Saudi Arabia. This *fatwa* was issued on October 1, 1964, and was based upon the preceding *fatwa* issued on March 29, 1964, upon realistic and convincing analysis of the situation and upon theological foundations. In this *fatwa*, it was decided:

1. To depose Saud bin Abdul Aziz bin Abdul Rahman bin Faisal al Saud from the throne.

2. To invest Crown Prince Faisal bin Abdul Aziz bin Abdul Rahman bin Faisal as legal King of Saudi Arabia, in which position he must respect God, use His Law for arbitration in all matters and enforce His Law among his subjects.

The members of the two Councils unanimously supported the decision of the Saud family and agreed to act in accordance with the *fatwa* of June 26, 1964. Therefore, they decided:

1. To invest Crown Prince Faisal bin Abdul Aziz bin Abdul Rahman bin Faisal al Saud as legal King of Saudi Arabia and Imam of the Moslems.

2. To request His Majesty King Faisal to accept and proclaim this

Statement by Shaikh Jamil Hujaylan, Saudi Minister of Information, proclaiming Prince Faisal as King of Saudi Arabia, Riyad, November 2, 1964 (*Um-Al-Qura*, November 2, 1964). From *Arab Political Documents 1964*, ed. Walid Khalidi and Yusuf Ibish (Beirut, Lebanon: Political Studies and Public Administration Department of the American University of Beirut, n.d.), p. 441.

investiture. We pray that God will prosper his reign and help him in serving and strengthening Canonical Law.

Text of King Faisal's Acceptance, Riyad, November 2, 1964
(*Al-Medina*, November 3, 1964)

I undertake to act in accordance with the Koran and to use it in all arbitration, to serve canonical law in all matters and to do my utmost to protect national sovereignty and to serve the citizens in whatever is of benefit to them, in both secular and sacred matters. I pray that God will guide us all to follow in the path of righteousness and to be faithful to Islam.

FURTHER READINGS

The Area in General

Anshen, Ruth N., ed., *Mid-East: World Center*. New York: Harper & Row, Publishers, Inc., 1956.

Berger, Morroe, *The Arab World Today*. Garden City, N. Y.: Doubleday & Company, Inc., 1962.

Coon, Carleton S., *Caravan: The Story of the Middle East*. London: Jonathan Cape, Ltd., 1952.

Halpern, Manfred, *The Politics of Social Change in the Middle East and North Africa*. Princeton, N.J.: Princeton University Press, 1963.

Harari, Maurice, *Government and Politics of the Middle East*. Englewood Cliffs, N. J.: Prentice-Hall, Inc., 1962.

Hottinger, Arnold, *The Arabs*. Berkeley and Los Angeles: University of California Press, 1963.

Karpat, Kemal H., ed., *Political and Social Thought in the Contemporary Middle East*. New York: Frederick A. Praeger, Inc., 1968.

Kirk, George E., *A Short History of the Middle East: From the Rise of Islam to Modern Times*. New York: Frederick A. Praeger, Inc., 1959.

Lenczowski, George, *The Middle East in World Affairs*, 3d ed. Ithaca, N. Y.: Cornell University Press, 1962.

Lewis, Bernard, *The Middle East and the West*. New York: Harper & Row, Publishers, Inc., 1966.

Peretz, Don, *The Middle East Today*. New York: Holt, Rinehart and Winston, Inc., 1963.

Rivlin, Benjamin, and Joseph Szyliowicz, eds., *The Contemporary Middle East: Tradition and Innovation*. New York: Random House, Inc., 1965.

175

Sharabi, H. B., *Governments and Politics of the Middle East in the Twentieth Century.* Princeton, N. J.: D. Van Nostrand Company, Inc., 1962.

Spencer, William, *Political Evolution in the Middle East.* Philadelphia and New York: J. B. Lippincott Company, 1962.

Thompson, J. H., and Reischauer, R. D., *Modernization of the Arab World.* Princeton, N. J.: D. Van Nostrand Company, Inc., 1966.

Administrative and Military Reform in the Nineteenth Century

Bailey, Frank E., *British Policy and the Turkish Reform Movement.* Cambridge, Mass.: Harvard University Press, 1942.

Creasy, Edward S., *History of the Ottoman Turks: From the Beginning of Their Empire to the Present Time.* London: R. Bentley, 1858; reprinted, Beirut: Khayat's, 1961.

Crouchley, A. E., *The Economic Development of Modern Egypt.* London: Longmans, Green, and Co., Ltd., 1938.

Davison, Roderic H., *Reform in the Ottoman Empire, 1856–1876.* Princeton, N. J.: Princeton University Press, 1963.

Dodwell, Henry, *The Founder of Modern Egypt: A Study of Muhammad Ali.* Cambridge: Cambridge University Press, 1931; reprinted 1967.

Eliot, Charles N. E., *Turkey in Europe.* London: E. Arnold, 1908.

Luke, Sir Harry, *The Old Turkey and the New: From Byzantium to Ankara,* rev. ed. London: Geoffrey Bles, 1955.

Mahomed Khan, ed., *The Life of Abdur Rahman.* London: John Murray, 1900.

Miller, W., *The Ottoman Empire and Its Successors.* Cambridge: Cambridge University Press, 1923.

Reform within Islam: Fundamentalism and Modernism

Adams, Charles C., *Islam and Modernism in Egypt: A Study of the Modern Reform Movement Inaugurated by Muhammad Abduh.* London: Oxford University Press, 1933.

Evans-Pritchard, E. E., *The Sanusi of Cyrenaica.* London: Oxford University Press, 1949.

Ghazzali, Muhammad al-, *Our Beginning in Wisdom.* Washington, D. C.: American Council of Learned Societies, 1953.

Gibb, H. A. R., *Modern Trends in Islam*. Chicago: University of Chicago Press, 1947.

Grunebaum, G. E. von, *Modern Islam: The Search for Cultural Identity*. Berkeley and Los Angeles: University of California Press, 1962.

Harris, Christina Phelps, *Nationalism and Revolution in Egypt: The Role of the Muslim Brotherhood*. The Hague: Mouton & Co., 1964.

Heyworth-Dunne, J., *Religious and Political Trends in Modern Egypt*. Washington, D. C.: "Near and Middle East Monographs," No. 1, 1950.

Husaini, Ishak Musa, *The Moslem Brethren*. Beirut: Khayat's, 1956.

Kerr, Malcolm H., *Islamic Reform: The Political and Legal Theories of Muhammad Abduh and Rashid Rida*. Berkeley and Los Angeles: University of California Press, 1966.

Kotb, Sayed, *Social Justice in Islam*. Washington, D. C.: American Council of Learned Societies, 1953.

Lichtenstadter, Ilse, *Islam and the Modern Age*. New York: Bookman Associates, 1958.

Philby, H. St. John, *Saʿudi Arabia*. London: Ernest Benn, Ltd., 1955.

———, *Arabia of the Wahhabis*. London: Constable and Company, Ltd., 1928.

Rosenthal, E. J. J., *Islam in the Modern National State*. Cambridge: Cambridge University Press, 1965.

Smith, Wilfred C., *Islam in Modern History*. Princeton, N. J.: Princeton University Press, 1957.

Ziadeh, Nicola A., *Sanusiyah: A Study of a Revivalist Movement in Islam*. Leiden: Brill, 1958.

Early Constitutionalism and Nationalism

Antonius, George, *The Arab Awakening*. New York: Capricorn Books, 1965.

Berkes, Niyazi, ed., *Turkish Nationalism and Western Civilization: Selected Essays of Ziya Gökalp*. New York: Columbia University Press, 1959.

Browne, Edward G., *The Persian Revolution of 1905–1909*. New York: Barnes & Noble, Inc., 1966.

Haim, Sylvia, ed., *Arab Nationalism: An Anthology*. Berkeley and Los Angeles: University of California Press, 1962.

Heyd, Uriel, *Foundations of Turkish Nationalism: The Life and Teachings of Ziya Gökalp*. London: Luzac & Co. and the Harvill Press, 1950.

Izzeddin, Nejla, *The Arab World: Past, Present, and Future*. Chicago: Henry Regnery Company, 1953.

Lewis, Bernard, *The Emergence of Modern Turkey*. London: Oxford University Press, 1961.

Mardin, Serif, *The Genesis of Young Ottoman Thought: A Study in the Modernization of Turkish Political Ideas*. Princeton, N. J.: Princeton University Press, 1962.

Ramsaur, Ernest E., *The Young Turks: Prelude to the Revolution of 1908*. Princeton, N. J.: Princeton University Press, 1957.

Zeine, Zeine N., *Arab-Turkish Relations and the Emergence of Arab Nationalism*. Beirut: Khayat's, 1958.

———, *The Struggle for Arab Independence: Western Diplomacy and the Rise and Fall of Faisal's Kingdom in Syria*. Beirut: Khayat's, 1960.

Modernization and Tutelage: Turkey and Iran between Two Wars

Allen, Henry E., *The Turkish Transformation*. Chicago: University of Chicago Press, 1935.

Armstrong, Harold C., *Grey Wolf, Mustafa Kemal: An Intimate Study of a Dictator*. London: Arthur Barker, Ltd., 1932.

Banani, Amin, *The Modernization of Iran, 1921–1941*. Stanford, Calif.: Stanford University Press, 1961.

Binder, Leonard, *Iran: Political Development in a Changing Society*. Berkeley and Los Angeles: University of California Press, 1962.

Cottam, Richard W., *Nationalism in Iran*. Pittsburgh, Pa.: University of Pittsburgh Press, 1964.

Frey, Frederick W., *The Turkish Political Elite*. Cambridge, Mass.: The M.I.T. Press, 1965.

Karpat, Kemal H., *Turkey's Politics: The Transition to a Multi-Party System*. Princeton, N. J.: Princeton University Press, 1959.

Kemal, Ghazi Mustapha, *A Speech Delivered by Ghazi Mustapha Kemal, President of the Turkish Republic, October 1927*. Leipzig: K. F. Koehler, 1929.

Lenczowski, George, *Russia and the West in Iran, 1918–1948: A Study in Big Power Rivalry*. Ithaca, N. Y.: Cornell University Press, 1949.

Lewis, Geoffrey L., *Turkey*. London: Ernest Benn, Ltd., 1955.

Pahlavi, Mohammed Reza Shah, *Mission for My Country*. New York: McGraw-Hill, Inc., 1961.

Thomas, Lewis V., and Richard N. Frye, *The United States and Turkey and Iran*. Cambridge, Mass.: Harvard University Press, 1951.

Upton, Joseph M., *The History of Modern Iran: An Interpretation*. Cambridge, Mass.: Harvard University Press, 1960.

Webster, Donald E., *Turkey of Ataturk*. Philadelphia: American Academy of Political and Social Science, 1939.

Liberal Democracy in the Arab World

Ahmed, Jamal M., *The Intellectual Origins of Egyptian Nationalism*. London: Oxford University Press, 1960.

Ghali, Mirrit Boutros, *The Policy of Tomorrow*. Washington, D. C.: American Council of Learned Societies, 1953.

Hourani, Albert, *Arabic Thought in the Liberal Age, 1798–1939*. London: Oxford University Press, 1962.

Hussein, Taha, *The Future of Culture in Egypt*. Washington, D. C.: American Council of Learned Societies, 1954.

Khalid, Khalid M., *From Here We Start*. Washington, D. C.: American Council of Learned Societies, 1953.

Nuseibeh, Hazem Zaki, *The Ideas of Arab Nationalism*. Ithaca, N. Y.: Cornell University Press, 1956.

Safran, Nadav, *Egypt in Search of Political Community: An Analysis of the Intellectual and Political Evolution of Egypt, 1804–1952*. Cambridge, Mass.: Harvard University Press, 1961.

Radical Arab Nationalism

Abu Jaber, Kamel S., *The Arab Ba'th Socialist Party: History, Ideology, and Organization*. Syracuse, N. Y.: Syracuse University Press, 1966.

Arab Political Documents, 1963 [and successive years]. Beirut: American University of Beirut.

Binder, Leonard, *The Ideological Revolution in the Middle East.* New York: John Wiley & Sons, Inc., 1964.

Cremeans, Charles D., *The Arabs and the World: Nasser's Arab Nationalist Policy.* New York: Frederick A. Praeger, Inc., 1963.

Fisher, Sydney N., ed., *The Military in the Middle East: Problems in Society and Government.* Columbus, Ohio: Ohio State University Press, 1963.

————, ed., *Social Forces in the Middle East.* Ithaca, N. Y.: Cornell University Press, 1955.

Kerr, Malcolm, *The Arab Cold War, 1958–1967: A Study of Ideology in Politics,* 2nd ed. London: Oxford University Press, 1967.

Kirk, George E., *Contemporary Arab Politics: A Concise History.* New York: Frederick A. Praeger, Inc., 1961.

Nasser, Gamal Abdel, *Egypt's Liberation: The Philosophy of the Revolution.* Washington, D. C.: Public Affairs Press, 1955.

Neguib, Mohammed, *Egypt's Destiny.* London: Victor Gollancz, Ltd., 1955.

Sadat, Anwar el-, *Revolt on the Nile.* London: Allan Wingate, 1957.

Sayegh, Fayez A., *Arab Unity: Hope and Fulfillment.* New York: Devin-Adair Co., 1958.

Sayegh, Fayez A., ed., *The Dynamics of Neutralism in the Arab World.* San Francisco: Chandler Publishing Company, 1964.

Tütsch, Hans E., *Facets of Arab Nationalism.* Detroit: Wayne State University Press, 1965.

Yamak, Labib Zuwiyya, *The Syrian Social Nationalist Party: An Ideological Analysis.* Cambridge, Mass.: Harvard University Press, 1966.

The White Revolutions

Bayne, E. A., *Persian Kingship in Transition.* New York: American Universities Field Staff, 1968.

De Gaury, Gerald, *Faisal, King of Saudi Arabia.* New York: Frederick A. Praeger, Inc., 1967.

Pahlavi Aryamehr Shahanshah of Iran, Mohammed Reza, *The White Revolution,* 2nd ed. Tehran: The Imperial Pahlavi Library, 1967.

Wilber, Donald, *Iran: Past and Present.* Princeton, N. J.: Princeton University Press, 1967.